digits™

Student Companion

Grade 8

PEARSON

Boston, Massachusetts • Chandler, Arizona • Glenview, Illinois • Upper Saddle River, New Jersey

Acknowledgments for illustrations and composition: Rory Hensley, David Jackson, Jim Mariano, Rich McMahon, Lorie Park, Ted Smykal, Ralph Voltz, and Laserwords

PEARSON

ISBN-13: 978-0-13-327627-5
ISBN-10: 0-13-327627-9
9 10 V001 17 16

digits™ System Requirements

◗ Supported System Configurations

	Operating System (32-bit only)	Web Browser* (32-bit only)	Java® Version**
PC	Windows® XP (SP3) Windows Vista (SP1) Windows 7	Internet Explorer® 7 Internet Explorer 8 Internet Explorer 9 Mozilla Firefox® 11 Google Chrome™	1.4.2 1.5 [5.0 Update 11 or higher] 1.6 [6.0 through Update 18]
Mac	Macintosh® OS 10.6.x, 10.7.x	Safari® 5.0 Safari 5.1 Google Chrome™	1.5 [5.0 Update 16 or higher]

* Pop-up blockers must be disabled in the browser.
** Java (JRE) plug-in must be installed and JavaScript® must be enabled in the browser.

◗ Additional Requirements

Software	Version
Adobe® Flash®	Version 10.4 or higher
Adobe Reader® (required for PC*)	Version 8 or higher
Word processing software	Microsoft® Word®, Open Office, or similar application to open ".doc" files

* Macintosh® OS 10.6 has a built-in PDF reader, Preview.

Screen Resolution
PC
Minimum: 1024 x 768*
Maximum: 1280 x 1024
Mac
Minimum: 1024 x 768*
Maximum: 1280 x 960
*recommended for interactive whiteboards

Internet Connection
Broadband (cable/DSL) or greater is recommended.

AOL® and AT&T™ Yahoo!® Users
You cannot use the AOL or AT&T Yahoo! browsers. However, you can use AOL or AT&T as your Internet Service Provider to access the Internet, and then open a supported browser.

The trademarks referred to above are the property of their respective owners, none of whom have authorized, approved, or otherwise sponsored this product.

◗ For *digits*™ Support

go to **http://support.pearsonschool.com/index.cfm/digits**

digits™ Learning Team

My Name: _____

My Teacher's Name: _____

My School: _____

Lisa Jay Andie Kamal

Francis (Skip) Fennell
digits Author

Approaches to mathematics content and curriculum, educational policy, and support for intervention

Eric Milou
digits Author

Approaches to mathematical content and the use of technology in middle grades classrooms

Art Johnson
digits Author

Approaches to mathematical content and support for English language learners

William F. Tate
digits Author

Approaches to intervention, and use of efficacy and research

Helene Sherman
digits Author

Teacher education and support for struggling students

Grant Wiggins
digits Consulting Author

Understanding by Design

Stuart J. Murphy
digits Author

Visual learning and student engagement

Randall I. Charles
digits Advisor

Janie Schielack
digits Author

Approaches to mathematical content, building problem solvers, and support for intervention

Jim Cummins
digits Advisor

Supporting English Language Learners

Jacquie Moen
digits Advisor

Digital Technology

myMATH
universe ● com

Go online for all your cool digits™ stuff!

Be sure to save your login information by writing it here.

> **My Username:** _____
>
> **My Password:** _____

First, go to **MyMathUniverse.com**. From there you can explore the **Channel List**, which includes fun and interactive games and videos, or select your program and log in.

Play some cool math **games!**

Complete your **homework** online**!**

Discover math **tricks** and **tips!**

Check out fun **videos!**

ACTIVe-book

No more pencils! No more books! Why? Because the Student Companion you have in front of you can also be found online in ACTIVe-book format. You can access your ACTIVe-book on a tablet or on a computer, so any questions you can answer in your Student Companion you can also master online.

1-1

Equivalent Ratios

CCSS: 7.RP.A.1: Compute unit rates associated with ratios of fractions, including ratios of lengths, areas and other quantities measured in like or different units.

Digital Resources

Launch

Your friend can't help but compare. During a game of stickball in the street, you notice him making all sorts of number comparisons. He asks for help making number comparisons on one building.

MP2, MP6

Name at least five number comparisons you can make by looking at the building.

Reflect Do you make number comparisons? Provide an example of a number comparison you've made and why you made it.

vii

Contents

Welcome to digits

Using the Student Companion

digits is designed to help you master mathematics skills and concepts in a way that's relevant to you. As the title *digits* suggests, this program takes a digital approach. The Student Companion supports your work on *digits* by providing a place to demonstrate your understanding of lesson skills and concepts in writing.

Your companion supports your work on *digits* in so many ways!

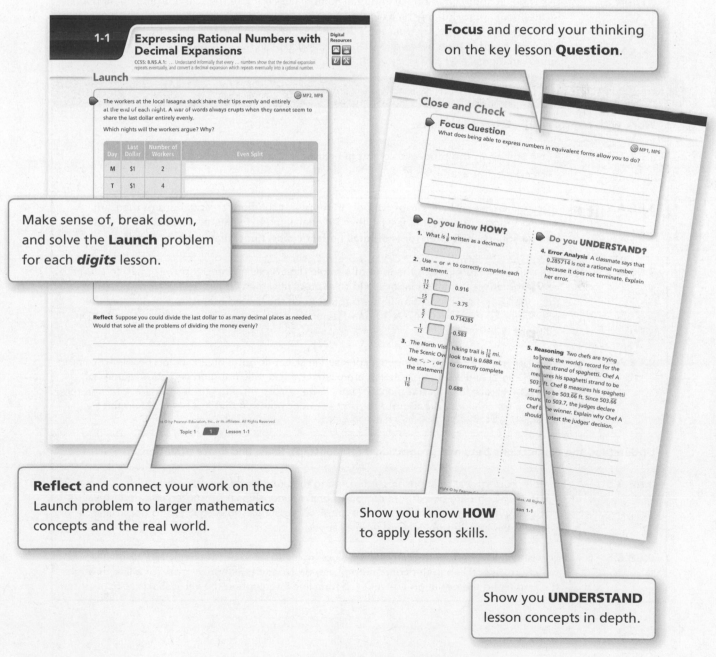

Focus and record your thinking on the key lesson **Question**.

Make sense of, break down, and solve the **Launch** problem for each *digits* lesson.

Reflect and connect your work on the Launch problem to larger mathematics concepts and the real world.

Show you know **HOW** to apply lesson skills.

Show you **UNDERSTAND** lesson concepts in depth.

Number	Standard for Mathematical Content

8.NS   The Number System

Know that there are numbers that are not rational, and approximate them by rational numbers.

8.NS.A.1	Know that numbers that are not rational are called irrational. Understand informally that every number has a decimal expansion; for rational numbers show that the decimal expansion repeats eventually, and convert a decimal expansion which repeats eventually into a rational number.
8.NS.A.2	Use rational approximations of irrational numbers to compare the size of irrational numbers, locate them approximately on a number line diagram, and estimate the value of expressions (e.g., π^2). For example, by truncating the decimal expansion of $\sqrt{2}$, show that $\sqrt{2}$ is between 1 and 2, then between 1.4 and 1.5, and explain how to continue on to get better approximations.

8.EE   Expressions and Equations

Work with radicals and integer exponents.

8.EE.A.1	Know and apply the properties of integer exponents to generate equivalent numerical expressions. For example, $3^2 \times 3^{(-5)} = 3^{(-3)} = \frac{1}{(3^3)} = \frac{1}{27}$.
8.EE.A.2	Use square root and cube root symbols to represent solutions to equations of the form $x^2 = p$ and $x^3 = p$, where p is a positive rational number. Evaluate square roots of small perfect squares and cube roots of small perfect cubes. Know that $\sqrt{2}$ is irrational.
8.EE.A.3	Use numbers expressed in the form of a single digit times an integer power of 10 to estimate very large or very small quantities, and to express how many times as much one is than the other. For example, estimate the population of the United States as 3×10^8 and the population of the world as 7×10^9, and determine that the world population is more than 20 times larger.
8.EE.A.4	Perform operations with numbers expressed in scientific notation, including problems where both decimal and scientific notation are used. Use scientific notation and choose units of appropriate size for measurements of very large or very small quantities (e.g., use millimeters per year for seafloor spreading). Interpret scientific notation that has been generated by technology.

Understand the connections between proportional relationships, lines, and linear equations.

8.EE.B.5	Graph proportional relationships, interpreting the unit rate as the slope of the graph. Compare two different proportional relationships represented in different ways. For example, compare a distance-time graph to a distance-time equation to determine which of two moving objects has greater speed.
8.EE.B.6	Use similar triangles to explain why the slope m is the same between any two distinct points on a non-vertical line in the coordinate plane; derive the equation $y = mx$ for a line through the origin and the equation $y = mx + b$ for a line intercepting the vertical axis at b.

Number	Standard for Mathematical Content

8.EE Expressions and Equations (continued)

Analyze and solve linear equations and pairs of simultaneous linear equations.

Number	Standard for Mathematical Content
8.EE.C.7	Solve linear equations in one variable.
8.EE.C.7a	Give examples of linear equations in one variable with one solution, infinitely many solutions, or no solutions. Show which of these possibilities is the case by successively transforming the given equation into simpler forms, until an equivalent equation of the form $x = a$, $a = a$, or $a = b$ results (where a and b are different numbers).
8.EE.C.7b	Solve linear equations with rational number coefficients, including equations whose solutions require expanding expressions using the distributive property and collecting like terms.
8.EE.C.8	Analyze and solve pairs of simultaneous linear equations.
8.EE.C.8a	Understand that solutions to a system of two linear equations in two variables correspond to points of intersection of their graphs, because points of intersection satisfy both equations simultaneously.
8.EE.C.8b	Solve systems of two linear equations in two variables algebraically, and estimate solutions by graphing the equations. Solve simple cases by inspection. For example, $3x + 2y = 5$ and $3x + 2y = 6$ have no solution because $3x + 2y$ cannot simultaneously be 5 and 6.
8.EE.C.8c	Solve real-world and mathematical problems leading to two linear equations in two variables. For example, given coordinates for two pairs of points, determine whether the line through the first pair of points intersects the line through the second pair.

8.F Functions

Define, evaluate, and compare functions.

Number	Standard for Mathematical Content
8.F.A.1	Understand that a function is a rule that assigns to each input exactly one output. The graph of a function is the set of ordered pairs consisting of an input and the corresponding output.
8.F.A.2	Compare properties of two functions each represented in a different way (algebraically, graphically, numerically in tables, or by verbal descriptions). For example, given a linear function represented by a table of values and a linear function represented by an algebraic expression, determine which function has the greater rate of change.
8.F.A.3	Interpret the equation $y = mx + b$ as defining a linear function, whose graph is a straight line; give examples of functions that are not linear. For example, the function $A = s^2$ giving the area of a square as a function of its side length is not linear because its graph contains the points (1,1), (2,4) and (3,9), which are not on a straight line.

Use functions to model relationships between quantities.

Number	Standard for Mathematical Content
8.F.B.4	Construct a function to model a linear relationship between two quantities. Determine the rate of change and initial value of the function from a description of a relationship or from two (x, y) values, including reading these from a table or from a graph. Interpret the rate of change and initial value of a linear function in terms of the situation it models, and in terms of its graph or a table of values.
8.F.B.5	Describe qualitatively the functional relationship between two quantities by analyzing a graph (e.g., where the function is increasing or decreasing, linear or nonlinear). Sketch a graph that exhibits the qualitative features of a function that has been described verbally.

Grade 8 Common Core State Standards *continued*

Number	Standard for Mathematical Content
8.G Geometry	
Understand congruence and similarity using physical models, transparencies, or geometry software.	
8.G.A.1	Verify experimentally the properties of rotations, reflections, and translations:
8.G.A.1a	Verify experimentally the properties of rotations, reflections, and translations: Lines are taken to lines, and line segments to line segments of the same length.
8.G.A.1b	Verify experimentally the properties of rotations, reflections, and translations: Angles are taken to angles of the same measure.
8.G.A.1c	Verify experimentally the properties of rotations, reflections, and translations: Parallel lines are taken to parallel lines.
8.G.A.2	Understand that a two-dimensional figure is congruent to another if the second can be obtained from the first by a sequence of rotations, reflections, and translations; given two congruent figures, describe a sequence that exhibits the congruence between them.
8.G.A.3	Describe the effect of dilations, translations, rotations, and reflections on two-dimensional figures using coordinates.
8.G.A.4	Understand that a two-dimensional figure is similar to another if the second can be obtained from the first by a sequence of rotations, reflections, translations, and dilations; given two similar two- dimensional figures, describe a sequence that exhibits the similarity between them.
8.G.A.5	Use informal arguments to establish facts about the angle sum and exterior angle of triangles, about the angles created when parallel lines are cut by a transversal, and the angle-angle criterion for similarity of triangles.
Understand and apply the Pythagorean Theorem.	
8.G.B.6	Explain a proof of the Pythagorean Theorem and its converse.
8.G.B.7	Apply the Pythagorean Theorem to determine unknown side lengths in right triangles in real-world and mathematical problems in two and three dimensions.
8.G.B.8	Apply the Pythagorean Theorem to find the distance between two points in a coordinate system.
Solve real-world and mathematical problems involving volume of cylinders, cones, and spheres.	
8.G.C.9	Know the formulas for the volumes of cones, cylinders, and spheres and use them to solve real-world and mathematical problems.

Number	Standard for Mathematical Content

8.SP Statistics and Probability

Investigate patterns of association in bivariate data.

8.SP.A.1	Construct and interpret scatter plots for bivariate measurement data to investigate patterns of association between two quantities. Describe patterns such as clustering, outliers, positive or negative association, linear association, and nonlinear association.
8.SP.A.2	Know that straight lines are widely used to model relationships between two quantitative variables. For scatter plots that suggest a linear association, informally fit a straight line, and informally assess the model fit by judging the closeness of the data points to the line.
8.SP.A.3	Use the equation of a linear model to solve problems in the context of bivariate measurement data, interpreting the slope and intercept.
8.SP.A.4	Understand that patterns of association can also be seen in bivariate categorical data by displaying frequencies and relative frequencies in a two-way table. Construct and interpret a two-way table summarizing data on two categorical variables collected from the same subjects. Use relative frequencies calculated for rows or columns to describe possible association between the two variables.

Number	Standard for Mathematical Practice
MP1	Make sense of problems and persevere in solving them.
MP2	Reason abstractly and quantitatively.
MP3	Construct viable arguments and critique the reasoning of others.
MP4	Model with mathematics.
MP5	Use appropriate tools strategically.
MP6	Attend to precision.
MP7	Look for and make use of structure.
MP8	Look for and express regularity in repeated reasoning.

Vocabulary

Language of Math for Topic 1

Lesson	Vocabulary	
	New	**Review**
Readiness 1 Skyscrapers		decimals order rational numbers
1-1 Expressing Rational Numbers with Decimal Expansions	repeating decimal terminating decimal	rational numbers
1-2 Exploring Irrational Numbers	irrational numbers perfect square real numbers square root	integer natural numbers whole numbers
1-3 Approximating Irrational Numbers		estimate
1-4 Comparing and Ordering Rational and Irrational Numbers		order
1-5 Problem Solving		natural numbers rational numbers repeating decimal
Topic 1 Topic Review	irrational numbers perfect square real numbers repeating decimal square root terminating decimal	integer natural numbers rational numbers whole numbers

Vocabulary

Language of Math for Topic 2

Lesson	Vocabulary	
	New	**Review**
Readiness 2 Auto Racing		Distributive Property one-step equations two-step equations
2-1 Solving Two-Step Equations		Commutative Property Distributive Property isolate the variable order of operations
2-2 Solving Equations with Variables on Both Sides		solution of an equation
2-3 Solving Equations Using the Distributive Property		Distributive Property least common multiple
2-4 Solutions – One, None, or Infinitely Many	infinitely many solutions no solution	solution of an equation
2-5 Problem Solving		equation
Topic 2 Topic Review	infinitely many solutions no solution	Commutative Property Distributive Property least common multiple order of operations solution of an equation

Vocabulary

Language of Math for Topic 3

Lesson	Vocabulary	
	New	**Review**
Readiness 3 Ocean Waves		perfect square square root squaring
3-1 Perfect Squares, Square Roots, and Equations of the form $x^2 = p$		inverse operations perfect square square root
3-2 Perfect Cubes, Cube Roots, and Equations of the form $x^3 = p$	cube root perfect cube	inverse operations
3-3 Exponents and Multiplication		base exponent power
3-4 Exponents and Division		base exponent power
3-5 Zero and Negative Exponents	Negative Exponent Property Zero Exponent Property	base exponent
3-6 Comparing Expressions with Exponents		base equivalent expressions exponent
3-7 Problem Solving		algebraic expression
Topic 3 Topic Review	cube root Negative Exponent Property perfect cube Zero Exponent Property	base exponent inverse operations perfect square power square root

Vocabulary

Language of Math for Topic 4

Lesson	Vocabulary	
	New	**Review**
Readiness 4 The Mathematics of Sound		negative exponent positive exponent power
4-1 Exploring Scientific Notation	scientific notation	base exponent power standard form
4-2 Using Scientific Notation to Describe Very Large Quantities		base exponent power scientific notation standard form
4-3 Using Scientific Notation to Describe Very Small Quantities		base exponent power scientific notation standard form
4-4 Operating with Numbers Expressed in Scientific Notation		base exponent power scientific notation
4-5 Problem Solving		scientific notation
Topic 4 Topic Review	scientific notation	base exponent power standard form

Vocabulary

Language of Math for Topic 5

Lesson	Vocabulary	
	New	**Review**
Readiness 5 High-Speed Trains		equation in two variables proportional relationship unit rate
5-1 Graphing Proportional Relationships		constant of proportionality proportional relationship
5-2 Linear Equations: $y = mx$	linear equation	proportional relationship
5-3 The Slope of a Line	slope slope of a line	x-coordinate y-coordinate
5-4 Unit Rates and Slope		rate slope unite rate
5-5 The y-intercept of a Line	y-intercept	y-axis
5-6 Linear Equations: $y = mx + b$		slope slope-intercept form y-intercept
5-7 Problem Solving		equation proportional relationship
Topic 5 Topic Review	linear equation slope y-intercept	constant of proportionality proportional relationship rate unit rate

Vocabulary

Language of Math for Topic 6

Lesson	Vocabulary	
	New	**Review**
Readiness 6 Owning a Pet		equations in one variable equations in two variables
6-1 What is a System of Linear Equations in Two Variables?	solution of a system of linear equations system of linear equations	linear equation ordered pair
6-2 Estimating Solutions of Linear Systems by Inspection		parallel lines solution of a system of linear equations system of linear equations
6-3 Solving Systems of Linear Equations by Graphing		solution of a system of linear equations system of linear equations
6-4 Solving Systems of Linear Equations Using Substitution		substitution method
6-5 Solving Systems of Linear Equations Using Addition		addition method substitution method
6-6 Solving Systems of Linear Equations Using Subtraction		addition method substitution method subtraction method
6-7 Problem Solving		addition method graphing method substitution method subtraction method system of linear equations
Topic 6 Topic Review	solution of a system of linear equations system of linear equations	addition method graphing method linear equation ordered pair substitution method subtraction method

Vocabulary

Language of Math for Topic 7

Lesson	Vocabulary	
	New	**Review**
Readiness 7 Skydiving		dependent variable independent variable linear equations in two variables
7-1 Recognizing a Function	function mapping diagram relation vertical-line test	ordered pair
7-2 Representing a Function		function
7-3 Linear Functions	linear function rate of change	slope
7-4 Nonlinear Functions	nonlinear function	linear function rate of change
7-5 Increasing and Decreasing Intervals	interval	label
7-6 Sketching a Function Graph		sketch
7-7 Problem Solving		linear function sketch
Topic 7 Topic Review	function interval linear function nonlinear function rate of change relation vertical-line test	ordered pair slope

Vocabulary

Language of Math for Topic 8

Lesson	Vocabulary	
	New	**Review**
Readiness 8 Snowboarding Competitions		functions linear equations in two variables proportional relationships
8-1 Defining a Linear Function Rule	linear function rule	linear function
8-2 Rate of Change		linear function rate of change
8-3 Initial Value	initial value	linear function rate of change slope y-intercept
8-4 Comparing Two Linear Functions		initial value linear function rate of change
8-5 Constructing a Function to Model a Linear Relationship		initial value linear function linear function rule rate of change
8-6 Problem Solving		linear function
Topic 8 Topic Review	initial value linear function rule	linear function rate of change slope y-intercept

Vocabulary

Language of Math for Topic 9

Lesson	Vocabulary	
	New	**Review**
Readiness 9 Computer-Aided Design		coordinate plane polygons reflect *x*-axis *y*-axis
9-1 Translations	image rigid motion transformation translation	vertex of a polygon
9-2 Reflections	line of reflection reflection	rigid motion transformation
9-3 Rotations	angle of rotation center of rotation rotation	rigid motion transformation
9-4 Congruent Figures	congruent figures	rigid motion
9-5 Problem Solving		rigid motion
Topic 9 Topic Review	congruent figures image reflection rigid motion rotation transformation translation	vertex of a polygon

Vocabulary

Language of Math for Topic 10

Lesson	Vocabulary	
	New	**Review**
Readiness 10 Air Travel		constant of proportionality scale drawing slope
10-1 Dilations	dilation enlargement reduction scale factor	transformation
10-2 Similar Figures	similar figures	dilation rigid motion
10-3 Relating Similar Triangles and Slope		similar figures slope
10-4 Problem Solving		dilation scale drawing rigid motion
Topic 10 Topic Review	dilation scale factor similar figures	rigid motion slope transformation

Vocabulary

Language of Math for Topic 11

Lesson	Vocabulary	
	New	Review
Readiness 11 Photography		parallel similar
11-1 Angles, Lines, and Transversals	alternate interior angles corresponding angles transversal	congruent parallel lines
11-2 Reasoning and Parallel Lines	deductive reasoning	alternate interior angles corresponding angles parallel lines transversal
11-3 Interior Angles of Triangles		angle
11-4 Exterior Angles of Triangles	exterior angle of a triangle remote interior angles	straight angle
11-5 Angle-Angle Triangle Similarity		similar
11-6 Problem Solving		similar
Topic 11 Topic Review	alternate interior angles corresponding angles deductive reasoning exterior angle of a triangle remote interior angles transversal	angle congruent parallel lines straight angle

Vocabulary

Language of Math for Topic 12

Lesson	Vocabulary	
	New	**Review**
Readiness 12 Designing a Billboard		distance on the coordinate plane squared numbers
12-1 Reasoning and Proof	proof theorem	conjecture
12-2 The Pythagorean Theorem	hypotenuse leg of a right triangle Pythagorean Theorem	pyramid slant height
12-3 Finding Unknown Leg Lengths		hypotenuse leg of a right triangle pyramid Pythagorean Theorem slant height
12-4 The Converse of the Pythagorean Theorem	Converse of the Pythagorean Theorem	hypotenuse leg of a right triangle Pythagorean Theorem
12-5 Distance in the Coordinate Plane		equilateral triangle isosceles triangle Pythagorean Theorem scalene triangle
12-6 Problem Solving		surface area of a pyramid
Topic 12 Topic Review	Converse of the Pythagorean Theorem hypotenuse leg of a right triangle proof Pythagorean Theorem theorem	conjecture pyramid slant height

Vocabulary

Language of Math for Topic 13

Lesson	Vocabulary	
	New	**Review**
Readiness 13 Sand Sculptures		area of a circle prism pyramid surface area volume
13-1 Surface Areas of Cylinders	base cylinder height lateral area lateral surface right cylinder surface area	net surface area
13-2 Volumes of Cylinders	volume	base cylinder height
13-3 Surface Areas of Cones	base cone height lateral area lateral surface right cone slant height surface area vertex	base area
13-4 Volumes of Cones	volume	base area cone height
13-5 Surface Areas of Spheres	radius sphere surface area	lateral area of a cylinder
13-6 Volumes of Spheres	volume of a sphere	volume of a cylinder
13-7 Problem Solving		cone cylinder
Topic 13 Topic Review	cone cylinder lateral area sphere surface area volume	net surface area

Vocabulary

Language of Math for Topic 14

Lesson	Vocabulary	
	New	**Review**
Readiness 14 Marching Bands		coordinate plane linear equations in two variables
14-1 Interpreting a Scatter Plot	scatter plot	ordered pair
14-2 Constructing a Scatter Plot		scatter plot
14-3 Investigating Patterns – Clustering and Outliers	cluster gap outlier	scatter plot
14-4 Investigating Patterns – Association		cluster outlier scatter plot
14-5 Linear Models – Fitting a Straight Line	trend line	scatter plot slope slope-intercept form y-intercept
14-6 Using the Equation of a Linear Model		scatter plot trend line
14-7 Problem Solving		outlier trend line
Topic 14 Topic Review	cluster gap outlier scatter plot trend line	ordered pair slope slope-intercept form y-intercept

Vocabulary

Language of Math for Topic 15

Lesson	Vocabulary	
	New	**Review**
Readiness 15 Road Trip!		histogram ratio
15-1 Bivariate Categorical Data	bivariate categorical data bivariate data categorical data measurement data	variable
15-2 Constructing Two-Way Frequency Tables	two-way frequency table two-way table	bivariate categorical data
15-3 Interpreting Two-Way Frequency Tables		two-way frequency table
15-4 Constructing Two-Way Relative Frequency Tables	two-way relative frequency table	population two-way frequency table
15-5 Interpreting Two-Way Relative Frequency Tables		two-way frequency table two-way relative frequency table
15-6 Choosing a Measure of Frequency		two-way frequency table two-way relative frequency table
15-7 Problem Solving		explain
Topic 15 Topic Review	bivariate categorical data bivariate data categorical data measurement data two-way frequency table two-way relative frequency table	variable population

This page intentionally left blank.

This page intentionally left blank.

Expressing Rational Numbers with Decimal Expansions

CCSS: 8.NS.A.1: ... Understand informally that every ... numbers show that the decimal expansion repeats eventually, and convert a decimal expansion which repeats eventually into a rational number.

Digital
Resources

Launch

MP2, MP8

The workers at the local lasagna shack share their tips evenly and entirely at the end of each night. A war of words always erupts when they cannot seem to share the last dollar entirely evenly.

Which nights will the workers argue? Why?

Day	Last Dollar	Number of Workers	Even Split
M	$1	2	
T	$1	4	
W	$1	3	
TH	$1	5	
F	$1	6	

Reflect Suppose you could divide the last dollar to as many decimal places as needed. Would that solve all the problems of dividing the money evenly?

_____

_____

_____

_____

_____

Got It?

PART 1 Got It

Wheels on some in-line skates can be removed using a $\frac{5}{32}$-in. Allen wrench. What is $\frac{5}{32}$ written as a decimal?

PART 2 Got It

Elena Kagan's confirmation to the U.S. Supreme Court was historic. For the first time, 3 of the 9 justices on the court were female. What is $\frac{3}{9}$ written as a decimal?

Got It?

PART 3 Got It

There are two parking lots near a concert hall. The covered parking lot is $\frac{5}{6}$ mi away. The open-air parking lot is 0.8 mi away. Which parking lot is closer to the concert hall? Explain.

Close and Check

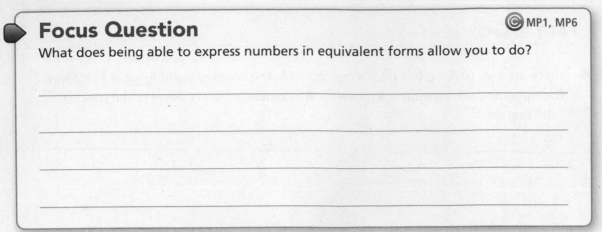

Focus Question

MP1, MP6

What does being able to express numbers in equivalent forms allow you to do?

_____

_____

_____

_____

Do you know HOW?

1. What is $\frac{1}{8}$ written as a decimal?

2. Use = or ≠ to correctly complete each statement.

$\frac{11}{12}$ ☐ 0.916

$-\frac{15}{4}$ ☐ −3.75

$\frac{5}{7}$ ☐ $0.\overline{714285}$

$-\frac{1}{12}$ ☐ $-0.58\overline{3}$

3. The North Vista hiking trail is $\frac{11}{16}$ mi. The Scenic Overlook trail is 0.688 mi. Use <, > , or = to correctly complete the statement.

$\frac{11}{16}$ ☐ 0.688

Do you UNDERSTAND?

4. Error Analysis A classmate says that $0.\overline{285714}$ is not a rational number because it does not terminate. Explain her error.

_____

_____

_____

_____

5. Reasoning Two chefs are trying to break the world's record for the longest strand of spaghetti. Chef A measures his spaghetti strand to be $503\frac{2}{3}$ ft. Chef B measures his spaghetti strand to be $503.\overline{66}$ ft. Since $503.\overline{66}$ rounds to 503.7, the judges declare Chef B the winner. Explain why Chef A should protest the judges' decision.

_____

_____

_____

_____

Exploring Irrational Numbers

Digital Resources

CCSS: 8.NS.A.1: Know that numbers that are not rational are called irrational. Understand informally that every number has a decimal expansion; for rational numbers show that the decimal expansion repeats eventually ... .

Launch

© MP1, MP6

Complete the table and then draw each square. Provide exact lengths. Describe any problems you have.

	Side Length	Area
Square 1		1 unit²
Square 2		2 units²
Square 3		4 units²

Square 1	Square 2	Square 3

Reflect Do you think you could find an exact side length for all of the squares if you kept trying? Explain.

_____

_____

_____

_____

Got It?

PART 1 Got It

Which numbers are irrational?

I. $\sqrt{25}$ II. $\sqrt{50}$ III. $\sqrt{125}$

PART 2 Got It

Which number is *not* irrational? Assume each pattern continues.

I.   3.202002000200002…
II. 3.213213213213…
III. 3.121221222…

PART 3 Got It

What are all the possible names for $1\frac{2}{9}$?

Close and Check

▶ Focus Question

What is the difference between an irrational number and a rational number? Can a number be both irrational and rational?

_____

_____

_____

_____

▶ Do you know HOW?

1. Circle the irrational numbers.

$\sqrt{111}$ $\sqrt{400}$ $\sqrt{160}$

$\sqrt{144}$ $\sqrt{220}$ $\sqrt{200}$

2. Circle the rational numbers. Assume each pattern continues.

4.014014   6.232342345

0.717717   1.594593592

12.12211222   9.96939693

3. Indicate all the possible names for each number.

	$\sqrt{36}$	$-\frac{1}{6}$	$\sqrt{11}$
Natural Number			
Whole Number			
Integer			
Rational Number			
Irrational Number			
Real Number			

▶ Do you UNDERSTAND?

4. Reasoning Can an irrational number ever be a natural number? A whole number? Explain.

_____

_____

_____

_____

5. Compare and Contrast What is the difference between locating $\frac{3}{5}$ on a number line and locating $\sqrt{5}$ on a number line?

_____

_____

_____

_____

_____

This page intentionally left blank.

Approximating Irrational Numbers

CCSS: 8.NS.A.2: Use rational approximations of irrational numbers to compare the size of irrational numbers, locate them approximately on a number line diagram, and estimate the value of expressions.

Launch

© MP1, MP2

Due to the sauciness of their sauce, the local lasagna shack decides to expand its old square napkin to a new square napkin.

Find the approximate side length of the new square napkin. Explain what you did.

Old Napkin
100 in.²

New Napkin
150 in.²

Reflect Why would it be useful to write the side length of the new square napkin as an approximate length instead of an exact length?

_____

_____

_____

_____

_____

Got It?

PART 1 Got It (1 of 2)

On a number line, between which two consecutive whole numbers would $\sqrt{70}$ be located?

PART 1 Got It (2 of 2)

The square root of an integer n is between 9 and 10. What are all the possible values for n? Explain.

PART 2 Got It (1 of 2)

What is $\sqrt{50}$ to the nearest tenth?

Got It?

Is it possible to find the exact decimal value for $\sqrt{50}$? Explain.

A square has an area of 112 cm². What is the approximate perimeter of the square?

You estimate $\sqrt{112}$ to the nearest tenth. Is the estimated value *rational* or *irrational*? Explain.

Discuss with a classmate
Read your explanation to this problem out loud.
Check for the following:
Is the explanation clear?
Are the key words, such as rational number, used correctly in the explanation?
If not, discuss how to improve the explanation.

Close and Check

Focus Question

How do you estimate an irrational number? Why might you need to be able to estimate an irrational number?

_____

_____

_____

_____

Do you know HOW?

1. On a number line, between which two whole numbers would $\sqrt{136}$ be located?

   [   ] and [   ]

2. The square root of an integer n is between 6 and 7. Write an inequality that expresses all the possible values for n.

   [   ]

3. Which value is farther to the right on a number line?

   2.5^2 $\sqrt{81}$

   [   ]

4. A square sandbox has an area of 42 ft². What is the approximate perimeter of the sandbox to the nearest hundredth?

   [   ]

Do you UNDERSTAND?

5. **Reasoning** Two classmates estimate the location of $\sqrt{60}$ on a number line. One student locates the point at 7.7. The other student says the point is located at 7.75. Can both students be correct? Explain.

   _____

   _____

   _____

   _____

6. **Writing** Pi (π) is an irrational number used to find the circumference and area of circles. Are the circumference and area of a circle actual or estimated measures? Explain.

   _____

   _____

   _____

   _____

Comparing and Ordering Rational and Irrational Numbers

CCSS: 8.NS.A.2: Use rational approximations of irrational numbers to compare the size of irrational numbers, locate them approximately on a number line diagram, and estimate the value of expressions.

Launch

MP4, MP7

For people who prefer pizza, the local lasagna shack also offers thin crust pizzas in three different shapes. Each costs $20.

Which deal is the best and which deal is the worst? Explain.

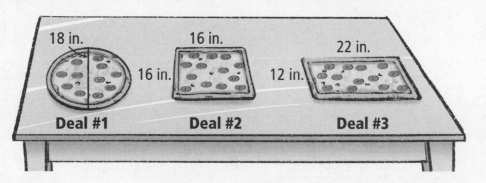

Reflect Do you think all the pizza areas are rational? Explain.

Got It?

PART 1 Got It (1 of 2)

What symbol correctly completes the statement?

$\frac{4}{3}$ ☐ $\sqrt{2}$

PART 1 Got It (2 of 2)

Your friend claims that for any positive real number a, $a > \sqrt{a}$. Is your friend correct? Explain. If your friend is incorrect, give a counterexample in your explanation.

Discuss with a classmate

Compare your explanations for this problem.

What does counterexample mean?

What does counterexample mean for a math problem?

Got It?

PART 2 Got It

Order the values from least to greatest.

π, $\sqrt{11}$, 3.4, 3.1

PART 3 Got It

Order the values from least to greatest.

$-\sqrt{16}$, $-\dfrac{16}{6}$, $\sqrt{8}$, 2.6, $-\sqrt{10}$

Close and Check

MP2, MP3

Focus Question

How can you compare rational and irrational numbers? Why might you want to?

_____

_____

_____

_____

Do you know HOW?

1. Use $<$, $>$, or $=$ to complete each statement.

7 ☐ $\sqrt{7}$

$\sqrt{121}$ ☐ 11

-16 ☐ $-\sqrt{225}$

$\sqrt{8}$ ☐ $\dfrac{21}{8}$

2. Order the values from least to greatest.

$\dfrac{25}{7}$ $\sqrt{3}$ 5.85 4^2 π

☐ ☐ ☐ ☐ ☐

3. Match each point on the number line to the nearest value.

$\sqrt{1}$ ☐ $\dfrac{19}{12}$ ☐

$\sqrt{3}$ ☐ $\dfrac{2}{11}$ ☐

Do you UNDERSTAND?

4. Reasoning The owners want to remake the pizza in Deal #3 of the Launch. Can they make a square pizza with exactly the same area? Explain.

_____

_____

_____

5. Writing What strategies can you use to order the numbers in Exercise 2 without changing them all to decimals?

_____

_____

_____

_____

_____

_____

_____

Problem Solving

CCSS: 8.NS.A.1: Know that numbers that are not rational are called irrational … and convert a decimal expansion which repeats eventually into a rational number. **8.NS.A.2:** Use rational approximations of irrational numbers to … estimate the value of expressions.

Launch

© MP5, MP6

Your friend said the square root of 14 is somewhere in between 3 and 4 as shown.

Explain whether you agree. Then show where would be a more precise spot to place the square root of 14 and tell why your estimate is better.

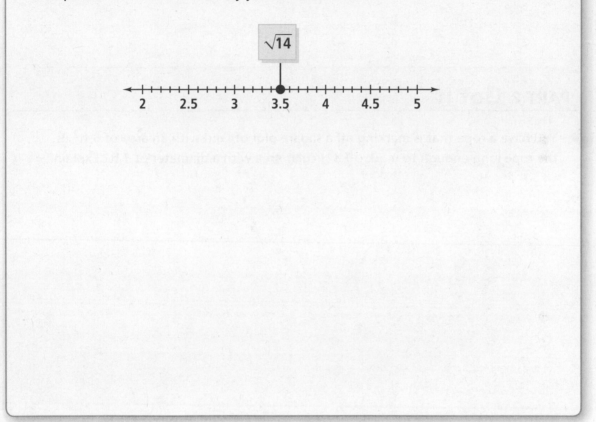

Reflect When is precision important and when is it not so important? Provide an example for each.

_____

_____

_____

_____

Got It?

PART 1 Got It

If $x = 12$, what is the smallest natural number y that makes $\sqrt{x^2 + y^2}$ rational?

PART 2 Got It

You have a rope that is marking off a square plot of land with an area of 6 ft². Is the rope long enough to mark off a circular area with a diameter of 3 ft? Explain.

Got It?

PART 3 Got It (1 of 2)

Write $0.\overline{24}$ as a fraction in simplest form.

PART 3 Got It (2 of 2)

Write $0.5\overline{3}$ as a fraction in simplest form.

Close and Check

How is solving a problem that includes rational numbers similar to solving a problem that includes irrational numbers? How is it different?

Do you know HOW?

1. If $x = 6$, what is the smallest natural number y that makes $\sqrt{x^2 + y^2}$ rational?

   $y = $

2. A carnival ride must be enclosed within a fence. The ride requires 676 ft² of space to operate. What is the minimum number of feet of fencing required to enclose the ride?

    ft

3. A square billboard is shown below. What is the approximate length and width of the billboard to the nearest hundredth?

   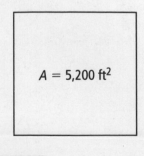

   $A = 5,200$ ft²

Do you UNDERSTAND?

4. **Reasoning** A square pool with side lengths of 16 ft sells for $\frac{2}{3}$ the price of a circular pool with a diameter of 18 ft. If the shape does not matter, which is the better deal? Explain.

5. **Error Analysis** Your friend says that 0.2 and $0.\overline{2}$ can both be written as the fraction $\frac{1}{5}$. Explain his mistake.

1-R Topic Review

New Vocabulary: irrational numbers, perfect square, real numbers, repeating decimal, square root, terminating decimal
Review Vocabulary: integer, natural numbers, rational numbers, whole numbers

Vocabulary Review

Identify two challenging vocabulary terms from this topic. Write one vocabulary term in the center oval, and fill in the surrounding boxes with details that will help you better understand the term.

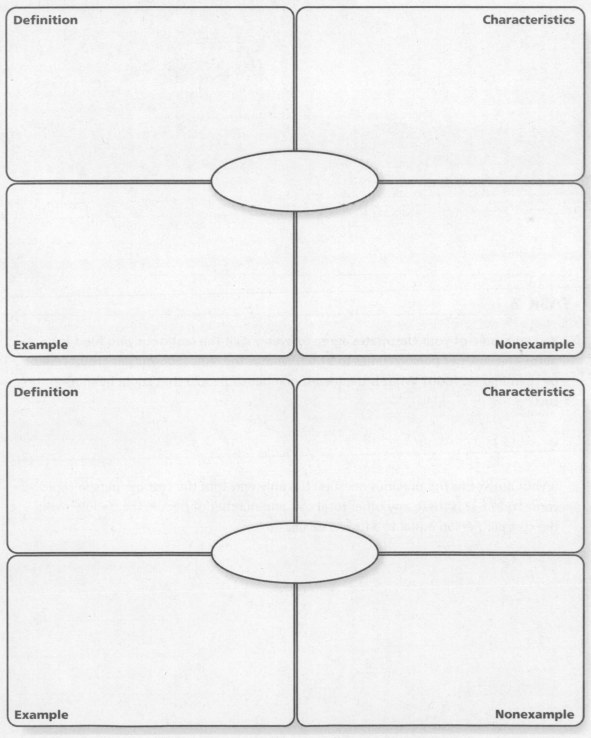

Definition

Characteristics

Example

Nonexample

Definition

Characteristics

Example

Nonexample

Pull It All Together

TASK 1

You want to fence in a square region with twice the area of the square garden shown. To the nearest foot, how much fencing will you need?

7 ft

7 ft

TASK 2

You and some of your classmates agree to evenly split the cost of buying food for a party. The cost per person comes to $1.$\overline{63}$. What is the least amount the group could be spending on food? What is the fewest number of people that could be sharing the cost?

Is your answer to the previous question the only way that the cost per person could come to $1.$\overline{63}$? Is there any other total cost and number of people that would make the cost per person equal to $1.$\overline{63}$? Explain.

Solving Two-Step Equations

CCSS: 8.EE.C.7: Solve linear equations in one variable. **8.EE.C.7b:** Solve linear equations with rational number coefficients, including equations whose solutions require expanding expressions using the distributive property and collecting like terms.

Launch

© MP2, MP4

Two friends shovel snow on a winter Saturday. Some people pay them their fee by handing them cash. Some give them their fee in an envelope. They split the money they make evenly.

What is their shoveling fee? Explain how you know.

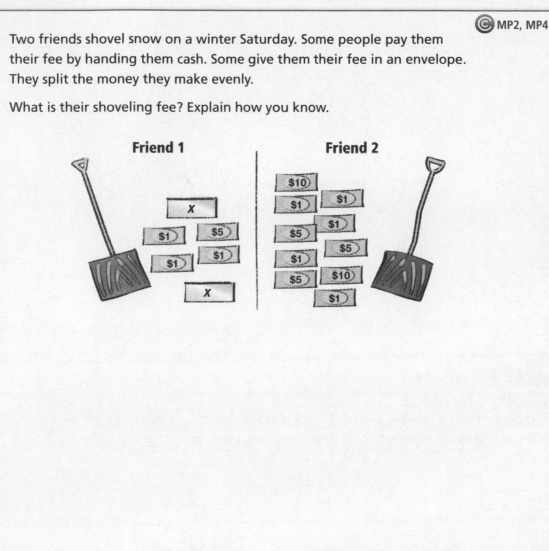

Friend 1   **Friend 2**

Reflect Could you write an equation for this problem? How might that help?

_____

_____

_____

_____

Got It?

PART 1 Got It

Solve $47 = -3 + 8y$.

PART 2 Got It

A family rents a moving van for $34.99 plus $.59 per mile. The bill is $148.86. Write and solve an equation to determine how many miles the family drove.

Discuss with a classmate

Compare the equations that you wrote for the problem.
How were they alike? How were they different?
Was one equation better than the other? What made it the better equation?

Got It?

PART 3 Got It

A plumber buys 20 feet of pipe in February and 35 feet of pipe in March. He spends a total of $384.45. What is the cost of the pipe, per foot?

Close and Check

Focus Question

What kinds of problems need two operations?

_____

_____

_____

_____

Do you know HOW?

1. Solve for x.

$$63 = 12x - 9$$

$x = \boxed{}$

2. A cell phone plan includes a monthly rate of $19.95 plus $0.55 per minute for international calls. The bill is $95.30. Write and solve an equation to determine how many minutes were spent on international calls.

3. A family buys 132 ft² of carpet for the guest bedroom and 270 ft² of carpet for the family room. They spend $1,201.98 on new carpet. What is the average cost per square foot for the new carpeting?

Do you UNDERSTAND?

4. Reasoning Which operation did you use first to solve Exercise 1? Explain.

_____

_____

_____

_____

_____

5. Error Analysis A classmate solves the equation shown. Explain his error and tell how you would solve it.

$$1.25x + 7.4 = 10.4$$
$$100(1.25x) + 10(7.4) = 10(10.4)$$
$$125x + 74 = 104$$
$$125x = 30$$
$$x = 0.24$$

_____

_____

_____

_____

Writing and Solving Equations with Variables on Both Sides

CCSS: 8.EE.C.7: Solve linear equations in one variable. **8.EE.C.7b:** Solve linear equations with rational number coefficients, including equations whose solutions require expanding expressions using the distributive property and collecting like terms.

Launch

© MP2, MP4

Two friends mow lawns on a spring Saturday. Some people pay them their fee by handing them cash. Some people give them their fee in an envelope. They split the money they make evenly.

What is their lawn-mowing fee? Explain how you know.

Friend 1

$1 $1
$5 $5
X
X

Friend 2

$10
$1 $1 $1
$10
$10 $1
$10 $1
$1
X

Reflect In the snow-shoveling problem in Lesson 2-1, only one friend had an envelope. The other friend had all cash. Was this problem more difficult because both friends had envelopes? Explain.

_____

_____

_____

_____

Got It?

PART 1 Got It

What is the value of x when the expression $12x + 7$ equals the expression $-8 + 13x$? Use algebra tiles to model the equation.

PART 2 Got It

A tree is 4 feet high when planted. It grows at a rate of 2.5 feet every year. A second tree is 6.5 feet high when planted. It grows at a rate of 2 feet every year. In how many years will the trees be equal in height?

PART 3 Got It

Solve $210t - 68 = 56t + 1{,}164$.

Close and Check

Focus Question

Why do some equations have the same variable on both sides?

_____

_____

_____

_____

Do you know HOW?

1. What is the value of x when the expression $3x + 6$ equals the expression $-15 + 6x$?

   $x = $ ☐

2. Two friends race. The first friend gets a head start and runs at a steady rate of 0.20 miles per minute. The second friend waits 1 minute and then runs at a steady rate of 0.25 miles per minute. How long will it take for the second runner to catch up with the first?

   ☐

3. Solve $72x + 436 = -96x + 1108$.

   ☐

4. You have $12.50 in a savings account. You deposit $7.25 more each week. Your friend has $32.50 in a savings account. She deposits $5.25 more each week. In how many weeks will the amount of money in the accounts be equal?

   ☐ weeks

Do you UNDERSTAND?

5. **Reasoning** If the two friends in Exercise 2 race for 4 miles at their constant rates, who will win the race? Explain.

   _____

   _____

   _____

   _____

6. **Compare and Contrast** How is solving an equation with the variable on both sides of the equation the same as and different from solving an equation with the variable on one side of the equation?

   _____

   _____

   _____

   _____

   _____

   _____

Solving Equations Using the Distributive Property

CCSS: 8.EE.C.7b: Solve linear equations with rational number coefficients, including equations whose solutions require expanding expressions using the distributive property and collecting like terms.

Launch

© MP2, MP6

Match the equivalent expressions. Tell how you know your matches are correct.

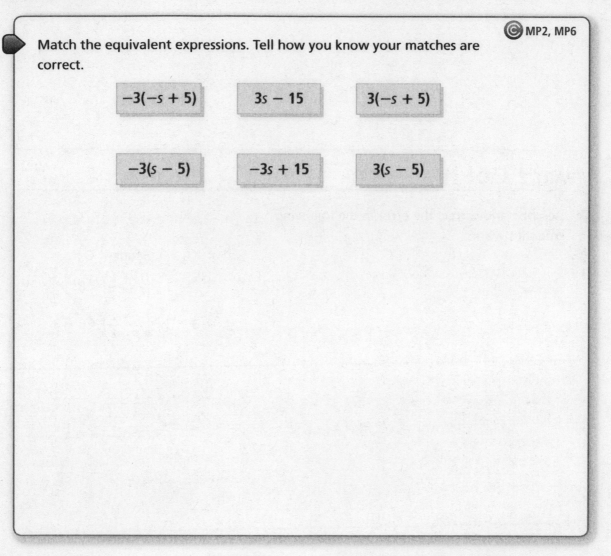

$-3(-s + 5)$ $3s - 15$ $3(-s + 5)$

$-3(s - 5)$ $-3s + 15$ $3(s - 5)$

Reflect Which expressions were the simplest to match? Which were the hardest to match? Explain.

_____

_____

_____

_____

Got It?

PART 1 Got It

Use the Distributive Property to solve $3e - 8 = 2(e - 4)$.

PART 2 Got It

Describe and correct the error in the following student's work.

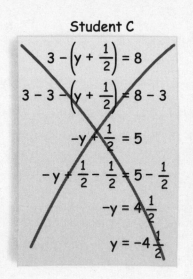

Student C

$$3 - \left(y + \frac{1}{2}\right) = 8$$

$$3 - 3 - \left(y + \frac{1}{2}\right) = 8 - 3$$

$$-y + \frac{1}{2} = 5$$

$$-y + \frac{1}{2} - \frac{1}{2} = 5 - \frac{1}{2}$$

$$-y = 4\frac{1}{2}$$

$$y = -4\frac{1}{2}$$

Got It?

The length of a rectangle is 7 ft longer than its width. The perimeter of the rectangle is 26 ft. Write an equation to represent the perimeter in terms of its width *w*. What is the length of the rectangle?

Discuss with a classmate

Draw a diagram of the rectangle and label all the given information from the problem. Then explain what information you used to write the equation to solve the problem. If your equations don't agree, find the error in the reasoning for the equation that contains an error.

Close and Check

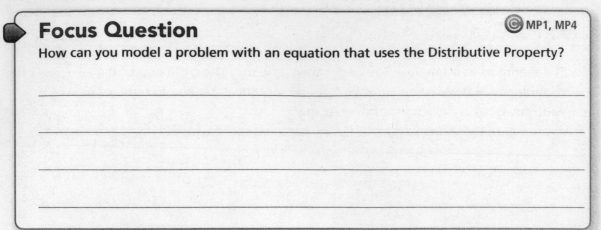

Focus Question

MP1, MP4

How can you model a problem with an equation that uses the Distributive Property?

_____

_____

_____

_____

 ## Do you know **HOW?**

1. Use the Distributive Property to solve $3(11r - 13) = -7r + 57 + 32r$.

   [ ]

2. Circle the correct solution to the equation $\frac{7}{9}x - 6 = 17$.

   A. $\frac{9}{7}\left(\frac{7}{9}x\right) - 6 = \frac{9}{7}(17)$

   $x - 6 = \frac{153}{7}$

   $x = \frac{153}{7} + \frac{42}{7}$

   $x = \frac{195}{7}$

   B. $\frac{7}{9}x = 17 + 6$

   $\frac{9}{7}\left(\frac{7}{9}x\right) = \frac{9}{7}(23)$

   $x = \frac{207}{7}$

3. The width of a rectangle is 17 yd shorter than the length. The perimeter of the rectangle is 126 yd. Find the width of the rectangle.

   [ ]

 ## Do you **UNDERSTAND?**

4. **Error Analysis** Explain the error made in the incorrect solution in Exercise 2.

   _____

   _____

   _____

   _____

   _____

5. **Reasoning** Write an equation for the perimeter of the rectangle in Exercise 3 in terms of the length ℓ. How is this equation different than an equation for the perimeter in terms of the width w?

   _____

   _____

   _____

   _____

   _____

   _____

Solutions – One, None, or Infinitely Many

CCSS: 8.EE.C.7: Solve linear equations in one variable. 8.EE.C.7a: Give examples of linear equations … with one solution, infinitely many solutions, or no solutions. Show which … is the case by successively transforming the given equation into simpler forms … .

Digital Resources

Launch

Evaluate each expression using different values for *s*. Then, tell what you know about the expressions.

© MP2, MP7, MP8

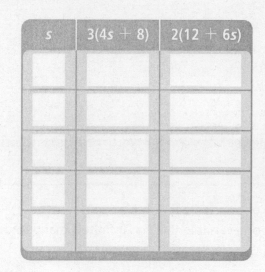

s	3(4s + 8)	2(12 + 6s)

Reflect Could you have reached the same conclusion about the expressions without trying different values for *s*? Explain.

_____

_____

_____

_____

_____

Got It?

PART 1 Got It (1 of 2)

What should you conclude if, after solving an equation, the result is $\frac{1}{2} = \frac{2}{3}$?

PART 1 Got It (2 of 2)

a. Write a linear equation in one variable that has no solution.

b. Write a linear equation in one variable that has infinitely many solutions.

PART 2 Got It (1 of 2)

Solve $4(n - 2) - 1 = 5n - n + 9$.

Got It?

At what point in the solution below do you first recognize that the equation has no solution? Explain.

Use the Distributive Property.

Combine like terms.

Subtract $4n$ from each side.

Combine like terms.

Simplify.

$$4(n - 2) - 1 = 5n - n + 9$$
$$4n - 8 - 1 = 5n - n + 9$$
$$4n - 9 = 4n + 9$$
$$4n - 4n - 9 = 4n - 4n + 9$$
$$0 - 9 = 0 + 9$$
$$-9 \neq 9$$

Solve $r = 5r - 3r - r$.

At what point in the solution below do you first recognize that the equation has infinitely many solution? Explain.

Use the Commutative Property.

Combine like terms.

Subtract $4p$ from each side.

Combine like terms.

$$9 + 4p - 2 = p + 3p + 7$$
$$9 - 2 + 4p = p + 3p + 7$$
$$7 + 4p = 4p + 7$$
$$7 + 4p - 4p = 4p - 4p + 7$$
$$7 = 7$$

Close and Check

Focus Question

What does it mean if an equation is simplified to $0 = 0$? Do all problems have exactly one solution?

_____

_____

_____

_____

▶ Do you know HOW?

1. Write *none*, *one*, or *many* to identify the number of solutions to each equation.

   $\frac{2}{3}x + 15 = \frac{4}{6}x + 15$ [____]

   $6 = 3^2$ [____]

   $2.7y - 9 = 18$ [____]

2. Solve $5(12 - d) + d = 2d - 6$.

   [____]

3. Solve $7t - (t + 5) = 6t + 5$.

   [____]

4. Solve $\frac{2}{3}\left(9s - \frac{3}{2}\right) = s(0.45 + 5) + 1.2$.

   [____]

▶ Do you UNDERSTAND?

5. **Writing** Explain how to identify whether an equation has no solution, one solution, or infinitely many solutions.

   _____

   _____

   _____

   _____

   _____

6. **Error Analysis** A classmate solves the equation $8 + 2(8r - 2r) = 4(3r + 2)$. She says $r = 0$ is the only solution. Is she correct? Explain.

   _____

   _____

   _____

   _____

   _____

Problem Solving

CCSS: 8.EE.C.7: Solve linear equations in one variable. **8.EE.C.7a:** Give examples of linear equations in one variable with one solution, infinitely many solutions, or no solutions … .

Launch

Two friends argue over how much to bill for a two-hour raking job. They charge their normal hourly rate plus $2.75 for lawn bags.

Write and solve equations to show how each friend could be correct. Then tell who you think is right and why.

MP3, MP4

Let's charge $36.

They only owe us $33.25.

Friend 1   **Friend 2**

Reflect How did the money problem context affect the solution to this problem? Explain.

_____

_____

_____

Got It?

PART 1 Got It

A small coffee distributor spends $7,860 per month on business expenses and $4.25 to produce each bag of coffee. It charges $12 for one bag of coffee. How many bags of coffee must the company sell in one month in order for its sales to equal its monthly costs?

PART 2 Got It

When you count by ones from any integer, you are counting consecutive integers. You can represent consecutive integers as x, $x + 1$, $x + 2$, $x + 3$, …

The sum of three consecutive integers is −255. What are the three integers?

PART 3 Got It

Health Club A charges a $160 sign-up fee and $25 per month. Health Club B charges a $40 sign-up fee and $65 per month. In how many months will the total cost of membership at Club A be equal to the total cost of membership at Club B?

Close and Check

Focus Question

 MP4, MP6

If you can describe a situation in two different ways, how do you use that information to solve a problem?

_____

_____

_____

_____

Do you know HOW?

1. A delivery driver earns $7.50 per hour and $2 per delivery. Each week, the driver spends $28 on vehicle maintenance and $86 on gas. If the driver works 40 hours per week, how many deliveries are needed each week to earn $300 a week after expenses?

    deliveries

2. The total cost, after additional fees, for three tickets to the dinner theater is $322.92. The fees include a 2% service charge and a 15% gratuity. What is the cost of one dinner theater ticket before the fees are added?

3. Craft club members pay $39 a year plus $9 for each craft kit. Non-members can buy craft kits for $12 each. How many kits will have to be bought for the price of membership and non-membership to be equal?

   [ ] kits

Do you UNDERSTAND?

4. **Writing** Two students solve the equation. Can both students be correct? Explain.

   $5(3r - 6) = 10r - 10$

Student A	Student B
$15r - 30 = 10r - 10$	$3r - 6 = 2r - 2$
$5r = 20$	$r = 4$
$r = 4$	

   _____

   _____

   _____

   _____

   _____

5. **Reasoning** Would Student B's method work if the equation were $5(3r - 6) = 11r - 14$? Explain.

   _____

   _____

   _____

   _____

This page intentionally left blank.

New Vocabulary: infinitely many solutions, no solution
Review Vocabulary: Commutative Property, Distributive Property, least common multiple, order of operations, solution of an equation

Vocabulary Review

 Identify two challenging vocabulary terms from this topic. Write one vocabulary term in the center oval, and fill in the surrounding boxes with details that will help you better understand the term.

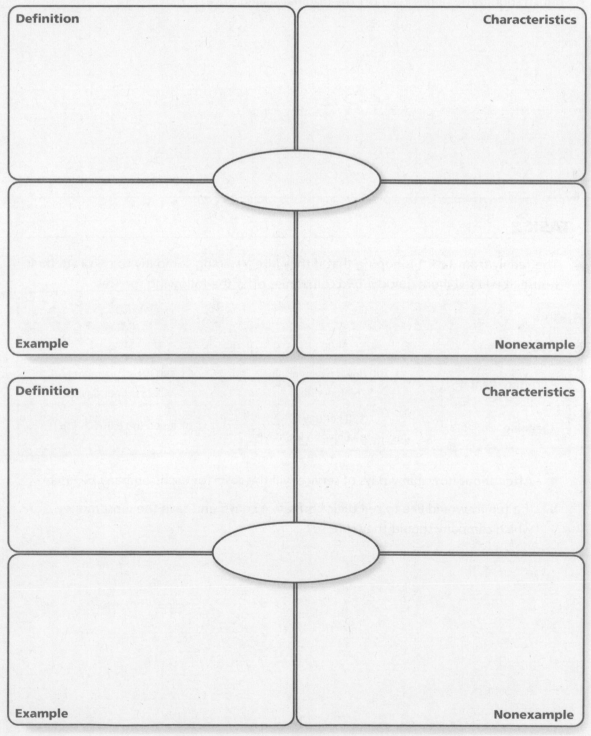

Definition

Characteristics

Example

Nonexample

Definition

Characteristics

Example

Nonexample

Pull It All Together

TASK 1

A family is selling their house and buying a new one. The asking price for their old house is $260,000. However, they would like to sell their house quickly, so they are willing to reduce the price.

20% of the new price must pay a $50,440 down payment on the new house. How much should the family take off the original selling price?

TASK 2

The family from Task 1 is hoping that if they hire a staging company to decorate their house, it will sell more quickly. Two companies offer the following services.

Service	Company A	Company B
Consultation	$600	$950
Furniture Rental	$1,200 down payment plus $26.66 per day	$1,350 down payment plus $23.33 per day
Cleaning	$30 per day (no charge first and last day)	Included (no extra charge)

a. After about how many days of service will the costs for each company be equal?

b. If a family would like to sell their house in 45 days, and save the most money, which company should they choose?

Perfect Squares, Square Roots, and Equations of the Form $x^2 = p$

CCSS: 8.EE.A.2: Use square root and cube root symbols to represent solutions to equations of the form $x^2 = p$ and x^3 and p, where p is a positive rational number. Evaluate square roots of small perfect squares and cube roots of small perfect cubes.

Launch

Ⓒ MP3, MP6

Your friend claims that x^2 is the same as $2x$. Tell how he could have come to that conclusion. Explain whether you agree.

They're the same, right?

x^2 $2x$

Reflect When have you used expressions with exponents like x^2 in mathematics before? Explain.

_____

_____

_____

_____

Got It?

PART 1 Got It

Solve $y^2 = 625$.

PART 2 Got It

Solve $y^2 = \frac{4}{9}$.

Got It?

PART 3 Got It

A square painting has an area of 460 cm². What is the length of one side of the painting to the nearest tenth of a centimeter?

Close and Check

 Focus Question   © MP7, MP8

How can you apply what you know about squares and square roots to write and solve equations of the form $x^2 = p$? How can you use equations in that form?

_____

_____

_____

_____

 ## Do you know HOW?

1. Solve each equation.

   A. $x^2 = 36$ ⬚

   B. $x^2 = 64$ ⬚

   C. $x^2 = 400$ ⬚

   D. $x^2 = 121$ ⬚

2. Solve $y^2 = \dfrac{144}{169}$.

   ⬚

3. A square flower garden has an area of 136 ft². Find the length of one side of the garden to the nearest tenth of a foot.

   ⬚ ft

4. A square playground has an area of 1,500 ft². Find the length of one side of the playground to the nearest tenth of a foot.

   ⬚ ft

Do you UNDERSTAND?

5. **Vocabulary** What is the relationship between perfect squares and square roots? Give an example.

   _____

   _____

   _____

   _____

   _____

6. **Error Analysis** The square-shaped downtown region of a town has an area of 144 km². Your friend says the length of one side can be represented by $\sqrt{144} = \pm 12$. Explain the error she made in her solution.

   _____

   _____

   _____

   _____

   _____

Perfect Cubes, Cube Roots, and Equations of the Form $x^3 = p$

CCSS: 8.EE.A.2: Use square root and cube root symbols to represent solutions to equations of the form $x^2 = p$ and $x^3 = p$, where p is a positive rational number. Evaluate square roots of small perfect squares and cube roots of small perfect cubes.

Launch

Ⓒ MP1, MP6

Draw a line from each measurement to the figure it could represent. Explain how you know you are correct.

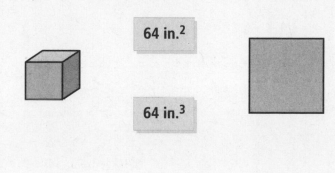

64 in.²

64 in.³

Reflect Could one of the measurements somehow represent something about both figures? Could the other?

_____

_____

_____

_____

Got It?

Solve $y^3 = -64$.

Solve $y^3 = \frac{1}{1000}$.

Got It?

PART 3 Got It

A mailing carton in the shape of a cube has a volume of 684 cubic inches. What is the length of one side of the carton to the nearest tenth of an inch?

Close and Check

Focus Question

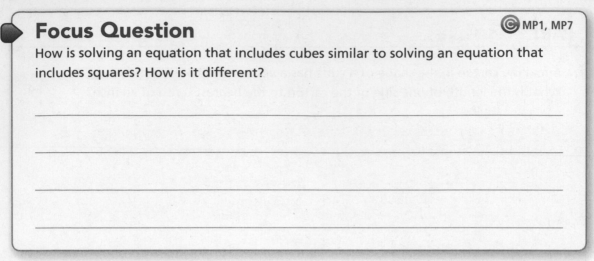

Ⓖ MP1, MP7

How is solving an equation that includes cubes similar to solving an equation that includes squares? How is it different?

_____

_____

_____

_____

▶ Do you know **HOW?**

1. Solve each equation.

   A. $x^3 = 343$ ☐

   B. $x^3 = -1,000$ ☐

   C. $x^3 = -729$ ☐

   D. $x^3 = 216$ ☐

2. Solve $y^3 = \frac{27}{512}$.

   ☐

3. A storage unit in the shape of a cube has a volume of 3,000 cubic feet. Find the length of one side of the storage unit to the nearest tenth of a foot.

   ☐ ft

4. An abstract sculpture in the shape of a cube has a volume of 925 ft³. Find the approximate length of one side of the sculpture to the nearest tenth of a foot.

   ☐ ft

▶ Do you **UNDERSTAND?**

5. **Error Analysis** A salesperson says the volume of a cube-shaped birdcage is 64 ft³. What error does the salesperson make when solving the equation? Write the correct solution and explain what it means.

$$x^3 = 64$$
$$\sqrt[3]{x^3} = \sqrt[3]{64}$$
$$x = \pm 4$$

_____

_____

_____

_____

6. **Reasoning** Can the cube root of a positive number ever be negative? Explain.

_____

_____

_____

_____

_____

Exponents and Multiplication

Digital Resources

CCSS: **8.EE.A.1:** Know and apply the properties of integer exponents to generate equivalent numerical expressions. *For example, $3^2 \times 3^{-5} = 3^{-3} = \frac{1}{3^3} = \frac{1}{27}$.*

Launch

Ⓒ MP3, MP7

The city's second-best scientist's first rocket fails to reach orbit. He promises his second rocket will fly twice as fast as his first and his third rocket will fly twice as fast as the second.

How fast will Rockets 2 and 3 fly? Show how you know.

Rocket 1
2^{14} mph

Rocket 2

Rocket 3

Reflect What do you know about the factors in the expression 2^{14}? Explain.

_____

_____

_____

_____

Got It?

PART 1 Got It (1 of 2)

Simplify the expression.

$3y^4 \cdot 5y^7$

PART 1 Got It (2 of 2)

Does $x^8 \cdot x^2$ have the same value as $x^5 \cdot x^5$? Justify your answer.

Discuss with a classmate

Compare your answers to this problem.

What steps did you take to justify your answers?

Test your answers using replacements for the variable x and see if your explanations are still valid. If they are not, revise them as needed.

Got It?

PART 2 Got It

Simplify the expression.

$(g^9)^6$

PART 3 Got It

Simplify the expression.

$(2s^5t^9)^4$

Close and Check

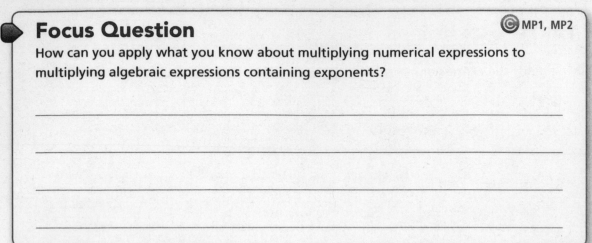

Focus Question

How can you apply what you know about multiplying numerical expressions to multiplying algebraic expressions containing exponents?

_____

_____

_____

_____

Do you know HOW?

1. Simplify the expression.
$4x^6 \cdot 12x^9$

2. Simplify the expression.
$(f^8)^3$

3. Simplify the expression.
$(4st)^4$

4. Simplify the expression.
$(7q^7r^3)^3$

5. Circle the expression(s) that is equivalent to $216a^9b^{15}c^{27}$.

A. $(72a^6b^{12}c^{24})^3$

B. $(72a^3b^5c^9)^3$

C. $(6a^6b^{12}c^{24})^3$

D. $(6a^3b^5c^9)^3$

Do you UNDERSTAND?

6. Writing Use arithmetic to prove it is incorrect to add the exponents of unlike bases. Use the equation $a^2b^2 \neq (ab)^4$.

_____

_____

_____

_____

7. Error Analysis A classmate says $3s^4 \cdot 5s^2 = (15s)^6$. Explain why your classmate is incorrect. Rewrite the equation to make a true statement.

_____

_____

_____

_____

_____

_____

_____

Exponents and Division

CCSS: 8.EE.A.1: Know and apply the properties of integer exponents to generate equivalent numerical expressions. *For example, $3^2 \times 3^{-5} = 3^{-3} = \frac{1}{3^3} = \frac{1}{27}$.*

Launch

© MP1, MP2, MP7

The city's second-best scientist likes to look overly complex. That's why he's second best. He presents the cost of a rocket bolt on Rocket 1 as shown.

How much does a bolt really cost? Show how you know.

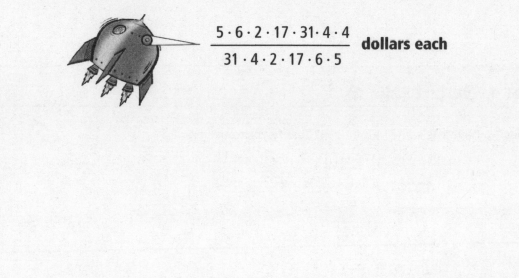

$$\frac{5 \cdot 6 \cdot 2 \cdot 17 \cdot 31 \cdot 4 \cdot 4}{31 \cdot 4 \cdot 2 \cdot 17 \cdot 6 \cdot 5} \textbf{ dollars each}$$

Reflect What was the key to solving this problem? Explain.

_____

_____

_____

_____

_____

Got It?

PART 1 Got It (1 of 2)

Simplify the expression $\dfrac{g^{35}}{g^{23}}$.

PART 1 Got It (2 of 2)

Does $\dfrac{a^{12}}{a^{8}}$ have the same value as $\dfrac{a^{6}}{a^{2}}$? Justify your answer.

PART 2 Got It

Simplify the expression $\left(\dfrac{a^{2}}{4b^{3}}\right)^{4}$.

Close and Check

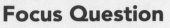
Do you know HOW?

1. Simplify the expression.

$$\frac{x^{27}}{x^{13}}$$

2. Simplify the expression.

$$\frac{r^{55}}{r^{32}}$$

3. Simplify the expression.

$$\left(\frac{2r^9}{3m}\right)^3$$

4. Simplify the expression.

$$\left(\frac{2d^3g^{12}}{4s^{12}w^6}\right)^5$$

Do you UNDERSTAND?

5. **Writing** Can the exponent in the denominator be subtracted from the exponent in the numerator when the bases are different? Explain.

_____

_____

_____

_____

6. **Error Analysis** When asked to simplify the expression, your classmate writes the following:

$$\left(\frac{c^3}{3d^5}\right)^2 = \frac{2c^5}{6d^7}$$

What errors did your classmate make? What should she have written?

_____

_____

_____

_____

This page intentionally left blank.

Zero and Negative Exponents

CCSS: 8.EE.A.1: Know and apply the properties of integer exponents to generate equivalent numerical expressions. *For example,* $3^2 \times 3^{-5} = 3^{-3} = \frac{1}{3^3} = \frac{1}{27}$.

Launch

Complete the table. Describe three patterns you see in the table.

MP7, MP8

2^x	10^x
$2^5 = 32$	$10^5 = 100{,}000$
$2^4 = 16$	$10^4 = 10{,}000$
$2^3 = 8$	$10^3 = 1{,}000$
$2^2 = 4$	$10^2 = 100$
$2^1 =$	$10^1 =$
$2^0 =$	$10^0 =$
$2^{-1} =$	$10^{-1} =$

Reflect Did you figure out the pattern in the left or right column first? Explain.

_____

_____

_____

_____

Got It?

PART 1 Got It

Simplify the expression $(-3.6)^0$.

PART 2 Got It (1 of 2)

Simplify the expression $\dfrac{m^2 n^4}{m^5 n^3}$.

Got It?

PART 2 Got It (2 of 2)

Is -3^{-2} *positive* or *negative*? Justify your answer.

PART 3 Got It

Is 4^{-3} greater than 1, equal to 1, or less than 1?

Close and Check

MP3, MP7

Focus Question

When do you need an exponent that is equal to zero? When do you need an exponent that is negative? What makes these exponents useful?

_____

_____

_____

_____

Do you know HOW?

1. Simplify the expression.

   $\dfrac{n^{15}}{n^{15}}$

2. Simplify the expression.

   $\dfrac{12k^{15}}{3k^{18}}$

3. Tell whether each expression is > 1, < 1, or $= 1$.

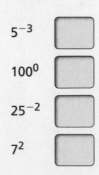

   5^{-3}

   100^{0}

   25^{-2}

   7^{2}

Do you UNDERSTAND?

4. **Reasoning** In the expression $\dfrac{a^3}{a^3}$, why can the variable *not* be equal to 0? Use substitution to justify your argument arithmetically.

   _____

   _____

   _____

   _____

5. **Error Analysis** Your classmate simplified the expression below. Explain his error and write the correct simplified expression.

   $$\frac{6w^{12}}{3w^{12}} = 2w^0 = 2 \cdot 0 = 0$$

   _____

   _____

   _____

   _____

Comparing Expressions with Exponents

CCSS: 8.EE.A.1: Know and apply the properties of integer exponents to generate equivalent numerical expressions. *For example, $3^2 \times 3^{-5} = 3^{-3} = \frac{1}{3^3} = \frac{1}{27}$.*

Launch

Ⓒ MP3, MP6

Use the tiles to create an expression with the least value and an expression with the greatest value. For each expression, you must use each number tile and the negative sign tile in only one location.

Tell how you decided the tile locations.

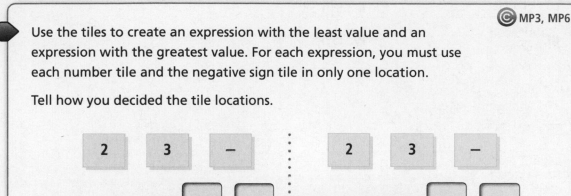

Least Value   Greatest Value

Reflect What did you decide first in solving the problem? Explain.

_____

_____

_____

Got It?

PART 1 Got It

Which expressions are equivalent to 5^8?

I. $5^1 \cdot 5^8$ II. $5^2 \cdot 5^6$

III. $\dfrac{5^{16}}{5^2}$ IV. $(5^2)^4$

PART 2 Got It

Use $<$, $>$, or $=$ to complete the statement.

9^{12} ☐ $\dfrac{9^{36}}{9^3}$

Got It?

PART 3 Got It

Use <, >, or = to complete the statement.

27^5 ☐ $\dfrac{9^8}{3^4}$

Close and Check

Focus Question

What does being able to write expressions with exponents in equivalent forms allow you to do?

_____

_____

_____

_____

Do you know HOW?

1. Which expression(s) is equivalent to 6^{12}?

   I. $2^{10} \cdot 3^2$

   II. $6^0 \cdot 6^{12}$

   III. $(6^{10})^2$

   IV. $(6^2)^6$

2. Use >, <, or = to complete each statement.

   8^0 ☐ $\dfrac{8^3}{1^3}$

   12^6 ☐ $(12^2)^3$

   25^8 ☐ 125^5

   27^{12} ☐ $(9^6)^3$

   $(8^6)^6$ ☐ $(4^4 \cdot 2^2)^6$

Do you UNDERSTAND?

3. **Compare and Contrast** What is the difference between comparing exponential numbers with like bases and comparing those with unlike bases?

   _____

   _____

   _____

   _____

   _____

   _____

4. **Error Analysis** A classmate writes equivalent expressions. Her work is shown below. Is she correct? Explain.

   $(4^2 \cdot 3^2)^6 = (12^4)^6 = 12^{24}$

   _____

   _____

   _____

   _____

Problem Solving

CCSS: 8.EE.A.1: Know and apply the properties of integer exponents to generate equivalent numerical expressions. *For example,* $3^2 \times 3^{-5} = 3^{-3} = \frac{1}{3^3} = \frac{1}{27}.$

Launch

© MP7, MP8

Look for a pattern in the table.

Based on the pattern, what value of x makes the statement $4^{15} = 2^x$ true?

Powers of 4	Powers of 2
$4^2 = 16$	$2^4 = 16$
$4^3 = 64$	$2^6 = 64$
$4^4 = 256$	$2^8 = 256$
$4^5 = 1024$	$2^{10} = 1024$

Reflect What property of exponents did you apply to help you solve this problem?

_____

_____

Did you use an equation to find the value of x? If so, what equation did you use?

_____

_____

_____

Got It?

PART 1 Got It

For what value(s) of m is the expression $3m^5$ reasonable in representing the area of a rectangle?

PART 2 Got It

For what values of a, if any, does $-3a^2 = -243$?
Explain your reasoning.

Close and Check

Do you know HOW?

1. Circle the value(s) of s for which the expression $-9s^3$ is reasonable for representing the volume of a cube.

   A. $s = 0$

   B. s can be any negative number.

   C. s can be any positive number.

2. Circle the value(s) of y for which the expression $35y^2$ is reasonable for representing the number of square yards your friend mows.

   A. $y = 0$

   B. y can be any negative number.

   C. y can be any positive number.

3. For what values of d, if any, will $2d^4 = 1,250$?

Do you UNDERSTAND?

4. **Reasoning** How would the solution to Exercise 3 change if the equation was $2d^4 = -1,250$? How do you know?

   _____

   _____

   _____

   _____

   _____

5. **Error Analysis** Your friend writes an expression to represent the score of a game. Is his expression useful? Explain.

   $$\frac{5p^6}{(p^2)^3}$$

   _____

   _____

   _____

   _____

This page intentionally left blank.

New Vocabulary: cube root, Negative Exponent Property, perfect cube, Zero Exponent Property
Review Vocabulary: base, exponent, inverse operations, perfect square, power, square root

Vocabulary Review

Identify two challenging vocabulary terms from this topic. Write one vocabulary term in the center oval, and fill in the surrounding boxes with details that will help you better understand the term.

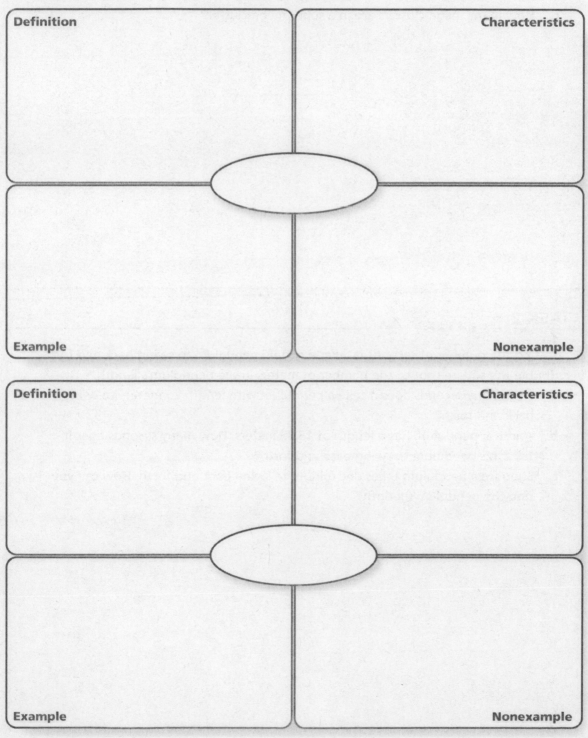

Definition

Characteristics

Example

Nonexample

Definition

Characteristics

Example

Nonexample

Pull It All Together

TASK 1

In a computer game, players collect objects. Objects come in clusters, mega-clusters, and super-mega-clusters. A cluster is 3^2 objects. A mega-cluster is 3^7 clusters. A super-mega-cluster is 3^{11} clusters.

a.   How many objects are in a mega-cluster?

b.   How many objects are in a super-mega-cluster?

c.   How many mega-clusters are in a super-mega-cluster?

TASK 2

To find the number of seconds it takes a certain pendulum to swing back and forth, double the square root of the number of meters in the pendulum's length.

a.   How many seconds does it take a pendulum with length 25 meters to swing back and forth?

b.   Another pendulum has a length of 15.85 meters. How many seconds does it take this pendulum to swing back and forth?

c.   Suppose a pendulum takes one minute to swing back and forth. How can you find the pendulum's length?

Exploring Scientific Notation

CCSS: 8.EE.A.3: Use numbers expressed in the form of a single digit times an integer power of 10 to estimate very large or very small quantities .... **8.EE.A.4:** Perform operations with numbers expressed in scientific notation ....

Launch

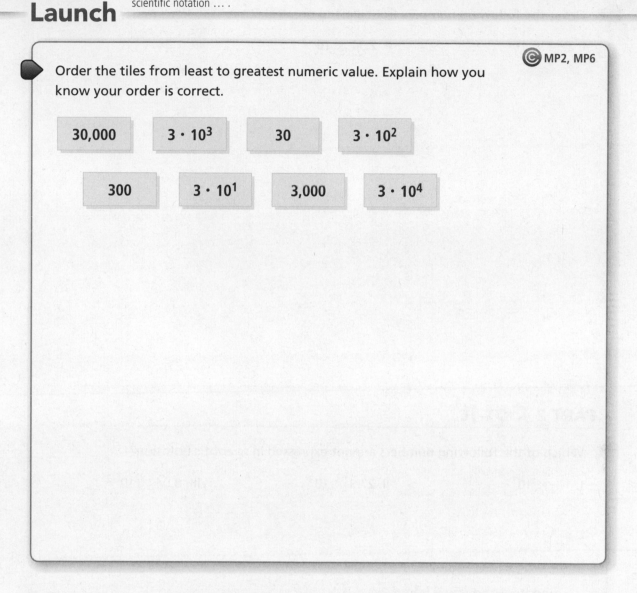

Ⓒ **MP2, MP6**

Order the tiles from least to greatest numeric value. Explain how you know your order is correct.

30,000	$3 \cdot 10^3$	30	$3 \cdot 10^2$

300	$3 \cdot 10^1$	3,000	$3 \cdot 10^4$

Reflect Is there a pattern between the numbers and the expressions? If so, describe it.

_____

_____

_____

_____

Got It?

PART 1 Got It

Order the following numbers from least to greatest.

I. 2.34×10^2

II. 2.34×10^{-2}

III. 2.34

PART 2 Got It

Which of the following numbers are not expressed in scientific notation?

I. 1.7×10^7

II. 27.3×10^3

III. 8.04×10^{-2}

Got It?

PART 3 Got It

Suppose your calculator display shows 7.7E–11. Express this result in scientific notation.

Close and Check

Focus Question
©MP3, MP8

Why might you use powers of 10 to write numbers?

_____

_____

_____

_____

Do you know HOW?

1. Order the numbers from least to greatest.

Least

7.29×10^0 [ ]

7.29×10^{-5} [ ]

7.29×10^3 [ ]

7.29×10^{-3} [ ]

Greatest

2. Circle the numbers that are expressed in scientific notation.

34.5×10^7 5.02×10^3

2×10^9 0.4×10^1

3. Write 745,000 in scientific notation.

[ ]

Do you UNDERSTAND?

4. Reasoning Explain the strategy you used to order the numbers in Exercise 1.

_____

_____

_____

_____

_____

_____

5. Vocabulary How is scientific notation useful in mathematics?

_____

_____

_____

_____

_____

_____

_____

Using Scientific Notation to Describe Quantities

Digital Resources

CCSS: 8.EE.A.3: Use numbers expressed in the form of a single digit times an integer power of 10 to estimate very large or very small quantities, and to express how many times as much one is than the other ... .

Launch

Your friend writes 5×2^6 as a shortcut for writing 1×10^6. Explain your friend's shortcut thinking. Is your friend's thinking more science or fiction?

Shorter is always better!

1×10^6 5×2^6

Reflect Why is it helpful to write numbers in scientific notation using powers of 10? Why is this better than using powers of 2? Explain.

_____

_____

_____

_____

_____

Got It?

PART 1 Got It

Light travels at a constant speed of 186,000 mi/s. Express the speed of light in scientific notation.

Discuss with a classmate

Take turns reading your response to this problem.
How did your prior experiences help you determine a large measurement that could be written in scientific notation? Did you both choose the same type of measurement? Can you think of another measurement different from either of the ones you wrote about?

PART 2 Got It (1 of 2)

The moon is about 2.4×10^5 miles from Earth. Express this distance in standard form.

PART 2 Got It (2 of 2)

Describe at least one large measurement (unrelated to astronomy) that you might want to write in scientific notation rather than in standard form.

Got It?

PART 3 Got It

A microbiologist observes two colonies of bacteria at the same time. The number of bacteria in each colony is shown. The number of bacteria in Colony A is how many times the number of bacteria in Colony B?

Colony A   Colony B

4×10^6 2×10^5

Close and Check

 Focus Question

MP6, MP8

How can positive powers of 10 make large and small numbers easier to write and compare?

_____

_____

_____

_____

Do you know HOW?

1. The X-15 aircraft holds the world speed record at 23,865,600 ft/hr. Express the world record speed in scientific notation.

   [   ]

2. The population on Earth increased by about 7.62×10^8 people during the first decade of the 21st century. Express the population growth in standard form.

    people

3. One giant ant colony is reported to have about 3.06×10^8 worker ants and 1.02×10^6 queen ants. The number of worker ants is how many times the number of queen ants?

   [   ]

Do you UNDERSTAND?

4. **Writing** Your best friend has never learned about scientific notation. Explain how to use scientific notation to rewrite very large numbers.

   _____

   _____

   _____

   _____

   _____

5. **Error Analysis** A friend says the average distance to the moon is 382,500 km. Is the number he wrote accurate? Explain.

   3.825×10^6

   _____

   _____

   _____

Using Scientific Notation to Describe Very Small Quantities

CCSS: 8.EE.A.3: Use numbers expressed in the form of a single digit times an integer power of 10 to estimate very large or very small quantities, and to express how many times as much one is than the other … .

Digital Resources

Launch

© MP2, MP4

Your friend says a zeptometer is 1×10^{-21} based on its standard form. Explain your friend's zepto-reasoning. Is your friend's thinking more science or fiction?

Unit	Scientific Notation (m)	Standard Form (m)
Meter	1×10^0	1
Decimeter	1×10^{-1}	0.1
Centimeter	1×10^{-2}	0.01
Millimeter	1×10^{-3}	0.001
Zeptometer		0.000000000000000000001

Reflect Does it make more sense to use scientific notation or standard form to represent 1 zeptometer?

_____

_____

_____

Got It?

An X-ray can have a wavelength of 0.00000001 m. Express this wavelength in scientific notation.

Wavelengths of visible light range from 0.0000004 m to 0.0000007 m. A nanometer is one-billionth of a meter. Which unit, meters or nanometers, might be more appropriate for measuring the wavelength of light? Explain your reasoning.

Got It?

PART 2 Got It

Express the diameter of the red blood cell shown in standard form.

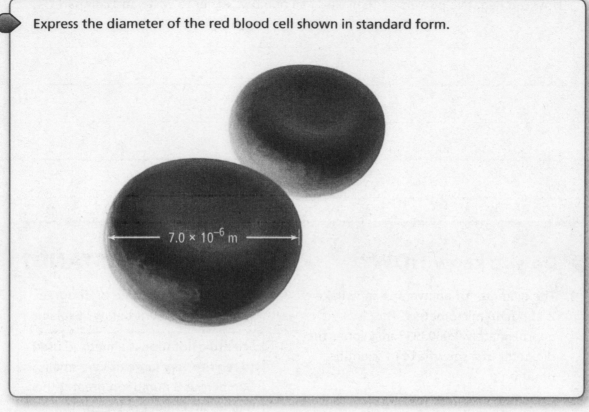

7.0×10^{-6} m

PART 3 Got It

The length of cell A is 3×10^{-4} m and the length of cell B is 3×10^{-5} m. How many times as long is cell A than cell B?

Close and Check

Focus Question

How can negative powers of 10 make small numbers easier to write and compare?

_____

_____

_____

_____

Do you know HOW?

1. The diameter of an average snowflake is about 10 micrometers. That is approximately 0.0003937 in. Express the diameter of a snowflake in scientific notation.

2. The diameters of atoms can vary. One particular atom has a diameter of 5.0×10^{-8} cm. Express the diameter of the atom in standard form.

3. The measurement 8.16 micrometers equals 8.16×10^{-6} meter. The measurement 2.04 centimeters equals 2.04×10^{-2} meter. How many times greater is the centimeter measurement than the micrometer measurement?

Do you UNDERSTAND?

4. **Writing** Do you agree or disagree with the statement below? Explain.

> Scientific notation is a method used to rewrite very large or very small numbers as a number n greater than 0 times an integer power of 10.

_____

_____

_____

_____

5. **Error Analysis** An earthworm travels 0.0000425 miles per second. A friend writes the rate as 4.25×10^5 mps. Explain her error. Write the correct rate in scientific notation.

_____

_____

_____

_____

Operating with Numbers Expressed in Scientific Notation

CCSS: 8.EE.A.3: Use numbers expressed in the form of a single digit times an integer power of 10 … . **8.EE.A.4:** Perform operations with numbers expressed in scientific notation, including problems where both decimal and scientific notation are used.

Launch

MP1, MP6

The scientific notation cards shown represent place values. Arrange at least six of the cards in place-value order to represent a three-digit number.

Then write your number in standard form and explain why the cards you chose represent your number.

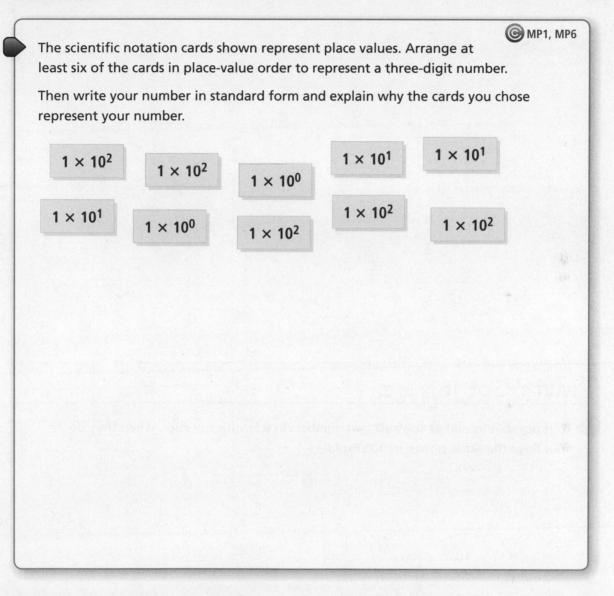

1×10^2 1×10^2 1×10^0 1×10^1 1×10^1

1×10^1 1×10^0 1×10^2 1×10^2 1×10^2

Reflect How is using the cards the same as using place value blocks? How is it different?

Got It?

Simplify $(5.9 \times 10^5) + (4.3 \times 10^5) - (2.2 \times 10^5)$.

Is it possible to add or subtract two numbers in scientific notation when they do not have the same power of 10? Explain.

Got It?

PART 2 Got It

About 1.0×10^8 bacteria live in a human body. If there are 2,000 spectators at a football game, how many bacteria are living in the spectators?

PART 3 Got It

The biggest stars are known as red supergiants. One example, Betelgeuse, is about 300 million miles wide. One AU is about 93,000,000 miles. What is the width of Betelgeuse in AU?

Close and Check

Focus Question

You previously learned how to multiply and divide expressions with exponents. How can you apply what you know to operations with numbers in scientific notation?

_____

_____

_____

_____

 Do you know HOW?

1. Simplify.

   $(6.9 \times 10^{12}) - (2.6 \times 10^{12}) + (3.4 \times 10^{12})$

   [_____]

2. One gram of dust can contain 2.5×10^5 dust mite droppings. The average six-room home collects about 1.5×10^3 grams of dust each month. In scientific notation, how many dust mite droppings can be found in an average home each month?

   [_____] droppings

3. The smallest ant is about 4.9×10^{-4} m in length. The distance around the earth at the equator is about 4×10^7 m. In scientific notation to the nearest tenth, how many of these small ants would it take to circle the earth at the equator?

   [_____] ants

Do you UNDERSTAND?

4. **Compare and Contrast** How are the processes for multiplying and dividing numbers written in scientific notation alike and different?

   _____

   _____

   _____

   _____

5. **Error Analysis** Your friend says this problem has no solution because 8.3 cannot be subtracted from 2.5. Do you agree? Explain.

   > Statistically, 2.5×10^7 plastic beverage bottles are used each day. If 8.3×10^6 bottles are recycled, how many end up in landfills?

   _____

   _____

Problem Solving

CCSS: 8.EE.A.4: Perform operations with numbers expressed in scientific notation .... Use scientific notation and choose units of appropriate size for measurements of very large or very small quantities .... Also, 8.EE.A.1 and 8.EE.A.3.

Launch

MP4, MP7

Approximate population data for adults and children in the most and least populous U.S. states in one year, according to the U.S. Census Bureau, are shown.

What is the total population for each state in scientific notation? Justify your answers.

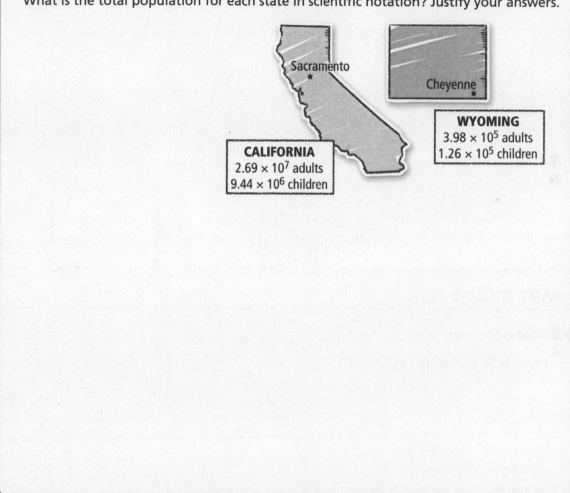

Sacramento

Cheyenne

WYOMING
3.98×10^5 adults
1.26×10^5 children

CALIFORNIA
2.69×10^7 adults
9.44×10^6 children

Reflect How can you tell that California has more people than Wyoming just by comparing the adult and children populations?

_____

_____

_____

_____

Got It?

PART 1 Got It

Which of the following is the most appropriate way to represent the distance from our solar system to our nearest star, Proxima Centauri?

I. 1.3×10^{17} feet   **II.** 4.22 light-years   **III.** 3.97×10^{16} m

PART 2 Got It

What is the value of n?

$1.5 \times 10^{21} = (3 \times 10^{14})(5 \times 10^{n})$

Close and Check

▶ Do you know HOW?

1. It takes light 8.5 minutes to travel from the sun to the earth. Light travels at 9.82×10^8 feet per second. How far does light travel from the sun to the earth? Express this distance in scientific notation using the most appropriate unit from the given list.

   5280 ft = 1760 yd
   1760 yd = 1 mi

2. The area of the world's largest country is about 6.6×10^6 mi². The area of the world's smallest country is about 1.7×10^{-1} mi². About how many times larger is the area of the largest country than the area of the smallest country? Express your answer in scientific notation.

3. Find the value of n.
   $1.887 \times 10^{12} = (5.1 \times 10^8)(3.7 \times 10^n)$

4. Find the value of n.
   $(4.5 \times 10^9) \div (9 \times 10^n) = 5 \times 10^2$

▶ Do you UNDERSTAND?

5. **Reasoning** Explain why you chose the unit of measure that you did in Exercise 1. Explain why you did not choose the others.

   _____

   _____

   _____

   _____

6. **Compare and Contrast** How can understanding operations on exponential numbers help you solve problems involving scientific notation?

   _____

   _____

   _____

   _____

   _____

This page intentionally left blank.

Topic Review

New Vocabulary: scientific notattion
Review Vocabulary: base, exponent, power, standard form

Vocabulary Review

 Identify two challenging vocabulary terms from this topic. Write one vocabulary term in the center oval, and fill in the surrounding boxes with details that will help you better understand the term.

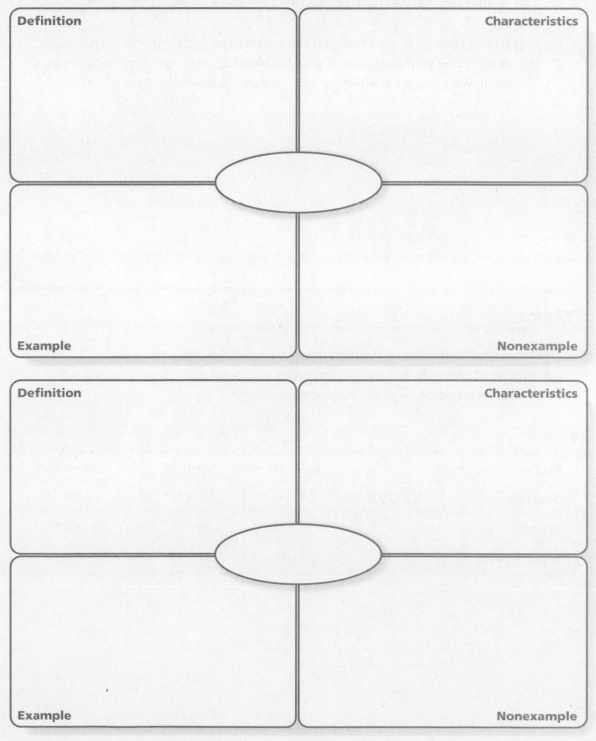

Definition

Characteristics

Example

Nonexample

Definition

Characteristics

Example

Nonexample

Pull It All Together

TASK 1

You want to download music on your computer. You decide that a song file should be 3.9×10^{-3} GB or less to preserve memory space. Your computer has 9 GB of memory space available for song files.

a. You want to download 2,500 songs of your preferred maximum size $(3.9 \times 10^{-3}$ GB). Do you have enough memory space on your computer? Explain.

b. You have a flash drive on which you can transfer the extra music files that might not fit on your computer. If you download 2,500 songs, how many songs will be on your computer and how many songs will be on the flash drive?

TASK 2

The table shows numbers of students in school in 4 states. Determine the percentage of students that are in elementary school for each state. Which state had the greatest percentage of elementary students?

	Elementary	High School	College	Total Students
Kansas		1.65×10^5	176,000	6.67×10^5
New York	2,210,000	1.1×10^6	1.3×10^6	
Oregon		1.91×10^5	2.05×10^5	7.81×10^5
South Carolina	4.74×10^5	230,000	2.17×10^5	

Graphing Proportional Relationships

CCSS: 8.EE.B.5: Graph proportional relationships, interpreting the unit rate as the slope of the graph. Compare two different proportional relationships represented in different ways.

Launch

© MP2, MP6

Make a graph based on the data in the table. Give the graph a title and label the axes so it's clear what the variables could represent.

Independent Variable	Dependent Variable
0	0
1	4
2	8
3	12
8	32

Reflect Does the table represent a proportional relationship? Explain.

_____

_____

_____

_____

_____

Got It?

PART 1 Got It

Your school is selling raffle tickets as a fundraiser. The raffle tickets are sold in groups of 4 for $3. Draw a graph to model this situation where the horizontal axis is the number of raffle tickets purchased and the vertical axis is the total cost.

You have $21. How many raffle tickets can you buy?

PART 2 Got It

At some airports you pay a tax of 14% on the cost of a car rental. Draw a graph to model this situation where the horizontal axis is the cost of the car rental and the vertical axis is the amount of the tax. Is the amount you pay in tax proportional to the cost of your car rental? How do you know?

Got It?

PART 3 Got It

A drill makes a well by tunneling down into the ground. A certain drill can tunnel down 10 m every 8 h. Draw a graph to model this situation where the horizontal axis is time and the vertical axis is the position of the drill head relative to the surface.

Is the position of the drill head relative to the surface proportional to time? How do you know?

Close and Check

Focus Question

© MP2, MP6

What does the graph of a proportional relationship look like? When and how can a graph of a proportional relationship be helpful?

_____

_____

_____

_____

▶ Do you know **HOW?**

1. You earn $4 in Bonus Bucks for each $50 you spend. Complete the graph to model this situation.

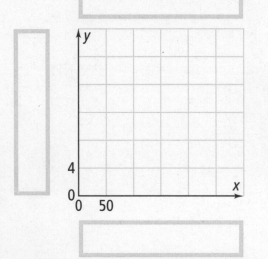

2. A scuba diver descends into the ocean from the surface at a rate of 65 feet per minute. Complete the table of the diver's position relative to the surface.

$$d = -65m$$

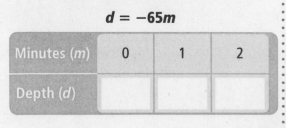

Minutes (*m*)	0	1	2
Depth (*d*)			

▶ Do you **UNDERSTAND?**

3. Writing Based on the graph in Exercise 1, is the relationship between the amount spent and the amount of bonus bucks earned proportional? Explain.

_____

_____

_____

_____

_____

4. Reasoning If the diver in Exercise 2 jumped off a boat into the ocean rather than descending from the surface of the ocean, would the relationship still be proportional?

_____

_____

_____

_____

_____

Linear Equations: $y = mx$

CCSS: 8.EE.B.5: Graph proportional relationships, interpreting the unit rate as the slope of the graph. Compare two different proportional relationships represented in different ways. **8.EE.B.6:** ... derive the equation $y = mx$ for a line through the origin ... .

Launch

© MP3, MP7

How are the lines similar? How are they different? Explain.

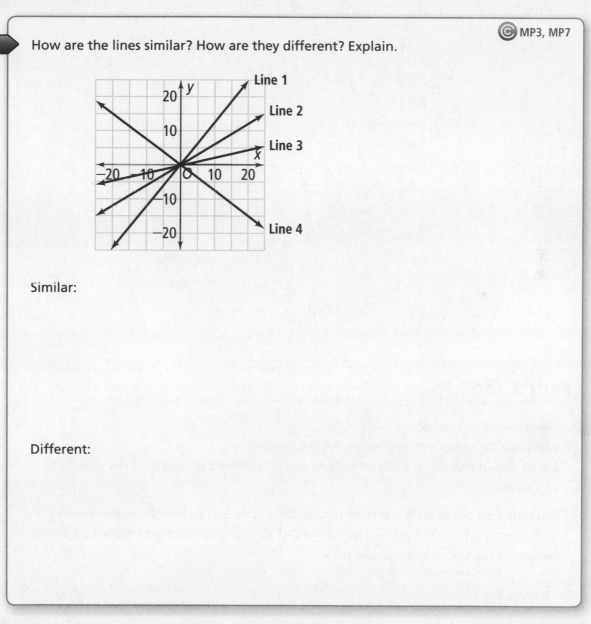

Similar:

Different:

Reflect Is one line more different than the others? Explain.

Got It?

PART 1 Got It

The graph shows the distance *d* a train travels in time *t* at a constant speed *r*.
Write an equation in $d = rt$ form that models the situation shown.

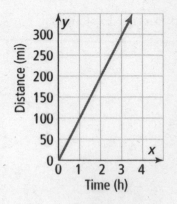

PART 2 Got It

Discuss with a classmate

Compare the equations you wrote for the problem.

Listen as you explain to each other how you determined the parts of the equation you wrote.

A hamburger made with a certain type of beef loses $\frac{1}{4}$ of its weight while cooking. Write an equation that models the weight of a cooked hamburger *y* based on the weight of the uncooked hamburger *x*.

Got It?

PART 3 Got It

The number of miles y a car travels in x hours can be modeled by the equation $y = 65x$. The graph shows the relationship between distance and time for a train. Which vehicle is traveling at a greater speed?

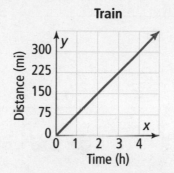

Train

Close and Check

Focus Question

What does it mean for an equation to be linear? What kind of relationships can be modeled by equations in the form $y = mx$?

_____

_____

_____

_____

Do you know HOW?

1. The graph shows the earnings e of an airplane mechanic for a number of weeks w at a constant rate r. Write an equation to model the situation shown.

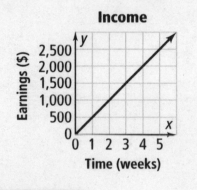

Income

Earnings ($) / Time (weeks)

[_____]

2. A machine manufactures a part in 11 minutes. A newer machine can manufacture the same part 1.5 minutes faster. Write an equation that models how many parts p each machine can manufacture in any number of minutes m.

Old Machine: [_____]

New Machine: [_____]

Do you UNDERSTAND?

3. Writing A diesel mechanic's earnings can be represented by the equation $e = 475w$. Who earns more, the airplane mechanic in Exercise 1 or the diesel mechanic? Explain.

_____

_____

_____

_____

_____

4. Reasoning Are all proportional equations linear? Are all linear equations proportional? Explain.

_____

_____

_____

_____

_____

_____

The Slope of a Line

CCSS: 8.EE.B.5: Graph proportional relationships, interpreting the unit rate as the slope of the graph. Compare two different proportional relationships represented in different ways.

Launch

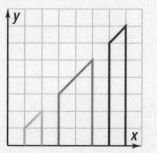

© MP3, MP7

An architect diagrams a series of skyscrapers on a coordinate grid. Tell how they are alike and different.

Alike:

Different:

Reflect Is one building more different than the others? Explain.

_____

_____

_____

_____

Got It?

PART 1 Got It (1 of 2)

What is the slope of the line?

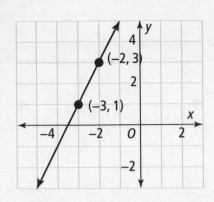

PART 1 Got It (2 of 2)

One of your friends describes the slope of a line: "as the *x*-coordinates increase by 2, the *y*-coordinates decrease by 5."

Your other friend describes the slope of a line: "as the *x*-coordinates decrease by 2, the *y*-coordinates increase by 5."

Is it possible for your friends to be describing the same line? Explain.

Got It?

PART 2 Got It (1 of 2)

What is the slope of the line that passes through the points (5, −3) and (−1, −2)?

PART 2 Got It (2 of 2)

The line shown has an *undefined* slope. Use the points shown to explain why.

PART 3 Got It

Which roof is steeper: Roof A with a rise of 12 and a run of 7 or Roof B with a rise of 8 and a run of 4? How do you know?

Close and Check

Focus Question

What does the slope of a line tell you about the line?

_____

_____

_____

_____

Do you know HOW?

1. What is the slope of the line?

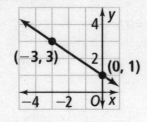

$(-3, 3)$ $(0, 1)$

Slope:

2. What is the slope of the line that passes through the points $(3, 3)$ and $(1, -2)$?

Slope: [ ]

3. Roof A has a rise of 11 and a run of 12. Roof B has a rise of 8 and a run of 9. Which roof is steeper?

4. Climber A climbs at a rate of 14 feet every 3 minutes. Climber B climbs 19 feet in 4 minutes. Which climber has the faster rate?

Do you UNDERSTAND?

5. Reasoning What is the slope of a horizontal line? Choose two points and show how you determined your solution.

_____

_____

_____

_____

6. Error Analysis A classmate finds the slope of a line containing the points $(-7, 5)$ and $(-3, 9)$. Explain the error she made in her calculations and find the correct slope.

$$\frac{9 - 5}{-7 - (-3)} = \frac{4}{-4} = -1$$

_____

_____

_____

_____

Unit Rates and Slope

Digital Resources

CCSS: 8.EE.B.5: Graph proportional relationships, interpreting the unit rate as the slope of the graph. Compare two different proportional relationships represented in different ways.

Launch

Ⓒ **MP4, MP6**

The graph shows the results of a plant-growing contest among three friends at a local plant club.

Which friend's plant grew the fastest? Explain how you know.

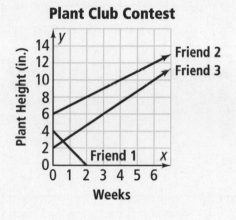

Reflect Is one line more different than the others? Explain.

_____

_____

_____

_____

Got It?

PART 1 Got It

The graph shows the amount of milk needed to make a quantity of butter. How many gallons of milk do you need per pound of butter?

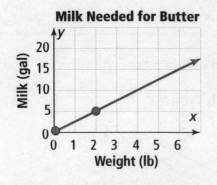

Milk Needed for Butter

PART 2 Got It

There is a proportional relationship between fathoms and feet. A depth of 6 fathoms is equivalent to a depth of 36 feet.

a. What is the unit rate of feet per fathom?

b. Use the unit rate to draw a graph that models this situation where the horizontal axis shows depth in fathoms and the vertical axis shows depth in feet. What is the slope of the line?

Got It?

PART 3 Got It

You friend has an automatic fish food dispenser. The graph shows how much food is left in the feeder after *x* days. How much food is being dispensed per day?

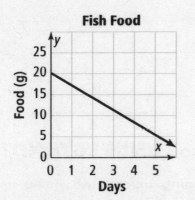

Fish Food

Close and Check

MP6, MP8

> ## Focus Question
>
> How are unit rates and slope related?
>
> _____
>
> _____
>
> _____
>
> _____

▶ Do you know HOW?

1. A caterer is preparing meatloaf for a large party. She needs 3 eggs for 2 pounds of ground beef. Graph the ratio of eggs to ground beef.

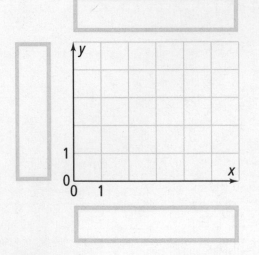

2. What is the slope of the line in the graph?

Slope: ⬜

3. Write an equation for Exercise 1 to find the number of eggs y for any number of pounds of ground beef x. How many eggs will be needed for 18 pounds of ground beef?

Equation: ⬜

 eggs

▶ Do you UNDERSTAND?

4. Reasoning Your creative writing teacher says you will have 15 short stories due over the next 12 weeks. What is the slope of the graph of number of papers due? Explain whether the graph represents a proportional relationship.

_____

_____

_____

_____

5. Writing Explain how to graph a line if you only know one point on the line and the slope of the line.

_____

_____

_____

_____

_____

_____

5-5 The y-intercept of a Line

Digital Resources

CCSS: 8.EE.B.6: … derive the equation $y = mx$ for a line through the origin and the equation $y = mx + b$ for a line intercepting the vertical axis at b.

Launch

© MP4, MP6

The graph shows the results of a plant-growing contest among three friends at a local plant club. The person with tallest plant after six weeks wins the contest.

Who won the contest? Do you think the contest was fair? Explain.

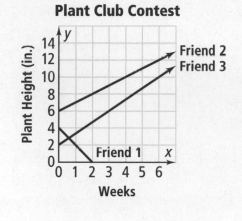

Plant Club Contest

Friend 2
Friend 3
Friend 1

Plant Height (in.)

Weeks

Reflect What do the lines all have in common?

_____

_____

_____

_____

_____

Got It?

PART 1 Got It

What is the *y*-intercept of the graph of the equation
$y = x + 6$?

PART 2 Got It (1 of 2)

What is the *y*-intercept of the graph of the equation
$y = -5x - 1$?

Discuss with a classmate

What is the *y*-intercept of a graph?

How do you recognize the *y*-intercept when given an equation?

Got It?

PART 2 Got It (2 of 2)

Your friend says that the graph of every linear equation must cross the y-axis. Provide a counterexample to your friend's statement.

PART 3 Got It

A bottle of dish soap starts to leak. The line models the total amount of dish soap in the bottle.

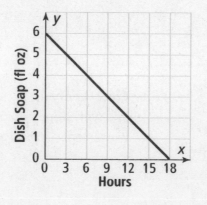

What is the y-intercept of the line? What does the y-intercept represent?

Close and Check

Focus Question

MP4, MP7

What is the *y*-intercept of a graph? What does the *y*-intercept tell you about the equation being graphed?

_____

_____

_____

_____

Do you know HOW?

1. You open a savings account with a $75 deposit. Then you deposit $25 each month. Complete the graph to model the situation.

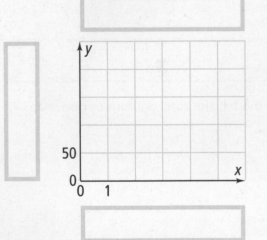

2. What does the *y*-intercept represent?

3. What is the slope of the line?

   Slope:

4. What does the slope represent?

Do you UNDERSTAND?

5. **Compare and Contrast** What about the graph in Exercise 1 would change if the initial deposit had been 0? What would stay the same? Explain.

_____

_____

_____

_____

_____

6. **Error Analysis** A classmate says a line with slope = 0 does not have a *y*-intercept. Do you agree? Explain.

_____

_____

_____

_____

_____

5-6

Linear Equations: $y = mx + b$

Digital Resources

CCSS: 8.EE.B.6: … derive the equation $y = mx$ for a line through the origin and the equation $y = mx + b$ for a line intercepting the vertical axis at b.

Launch

MP2, MP5

Complete the table. Describe any patterns you see between the slope and y-intercept for each line and the equation.

Equation	Slope	y-intercept
$y = 2x + 1$		
$y = 2x + 3$		
$y = -\frac{1}{3}x + 6$		
$y = x$		
$y = 1$		

$y = 2x + 3$ $y = 2x + 1$ $y = x$

$y = -\frac{1}{3}x + 6$

$y = 1$

Reflect Is it easier to spot the slope and y-intercept of a line from the graph or the equation of the line? Explain.

Got It?

PART 1 Got It

Write an equation in slope-intercept form for the line.

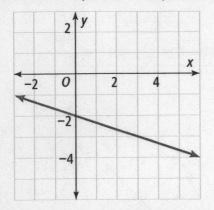

Discuss with a classmate

Compare your answers to the problem.

Take turns by choosing a part of the equation you wrote and explain
to your classmate how you used the graph to find that value.

Got It?

PART 2 Got It

The Kelvin scale for measuring temperature is often used in scientific calculations. The line models the relationship between a temperature in degrees Celsius and a temperature in kelvins.

Write an equation for the line where x is the temperature in degrees Celsius and y is the temperature in kelvins.

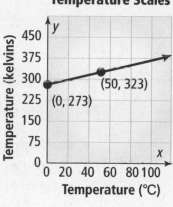

Temperature Scales

PART 3 Got It

What is the graph of the equation $y = -2x + 3$?

Close and Check

© MP4, MP7

Previously you studied equations in the form $y = mx$. How are equations in the form $y = mx$ similar to equations in the form $y = mx + b$? How do you know when to use each form?

_____

_____

_____

_____

Do you know **HOW?**

Use the graph for Exercises 1–4.

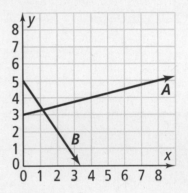

1. Write an equation in slope-intercept form for Line *A*.

   [   ]

2. Write an equation in slope-intercept form for Line *B*.

   [   ]

3. Graph and label Line *C* where $y = -\frac{2}{3}x + 7$.

4. Graph and label Line *D* where $y = \frac{7}{8}x + 1$.

Do you **UNDERSTAND?**

5. **Reasoning** You know the slope of a line and a point on the line that is not the *y*-intercept. Can you use a graph to write the equation of the line in slope-intercept form? Explain.

   _____

   _____

   _____

   _____

   _____

   _____

6. **Writing** Do the equations $y = \frac{5}{6}x + 2$ and $y = \frac{15}{18}x + 2$ represent two different lines? Explain.

   _____

   _____

   _____

   _____

   _____

   _____

Problem Solving

CCSS: 8.EE.B.5: … Compare two different proportional relationships represented in different ways.
8.EE.B.6: … derive the equation $y = mx$ for a line through the origin and the equation $y = mx + b$ for a line intercepting the vertical axis at b.

Launch

©MP4, MP6

Create your own graph and matching linear equation. Describe a situation that makes sense for each representation. Label your graph appropriately. Your situation must include the point (2, 4).

Equation:

Description of situation:

Reflect What did you do first—write an equation, complete the graph, or describe the situation? Why?

_____

_____

_____

Got It?

PART 1 Got It

Three stores are having a sale. Each store advertises its sale in a different way. Which store is offering the greatest discount?

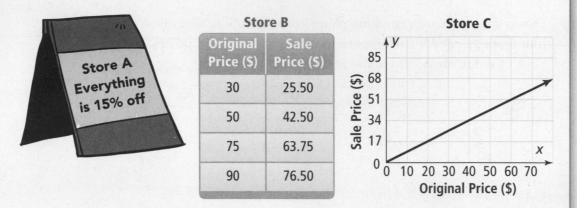

Store A Everything is 15% off

Store B

Original Price ($)	Sale Price ($)
30	25.50
50	42.50
75	63.75
90	76.50

Store C

Got It?

PART 2 Got It

Stores offer different rewards programs.

Store A:
You earn 3 points for every dollar spent.

Store B:
You start with 100 points and then earn 1 point for every dollar spent.

Store C:
The equation $y = 2x + 50$ models the rewards program, where y is the total number of points and x is the total dollars spent.

At each store you need 240 points to receive your first reward.
At which store do you need to spend the least amount of money to earn your first reward?

Discuss with a classmate

Choose one of the Stores' rewards programs.
Read the description of the program out loud, and then show how much you would need to spend in order to earn your first reward.
If you do not understand any of the descriptions, circle the word or phrase that is not clear to you and ask your teacher to help you.

Close and Check

Focus Question

You have studied the relationship between linear equations and proportional relationships. How and when can you use linear equations to solve problems?

_____

_____

_____

_____

 Do you know **HOW?**

1. To make a multi-age 800-meter race fair, Runner 1 gets a 100-meter head start. He runs 350 meters every 2 minutes. Represent on the graph how Runner 1 runs the race.

Runner 1

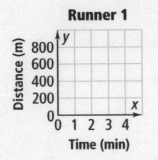

2. Runner 2 gets a 75-meter head start. Her rate is 210 meters per minute. Complete the table.

Time (min)	0	1	2	3	4
Distance (m)					

3. Runner 3 does not get a head start. He runs 750 meters every 3 minutes. Write an equation to represent Runner 3's distance y for x minutes.

[   ]

Do you UNDERSTAND?

4. **Writing** Which runner from Exercises 1–3 is ahead after 1 minute? Will that runner win the race? Explain.

_____

_____

_____

_____

_____

_____

5. **Reasoning** Which is most helpful in problem solving, a graph, a table, or an equation? Explain.

_____

_____

_____

_____

_____

_____

Topic Review

New Vocabulary: linear equation, slope, y-intercept
Review Vocabulary: constant of proportionality, proportional relationship, rate, unit rate

Vocabulary Review

Identify two challenging vocabulary terms from this topic. Write one vocabulary term in the center oval, and fill in the surrounding boxes with details that will help you better understand the term.

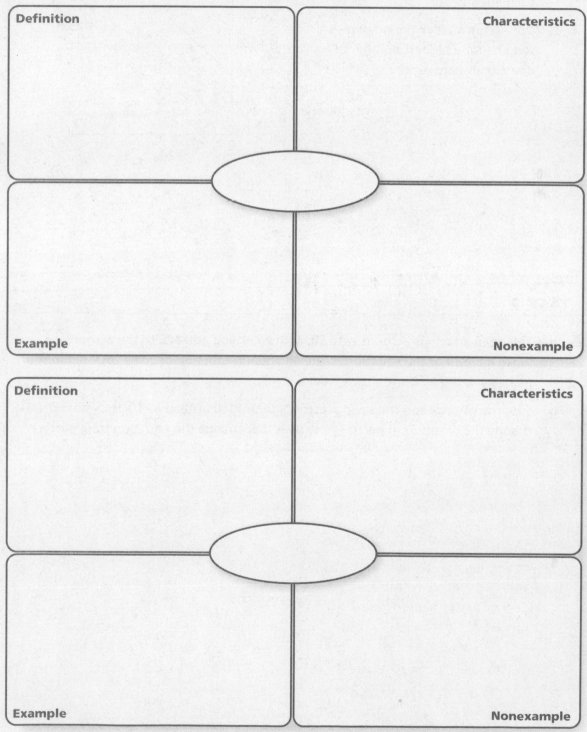

Definition

Characteristics

Example

Nonexample

Definition

Characteristics

Example

Nonexample

Pull It All Together

TASK 1

The graph shows the total number of downloads for three songs over a 4-week period.

a. Write an equation to represent each line shown.

b. During the 4-week period, which song had the highest number of downloads per week?

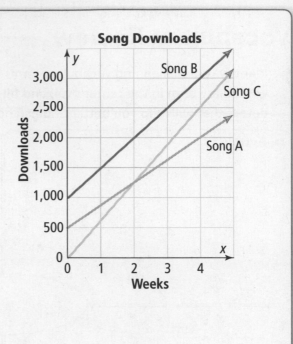

Song Downloads

TASK 2

a. You open a savings account with $0. Each week you add $25 to the account. Make a graph of the situation. Write an equation that models the total amount of money y in the account after x weeks.

b. Suppose you opened the savings account with $100 instead of $0. How does that change the graph from part a? How does that change the equation from part a?

What is a System of Linear Equations in Two Variables?

CCSS: **8.EE.C.8:** Analyze and solve pairs of simultaneous linear equations. **8.EE.C.8a:** Understand that solutions to a system of two linear equations in two variables correspond to points of intersection of their graphs, … . Also, **8.EE.C.8c.**

Launch

© MP1, MP4

Two runners run a 40-yd dash at speeds shown in the diagram. Runner 1 starts 4 seconds before Runner 2 to make the race more competitive. Will Runner 2 pass Runner 1? Tell how you know.

Runner 1
4 yd/s

Runner 2
8 yd/s

FREEZE

Reflect Do you think your method for solving the problem would be practical and easy to use for any race with runners who run any speed with any head start? Explain.

_____

_____

_____

_____

Got It?

PART 1 Got It

Which of the following represents a system of linear equations?

I. $14a + 9b = 36$

II. $x = 5$
$y = x + 1$

III. $y = 2x$
$y = 3.2x - 8$

PART 2 Got It

Is $(3, -4)$ a solution of the system?

$3x + y = 5$
$x - y = 7$

Got It?

PART 3 Got It

Marine biologists studied the lengths of two species of shark for several years. The initial length and growth rate of each species are shown in the table. Write a system of equations the biologists could use to compare the lengths of the two species.

	Greenland Shark	Spiny Dogfish Shark
Initial Length	37 cm	22 cm
Rate of Growth	0.75 cm per year	1.5 cm per year

Close and Check

Focus Question

What does a system of linear equations allow you to describe? What does the solution of a system represent?

_____

_____

_____

_____

Do you know **HOW?**

1. Circle the systems of equations.

   A. $7x - 5y = 16$ **B.** $2xy = 30$

   $\quad\quad\quad\quad\quad\quad\quad\quad\quad 7x - 1 = 4y$

   C. $y = 3x + 4$ **D.** $17 - xy$

   $\quad\quad y = 4x - 3$

2. Circle the ordered pair that is a solution to the system of equations.

   $$2y + 6 = 3x$$
   $$7x + 5 = 8y - 1$$

   (4, 3)   (4,4)   (6, 6)   (8, 9)

3. The table shows the initial height and growth rate of an apple tree and a cherry tree. Write a system of equations the gardener could use to determine the time t when the height h of the two trees will be the same.

	Apple	Cherry
Initial Height (ft)	2.75	2.12
Growth Rate (ft/yr)	1.2	1.38

Do you **UNDERSTAND?**

4. **Writing** Two brothers decide to save money. One starts with $10 and saves $2 each day. The other starts with none but saves $3 each day. What can a system of equations tell you about the situation?

   _____

   _____

   _____

   _____

5. **Error Analysis** A classmate uses the system of equations below to conclude that (2, 5) is a solution because $(3 \cdot 2) + (2 \cdot 5) = 16$. Explain why she is incorrect.

   $$3x + 2y = 16$$
   $$-xy + 5 = 15$$

   _____

   _____

   _____

   _____

Estimating Solutions of Systems by Inspection

CCSS: **8.EE.C.8:** Analyze and solve pairs of simultaneous linear equations. **8.EE.C.8b:** Solve systems of two linear equations in two variables algebraically, and estimate solutions by graphing the equations. Solve simple cases by inspection … .

Launch

Two runners run a 100-yd dash at speeds shown in the diagram. Runner 3 starts 4 seconds before Runner 2. Will Runner 2 pass Runner 3? Tell how you know.

MP2, MP4

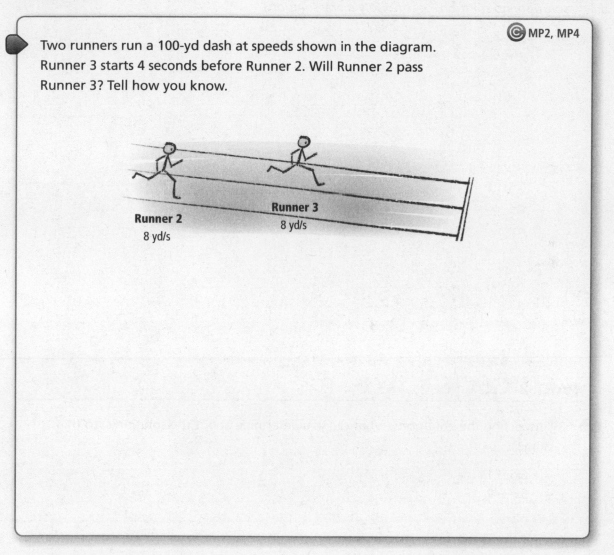

Runner 3
8 yd/s

Runner 2
8 yd/s

Reflect Do you need to set up a system of equations to solve the problem? Explain.

Got It?

PART 1 Got It

Without graphing, decide whether the system of linear equations has *one solution, no solution,* or *infinitely many solutions.*

$2x - 2y = 8$
$x - y = 6$

PART 2 Got It

By inspecting the equations, what can you determine about the solution(s) to this system?

$y = -6x + 15$
$y = -6x + 9$

Discuss with a classmate

What does it mean to "inspect" something?
Give some non-math examples of things that are inspected.
Why can inspecting something be helpful?

Close and Check

Focus Question

MP2, MP5

How can you find the solution of a system of linear equations just by inspecting the equations?

_____

_____

_____

_____

Do you know HOW?

1. Circle the system of equations that has no solution.

   A. $y = 3x - 3$ B. $2y = 7x + 2$
      $\dfrac{y}{3} = x - 1$ $y = 3.5x + 2$

   C. $2x - 5y = 7x + 5$ D. $y = 5x + 7$
         $y = x - 1$ $y = -5x + 7$

2. Circle the correct description of the system of equations.

   $$16x + 4 = 8y - 1$$
   $$3x + 0.5 = y$$

   A. one solution

   B. no solution

   C. infinite number of solutions

3. Which equation does NOT complete the system of equations with an infinite number of solutions?
   $$6x + 3y = 18$$

   A. $2x + y = 6$

   B. $y = -2x + 6$

   C. $-y = -2x - 6$

   D. $2y = -4x + 12$

Do you UNDERSTAND?

4. **Writing** Explain how to analyze a system of equations using the slope-intercept form of the equations of two lines.

   _____

   _____

   _____

   _____

   _____

5. **Error Analysis** A classmate concludes that the system of equations in Exercise 1D has infinitely many solutions. Explain why this is not true.

   _____

   _____

   _____

   _____

   _____

This page intentionally left blank.

Solving Systems of Linear Equations by Graphing

CCSS: 8.EE.C.8a: Understand that solutions to a system of two linear equations ... correspond to points of intersection of their graphs ... . 8.EE.C.8b: ... estimate solutions by graphing the equations. Also, 8.EE.C.8, 8.EE.C.8c.

Launch

© MP1, MP5

Spy 1 and Spy 2 hand off secret documents at point (1, 3), a park bench. Each spy walks past the bench in a different straight line so they can't be easily tracked.

Show each path by writing an equation and drawing them on the graph. Label each spy's path on the graph.

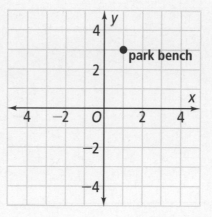

Reflect Did you write the equations or draw the paths first? Explain why.

_____

_____

_____

_____

_____

Got It?

What is the solution of the system equations represented by the graph?

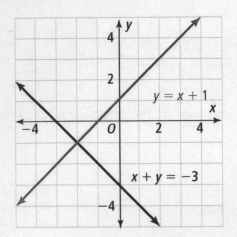

$y = x + 1$

$x + y = -3$

Got It?

PART 2 Got It

Estimate the solution of the system of equations by graphing the equations.

$y = 3x + 1$
$x - 3y = 1$

PART 3 Got It

Tickets for a concert cost $10 each if you order them online, but you must pay a service charge of $8 per order. The tickets are $12 each if you buy them at the door on the night of the concert. How many tickets must you buy for the costs to be the same?

Close and Check

Focus Question

©ᴹᴾ⁵, ᴹᴾ⁷ MP5, MP7

How can a graph help you find the solution of a system of linear equations?

_____

_____

_____

_____

Do you know HOW?

1. What is the solution of the system represented by the graph?

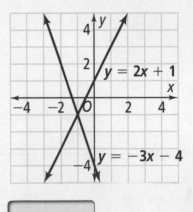

   y = 2x + 1

   y = −3x − 4

2. Estimate the solution of the system by graphing the equations.

$$3y = 2x + 1$$
$$-3y + 6x = 3$$

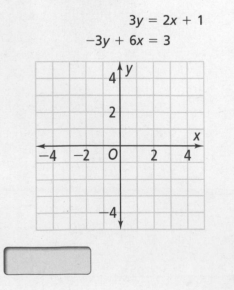

Do you UNDERSTAND?

3. **Writing** A GameSwap membership costs $20 and includes one game a month for $5. Non-members can get one game a month for $7. Explain how to use this information to decide whether to become a member.

   _____

   _____

   _____

   _____

4. **Error Analysis** A friend uses a graph to compare her commute to school with yours. She says the point at which the two lines intersect is when you both arrive at school. Is she correct? Explain.

   _____

   _____

   _____

   _____

Solving Systems of Linear Equations Using Substitution

CCSS: 8.EE.C.8b: Solve systems of two linear equations in two variables algebraically, and estimate solutions by graphing the equations. **8.EE.C.8c:** Solve real-world and mathematical problems leading to two linear equations in two variables. Also, **8.EE.C.8.**

Launch

© MP2, MP7

Solve the system of equations shown. Tell what you did.

$$y = x \qquad 3x - 2y = 3$$

Reflect What does the equal sign mean? How does that affect how you solve this problem?

_____

_____

_____

_____

_____

Got It?

PART 1 Got It

What is the solution of the system if the ordered pair is in the form (p, q)?
Use substitution.

$p = 4 - q$
$4p + q = 1$

Discuss with a classmate

Substitution involves replacing one thing with something else.
How did you decide what to substitute in order to solve this problem?
Compare the steps you took to solve the problem. If your steps do not match, discuss what makes them different and compare your solutions with another group of students.

PART 2 Got It

Marine biologists studied the lengths of two species of shark for several years. The initial length and growth rate of each species are shown in the table. If the growth rates stay the same, at what age would a Spiny Dogfish shark and a Greenland shark be the same length? What is the length?

	Greenland Shark	Spiny Dogfish Shark
Initial Length	37 cm	22 cm
Rate of Growth	0.75 cm per year	1.5 cm per year

Close and Check

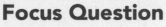

Focus Question

© MP5, MP7

Some systems cannot be solved by graphing. How can you use algebra to solve a system?

_____

_____

_____

_____

 Do you know HOW?

1. What is the solution of the system? Use substitution.

$$4x - y = 25$$
$$3y - 2 = x$$

[ ]

2. An air conditioner cools the inside of your home as it gets warmer outside. Use the table to write and solve a system of equations to determine the hour h when the temperatures t will be the same.

	Inside	Outside
Initial Temperature	77°F	65°F
Rate of Change	−1°F/hr	2°F/hr

System:

Solution:

[ ]

Do you UNDERSTAND?

3. **Reasoning** What is the meaning of the solution to Exercise 2?

_____

_____

_____

_____

4. **Writing** Why is it more accurate to solve a system of equations containing decimals by using algebra and substitution than by graphing the equations?

_____

_____

_____

_____

_____

_____

This page intentionally left blank.

Solving Systems of Linear Equations Using Addition

CCSS: 8.EE.C.8b: Solve systems of two linear equations in two variables algebraically, and estimate solutions by graphing the equations. **8.EE.C.8c:** Solve real-world and mathematical problems leading to two linear equations in two variables. Also, **8.EE.C.8, 8.EE.C.8a.**

Launch

© MP3, MP8

Each piece of paper shows a numerical expression or an algebraic expression. Can you show the same total value using fewer pieces of paper? Write your expressions and explain your reasoning.

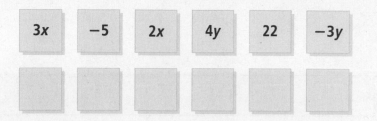

$3x$ -5 $2x$ $4y$ 22 $-3y$

Reflect How does equality help you solve this problem?

_____

_____

_____

_____

Got It?

PART 1 Got It

Is the addition method a good choice for solving the system of equations?

$-x + y = 4$
$x + 2y = 8$

PART 2 Got It

Solve the system of equations using addition.

$7x + 2y = 10$
$-7x + y = -16$

PART 3 Got It

Two buildings in an apartment complex, Building A and Building B, have a total of 120 apartments. The difference in the number of apartments between the two buildings is 16 apartments. How many apartments does each building have?

Close and Check

Focus Question

MP2, MP8

What kinds of systems are easiest to solve using addition?

_____

_____

_____

_____

Do you know **HOW?**

1. Solve the system of equations using addition.

   $$6x + 4y = 42$$
   $$3x - 4y = 3$$

2. A delivery truck's route is 588 miles long. The first part of the route is 148 miles longer than the second part. What is the distance of each part?

   First Part: _____

   Second Part: _____

3. There are 2,250 students enrolled in the middle school and high school. The middle school has 374 less students than the high school. How many students are enrolled in each school?

   Middle School: _____

   High School: _____

Do you **UNDERSTAND?**

4. **Compare and Contrast** Does it make a difference if a system is solved using the substitution method or the addition method? Explain.

   _____

   _____

   _____

   _____

   _____

5. **Error Analysis** A classmate says the system cannot be solved using the addition method. Explain how to solve this system using the addition method.

   $$4x + 2y = 5y + 7$$
   $$8x + 3y = 41$$

   _____

   _____

   _____

   _____

   _____

This page intentionally left blank.

Solving Systems of Linear Equations Using Subtraction

CCSS: 8.EE.C.8: Analyze and solve pairs of simultaneous linear equations. **8.EE.C.8b:** Solve systems of two linear equations in two variables algebraically .... **8.EE.C.8c:** Solve ... problems leading to two linear equations in two variables .... Also, **8.EE.C.8a.**

Launch

© MP1, MP8

Each friend has the same amount of money. Envelope x has one amount of money. Envelope y has a different amount of money.

Provide a possible amount of money for envelopes x and y. Tell how you decided.

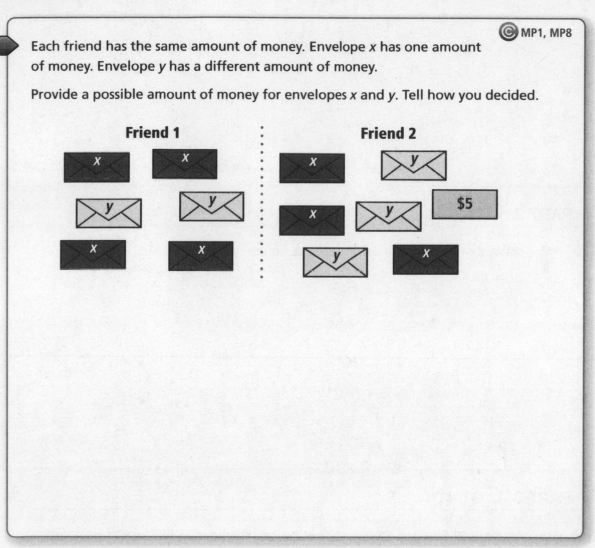

Reflect Does this problem have one answer? Explain.

_____

_____

_____

_____

_____

Got It?

Which system of equations can you solve most efficiently with the subtraction method?

I. $-x + y = 12$
  $x + 2y = 9$

II. $y = x - 15$
  $2y = 5x - 8$

III. $5x - y = 15$
  $5x + 2y = 20$

Solve the system of equations using subtraction.

$3x + 4y = 20$
$3x + 2y = 16$

You only have $1 bills and $5 bills in your wallet. You have 33 bills worth a total of $93. How many of each type of bill do you have?

Close and Check

Focus Question

What kinds of systems are easiest to solve using subtraction?

_____

_____

_____

_____

Do you know **HOW?**

1. Circle the system of equations that would be solved most efficiently by using the subtraction method.

   A. $x = 4y - 12$
      $x = 2(3y + 8)$

   B. $7r + 2s = 18$
      $5r - 9 = 2s$

   C. $6p + 2q = 4$
      $4p + 2q = 2$

   D. $9a + 8b = 15$
      $3a - 8b = 5$

2. Solve the system of equations by using subtraction.

   $$7s + 2t = 31$$
   $$5s + 2t = 25$$

   [ ]

3. The 8th grade class sells 275 magazine subscriptions and individual greeting cards for a fundraiser. The subscriptions cost $26 and cards cost $1 each. The students earn $2,875. How many of each item is sold?

   Magazines: Greeting Cards:

   [ ]   [ ]

Do you **UNDERSTAND?**

4. **Reasoning** Your friend says he would solve this system of equations by using the subtraction method. Why might that method be efficient in this case?

   $$12x - 5y = 73$$
   $$10x - 5y = 35$$

   _____

   _____

   _____

   _____

5. **Compare and Contrast** Explain how to determine whether the addition method or the subtraction method is most efficient for solving a system of equations.

   _____

   _____

   _____

   _____

   _____

   _____

This page intentionally left blank.

Problem Solving

CCSS: 8.EE.C.8b: Solve systems of two linear equations in two variables algebraically, and estimate solutions by graphing the equations. **8.EE.C.8c:** Solve real-world and mathematical problems leading to two linear equations in two variables. Also, **8.EE.C.8.**

Launch

© MP3, MP6

In each account, the sum of the envelopes results in the balance shown. You can take either the x envelopes or the y envelopes from each account. Use systems of equations to show which envelope type you would take.

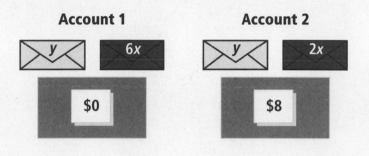

Account 1

y   6x

$0

Account 2

y   2x

$8

Reflect In the real world, what do you think each envelope could represent?

_____

_____

_____

_____

Got It?

PART 1 Got It

Which method would be the most efficient method to use to solve the system?

$x + y = 6$

$5x + 8y = 24$

PART 2 Got It

How can you change the equations to eliminate the b-terms?

$2a - 3b = 14$

$7a + 5b = 18$

Got It?

PART 3 Got It

A hotel offers two activity packages. One costs $192 and includes 3 hours of horseback riding and 2 hours of parasailing. The second costs $213 and includes 2 hours of horseback riding and 3 hours of parasailing. What is the cost for 1 hour of each activity?

Close and Check

Focus Question

In this topic, you learned how to solve systems of two linear equations in two variables using different methods. How do you build a solution strategy for a system of equations when the method of solving is left up to you?

_____

_____

_____

_____

Do you know HOW?

1. Write _substitution, addition,_ or _subtraction_ to tell which method is most efficient for finding the solution.

   A. $9j + 4k = 17$
      $5j + 4k = 13$

   B. $y = 7x - 3$
      $y = 6x + 5$

   C. $8v + 2w = 28$
      $5v - 2w = 23$

2. Solve the system of equations by multiplying one or both equations by a constant.

   $2a + 5b = 53$
   $8a - 3b = 5$

3. A store offers pens for $4/pack and day planners for $8 each. You spend $48 on these items. The next week the items go on sale. Pens cost $2/pack and day planners cost $6 each. The same purchase now costs $30. How many of each item did you buy?

   Packs of Pens: Day Planners:

Do you UNDERSTAND?

4. **Writing** How can solving systems of equations be helpful in real-life problem solving?

   _____

   _____

   _____

   _____

   _____

5. **Error Analysis** You have 3 coins and 4 bills totaling $16.75. Your friend has 12 coins and 3 bills totaling $7.98. Your friend says she can use a system of equations to figure out what bills and coins you have. What is the error in her reasoning?

   _____

   _____

   _____

   _____

New Vocabulary: solution of a system of linear equations, system of linear equations
Review Vocabulary: addition method, graphing method, linear equation, ordered pair, substitution method, subtraction method

Vocabulary Review

 Identify two challenging vocabulary terms from this topic. Write one vocabulary term in the center oval, and fill in the surrounding boxes with details that will help you better understand the term.

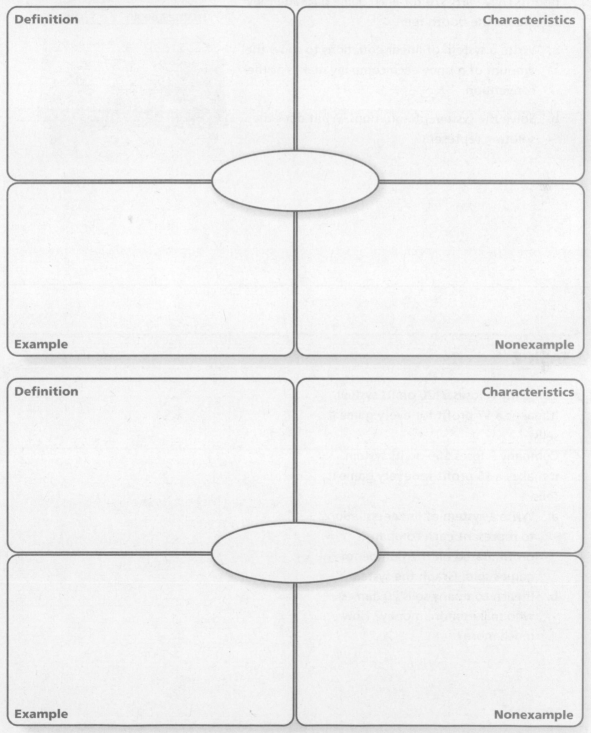

Definition	Characteristics
Example	Nonexample

Definition	Characteristics
Example	Nonexample

Pull It All Together

TASK 1

Company A is selling their new game at a Standard booth. They earn $50 for each game package they sell, minus the booth fee.

Company B is selling their new game at a Luxury booth. They earn $70 for each game package they sell, minus the booth fee.

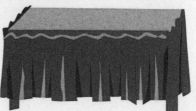

a. Write a system of linear equations to show the amount of money each company makes at the convention.

b. Solve the system of equations. What does the solution represent?

TASK 2

Company A loses $120 on its system. It makes a $7 profit for every game it sells.
Company B loses $50 on its system. It makes a $5 profit for every game it sells.

a. Write a system of linear equations to represent each company's profit, based on the number of games sold. Graph the system.

b. If each company sells 20 games, who makes more money? How much more?

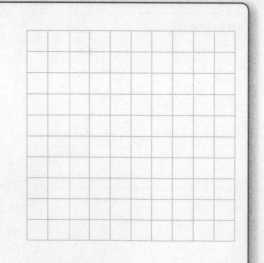

Recognizing a Function

CCSS: 8.F.A.1: Understand that a function is a rule that assigns to each input exactly one output. The graph of a function is the set of ordered pairs consisting of an input and the corresponding output.

Launch

© MP1, MP3

Two local dog-walking services scratch and claw for customers using sometimes unusual pay plans.

Which service would you use if you need a dog break for 2 hours on Friday, 3 hours on Saturday, and 1 hour on Sunday? Why?

Friendly Dog Walking

Flip-a-Coin Fees
1 hour $2 or $4
2 hours $3 or $6
3 hours $6 or $8

Dog Walk Friends

Fees
1 hour $3
2 hours $5
3 hours $7

Reflect Do companies usually have set prices or prices that can vary? Why?

_____

_____

_____

_____

Got It?

PART 1 Got It

Name the set of ordered pairs represented by the mapping diagram.

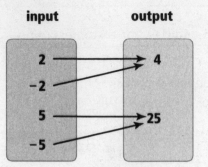

PART 2 Got It

Is the relation a function? Use a mapping diagram to explain your reasoning.

{(1, 3), (1, 2), (2, −4), (3, 2)}

Got It?

PART 3 Got It

Is the relation a function? Explain.

input	output
−5	−5
−3	−3
1	1
2	2

PART 4 Got It (1 of 2)

Use the vertical line test to determine which graphs represent functions.

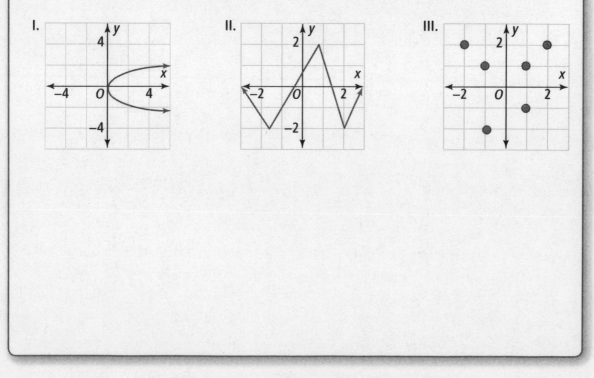

Got It?

Why does a horizontal line represent a function but a vertical line does not represent a function? Explain your reasoning using graphs.

Close and Check

MP2, MP6

Focus Question

How will you know a function when you see one?

_____

_____

_____

_____

Do you know HOW?

1. Name the set of ordered pairs represented by the mapping diagram.

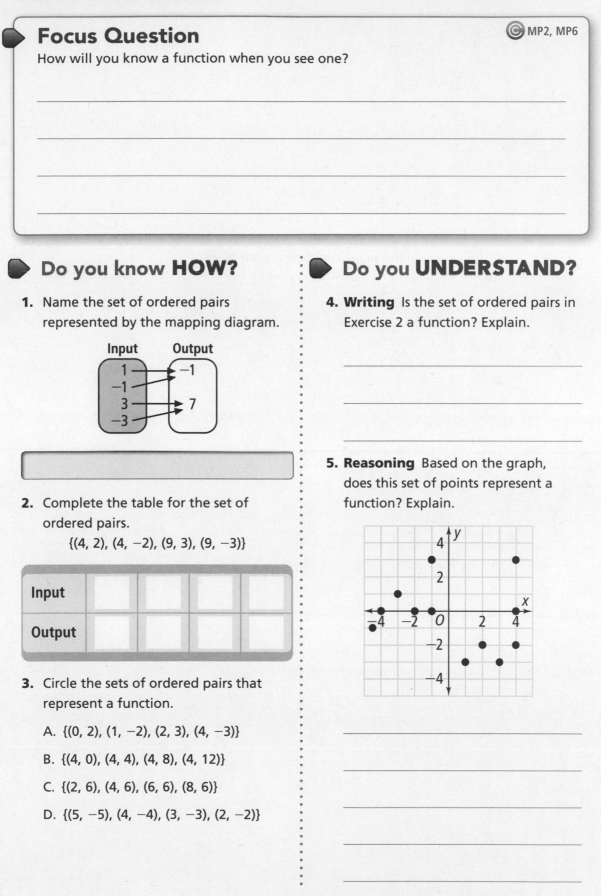

Input   Output

1 ⟶ −1
−1
3 ⟶ 7
−3

_____

2. Complete the table for the set of ordered pairs.

$\{(4, 2), (4, -2), (9, 3), (9, -3)\}$

Input				
Output				

3. Circle the sets of ordered pairs that represent a function.

A. $\{(0, 2), (1, -2), (2, 3), (4, -3)\}$

B. $\{(4, 0), (4, 4), (4, 8), (4, 12)\}$

C. $\{(2, 6), (4, 6), (6, 6), (8, 6)\}$

D. $\{(5, -5), (4, -4), (3, -3), (2, -2)\}$

Do you UNDERSTAND?

4. Writing Is the set of ordered pairs in Exercise 2 a function? Explain.

_____

_____

_____

5. Reasoning Based on the graph, does this set of points represent a function? Explain.

_____

_____

_____

_____

_____

This page intentionally left blank.

Representing a Function

CCSS: 8.F.A.1: Understand that a function is a rule that assigns to each input exactly one output. The graph of a function is the set of ordered pairs consisting of an input and the corresponding output.

Launch

Write some of the ordered pairs in the table to make a function.
Describe what the function could mean.

ⓒ MP2, MP3

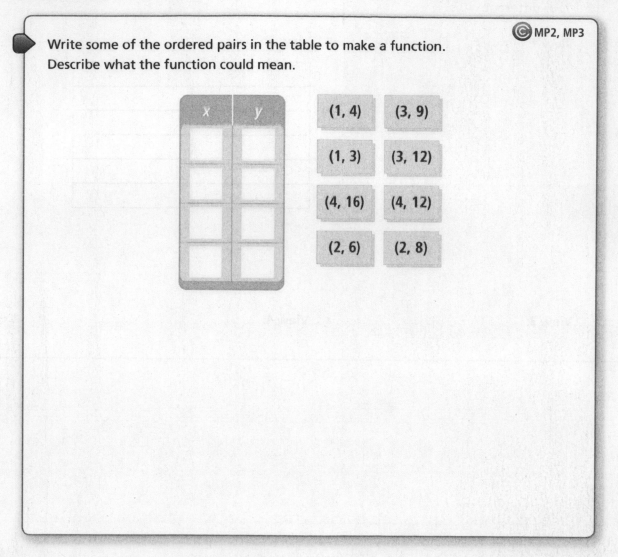

x	y

(1, 4)   (3, 9)

(1, 3)   (3, 12)

(4, 16)   (4, 12)

(2, 6)   (2, 8)

Reflect Name two ordered pairs that cannot belong to the same function. Explain.

_____

_____

_____

_____

_____

Got It?

PART 1 Got It

A freight train travels at 35 miles per hour. How can you represent this situation in four different ways?

View 1:

View 2:

View 3:

View 4:

Got It?

PART 2 Got It

Which equation could be a view of the function represented by the table?

I. $y = -2x$

II. $y = x - 2$

III. $y = -x + 2$

x	y
-4	-6
-2	-4
0	-2
2	0
4	2

Discuss with a classmate

Circle the key words in this problem: equation, function, table.
Choose a word and give its definition.
For any word that you cannot define, ask other classmates or your teacher.

Close and Check

Focus Question

© MP3, MP7

There are several ways to represent functions. What are the advantages of each of these ways?

_____

_____

_____

_____

Do you know HOW?

1. The earth travels 30 km/s in its orbit around the sun. Circle the correct representation(s) of this situation.

   A. $30x = y$

   B. $\{(0, 0), (1, 30), (3, 60)\}$

   C.

x	y
1	30
4	120
7	210
10	300

   D. **Earth's Orbit**

   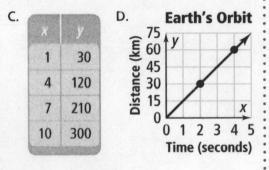

   Distance (km) vs Time (seconds)

2. Complete the table of values for $y = 3x - 2$.

   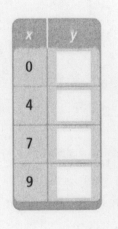

x	y
0	
4	
7	
9	

Do you UNDERSTAND?

3. **Reasoning** Consider a circle graphed on the coordinate plane with the center of the circle at the origin. Can the equation of a circle ever be a function? Explain.

   _____

   _____

   _____

   _____

4. **Writing** A friend says the equation $\sqrt{x} = y$ is not an example of a function because if $x = 16$, then $y = -4$ and 4. Explain whether this reasoning is always correct.

   _____

   _____

   _____

   _____

   _____

Linear Functions

CCSS: 8.F.A.3: Interpret the equation ... as defining a linear function, whose graph is a straight line .... **8.F.B.5:** Describe qualitatively the functional relationship between two quantities by analyzing a graph (e.g., where the function is ... linear or nonlinear).

Launch

© MP3, MP8

Draw lines to sort the graphs into two groups. Describe each of your groups.

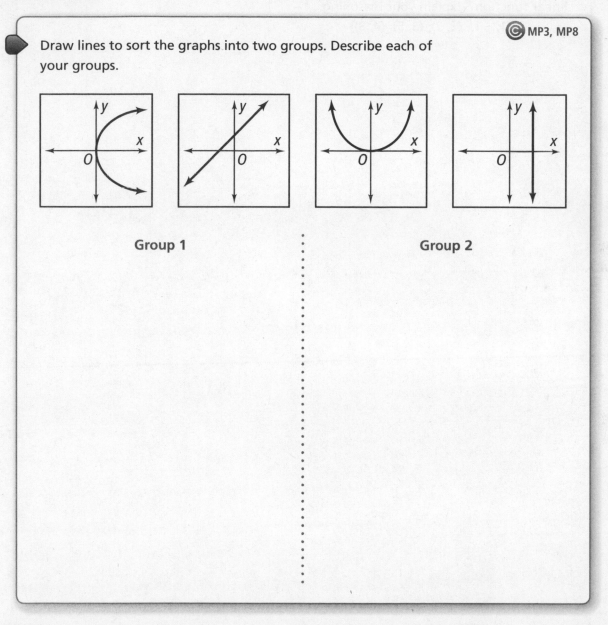

Group 1   Group 2

Reflect Could you have sorted the graphs in a different way? Explain.

_____

_____

_____

_____

Got It?

PART 1 Got It

Does the set of ordered pairs represent a
linear function? Explain your reasoning.

{(1, −1), (2, 2), (3, 5), (4, 8)}

Got It?

PART 2 Got It

Does the relation defined by the table represent a linear function?
Explain.

Input	Output
−10	8
−5	5
0	2
5	−1
10	−4

PART 3 Got It

The table shows the age and the length of a shark over a 15-year period.

a. What is the rate of change of this linear function? What does this rate of change represent in this situation?

b. Use the growth rate to predict the length of the shark when it is 25 years old and when it is 40 years old.

Length of a Shark

Age (years)	Length (cm)
5	40.75
10	44.5
15	48.25
20	52

Close and Check

Focus Question

MP1, MP4

What are linear functions? How are linear functions useful?

_____

_____

_____

_____

Do you know HOW?

1. Graph the set of ordered pairs.
   $\{(-3, -4), (-2, -2), (-1, 0), (0, 2), (1, 4)\}$

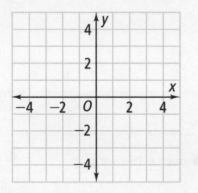

2. Do the ordered pairs in Exercise 1 represent a function?

   [ ]

3. Find the rate of change in the table.

Input	Output
−3	−5
−1	1
1	7
3	13

   [ ]

Do you UNDERSTAND?

4. **Writing** An ordered pair with the x-coordinate 2 is added to the set in Exercise 1. Explain how to find the y-coordinate of the ordered pair.

   _____

   _____

   _____

5. **Error Analysis** What mistake did your classmate make in determining the rate of change in the table below? Find the actual rate of change.

Input	Output	Rate of change = +6
−5	1	−5 + 6 = 1
−2	4	−2 + 6 = 4
1	7	1 + 6 = 7

   _____

   _____

   _____

   _____

Nonlinear Functions

CCSS: **8.F.A.3:** Interpret the equation … is a straight line; give examples of functions that are not linear. **8.F.B.5:** Describe qualitatively the functional relationship between two quantities by analyzing a graph (e.g., where the function is … linear or nonlinear). Also, **8.F.A.1.**

Launch

© MP1, MP3

Your friend designs a rectangular board game using 16 square pieces. Let *x* equal the number of rows of squares on the board and *y* equal the number of columns on the board.

Do the numbers of rows and columns represent a function? A linear function? Use a table or a graph to support your response.

Reflect Did you choose to support your response with a table or a graph? Explain your choice.

_____

_____

_____

_____

Got It?

PART 1 Got It

Which graph(s) represent a nonlinear function? Explain.

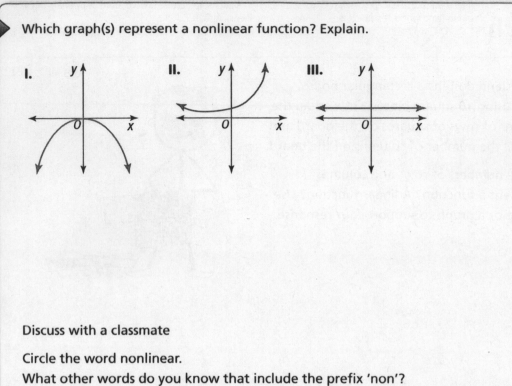

I. II. III.

Discuss with a classmate

Circle the word nonlinear.
What other words do you know that include the prefix 'non'?

PART 2 Got It

Does the table represent a linear or a nonlinear function? Explain.

Input	Output
1	5
2	6
3	9
4	14
5	21

Got It?

PART 3 Got It

The table shows the population of a species of brown bat in Missouri.

a. Is this relationship linear or nonlinear? Explain.

b. Why can't you use this table to predict the bat population in 2011?

Brown Bat Population

Year	Population
1999	19,900
2001	13,000
2003	14,100
2005	9,900
2007	8,600

Close and Check

Focus Question

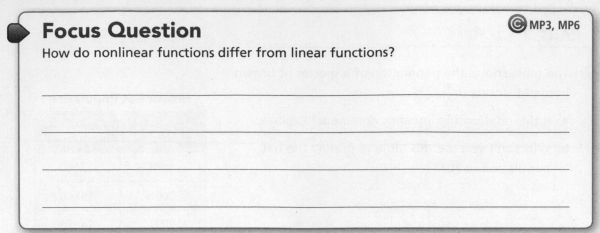

MP3, MP6

How do nonlinear functions differ from linear functions?

_____

_____

_____

_____

Do you know HOW?

1. Circle the graph(s) that represent a nonlinear function.

A.

B.

C.

D.

2. Complete the table of values for the equation $|x| - 2 = y$.

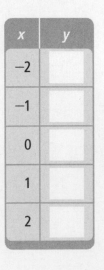

x	y
-2	
-1	
0	
1	
2	

Do you UNDERSTAND?

3. **Writing** Does the table in Exercise 2 represent a linear function? Explain.

_____

_____

_____

_____

_____

_____

4. **Error Analysis** A classmate says the equation $y = \frac{5}{3}x - 6$ is nonlinear. Do you agree? Explain.

_____

_____

_____

_____

_____

_____

Increasing and Decreasing Intervals

CCSS: 8.F.B.5: Describe qualitatively the functional relationship between two quantities by analyzing a graph (e.g., where the function is increasing or decreasing). Sketch a graph that exhibits the qualitative features of a function that has been described verbally.

Launch

© MP1, MP3

The graph represents the number of people in an outdoor stadium for a baseball game. Tell what the *x*- and *y*-axes represent. Tell what happens during parts A to E to the people at the game.

x:

y:

A:

B:

C:

D:

E:

Reflect How could a graph such as this be valuable to the owners of the baseball team? Explain.

_____

_____

_____

_____

Got It?

What type of interval is interval S?

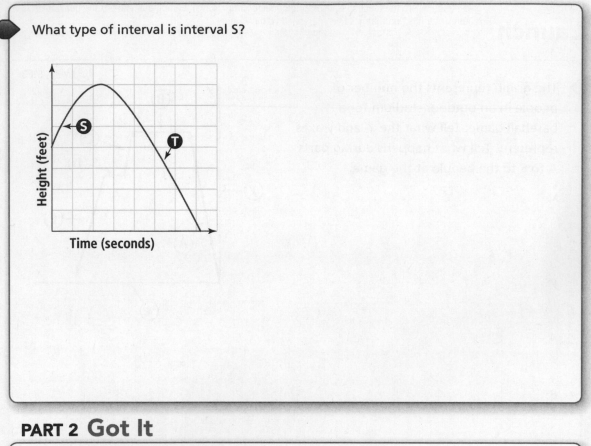

PART 2 Got It

Label the graph to indicate which intervals are increasing, decreasing, or constant.

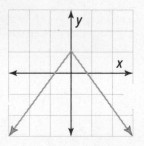

Got It?

The graph shows the speed of a commuter train as it makes a morning trip.

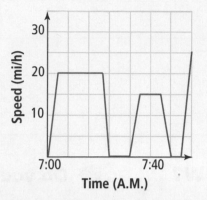

a. How many decreasing intervals are defined in the graph?

b. How are the decreasing intervals alike?

c. How are the decreasing intervals different?

Close and Check

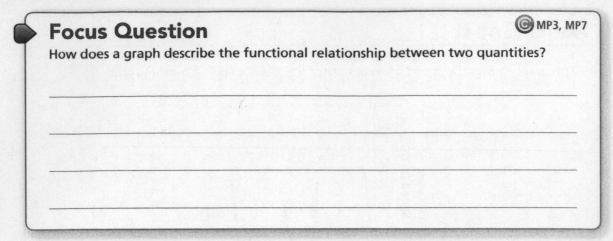

Focus Question
© MP3, MP7

How does a graph describe the functional relationship between two quantities?

_____

_____

_____

_____

Do you know HOW?

1. List the type of intervals on the graph by writing the letters under the correct heading below.

Sales Trends

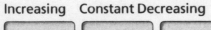

Increasing	Constant	Decreasing

2. Does the graph show more increasing or decreasing intervals?

3. What was the total change in income from the beginning of March through the end of April?

4. What was the total change in income from the beginning of March through the end of May?

Do you UNDERSTAND?

5. **Reasoning** Explain why intervals c and d in Exercise 1 are labeled separately rather than as one interval.

_____

_____

_____

_____

_____

_____

6. **Writing** Explain what the intervals b and f in Exercise 1 represent.

_____

_____

_____

_____

_____

Sketching a Function Graph

CCSS: 8.F.B.5: Describe qualitatively the functional relationship between two quantities by analyzing a graph (e.g., where the function is increasing or decreasing). Sketch a graph that exhibits the qualitative features of a function that has been described verbally.

Launch

© MP3, MP4

Your cousin keeps the hot dog supply stocked at a concession stand at the baseball game. Despite lots of hungry fans, the stand never runs out of hot hot dogs.

Sketch one possible graph of your cousin's efforts on the coordinate grid. Label the x- and y-axes and tell why your graph makes sense.

Reflect How could your cousin use a graph like the one you created?

_____

_____

_____

_____

_____

Got It?

PART 1 Got It

You have an empty bucket in your yard to collect rainwater. Rain falls for six hours and then stops. After five hours, the rain begins again and lasts for one more hour.

Sketch a graph to represent the volume of water in your bucket during this time.

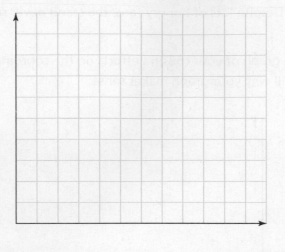

PART 2 Got It (1 of 2)

Each graph describes the height of a candle over a certain period of time. Which graph is *not* a reasonable description for this situation?

You light a candle and let it burn until it burns out.

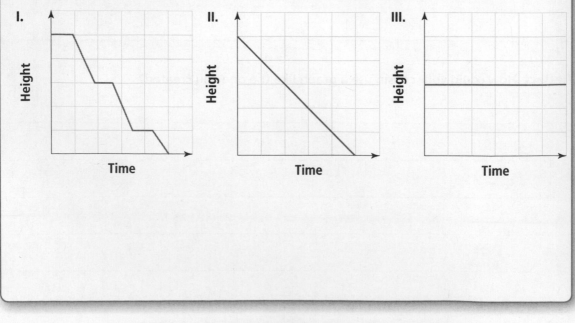

Got It?

You light a candle and let it burn until it burns out.

What additional information do you need to know in order to choose which graph better matches the situation?

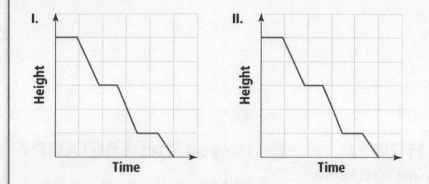

Close and Check

Focus Question

© MP2, MP5

How does sketching the graph of a function help you to determine the behavior of a function?

_____

_____

_____

_____

Do you know HOW?

Write the letter of the graph that matches each description in Exercises 1–3.

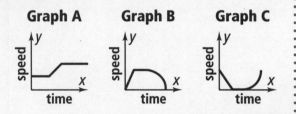

Graph A   Graph B   Graph C

1. A car starts from a complete stop and accelerates at a constant rate. Then it travels at a constant speed until the driver sees a stop sign and gradually slows down to a stop.

2. A car is traveling at a constant speed. It accelerates at a constant rate. Finally, it continues traveling at a constant speed.

3. A car slows down at a constant speed as it approaches a red light. After a short time, the light changes and the car gradually accelerates.

Do you UNDERSTAND?

4. **Writing** Sketch a graph, and then write a brief description of what the graph could represent.

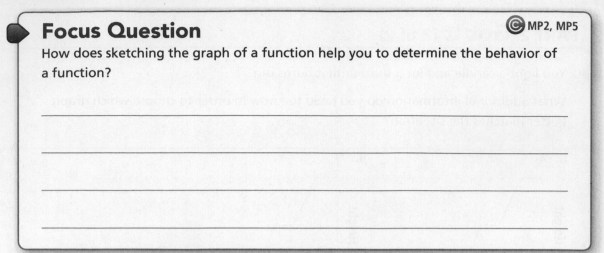

_____

_____

_____

_____

5. **Reasoning** Is it possible for a sketch of a graph to represent more than one situation? Explain.

_____

_____

_____

_____

Problem Solving

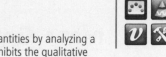
CCSS: 8.F.B.5: Describe qualitatively the functional relationship between two quantities by analyzing a graph (e.g., where the function is increasing or decreasing). Sketch a graph that exhibits the qualitative features of a function that has been described verbally.

Launch

MP1, MP4

The graphs represent ticket sales for three upcoming games with *x* representing time and *y* the rate of ticket sales.

Which game will be the easiest for your cousin to plan how many hot dog buns to buy? Which game will be the most challenging to plan for? Explain why.

Graph A

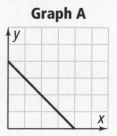

Graph B

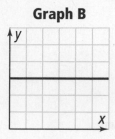

Graph C

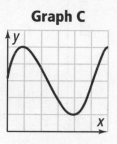

Easiest:

Most Challenging:

Reflect What value do the graphs have for your cousin? What other information might he want to make his plans?

_____

_____

_____

_____

Got It?

PART 1 Got It

You walk home from school, stopping at a friend's house on the way. Sketch a graph to describe the total distance you walked during the time you walked home.

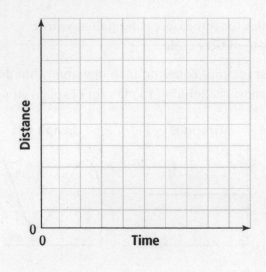

PART 2 Got It

Explain why $y = x^2 - 3$ is a nonlinear function using both a table and a graph.

Close and Check

Focus Question

How can you use different representations of a function to analyze a situation?

_____

_____

_____

_____

Do you know **HOW?**

1. Complete the table. Is the equation linear or nonlinear?

$$x^3 - 3 = y$$

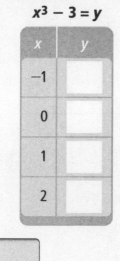

x	y
−1	
0	
1	
2	

2. Graph the equation from Exercise 1. Is the equation a function?

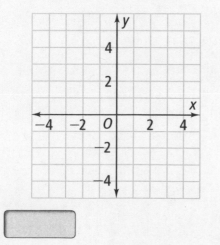

Do you **UNDERSTAND?**

3. **Writing** Explain how you determined whether the equation in Exercise 1 is linear or nonlinear.

_____

_____

_____

_____

_____

_____

4. **Reasoning** An interior designer wants to show her customers how the length of a square wall determines the total area. She uses the equation $x^2 = y$. Would you use the equation, a table, or a graph to share with the customers? Explain.

_____

_____

_____

_____

This page intentionally left blank.

New Vocabulary: function, interval, linear function, nonlinear function, rate of change, relation, vertical-line test
Review Vocabulary: ordered pair, slope

Vocabulary Review

Identify two challenging vocabulary terms from this topic. Write one vocabulary term in the center oval, and fill in the surrounding boxes with details that will help you better understand the term.

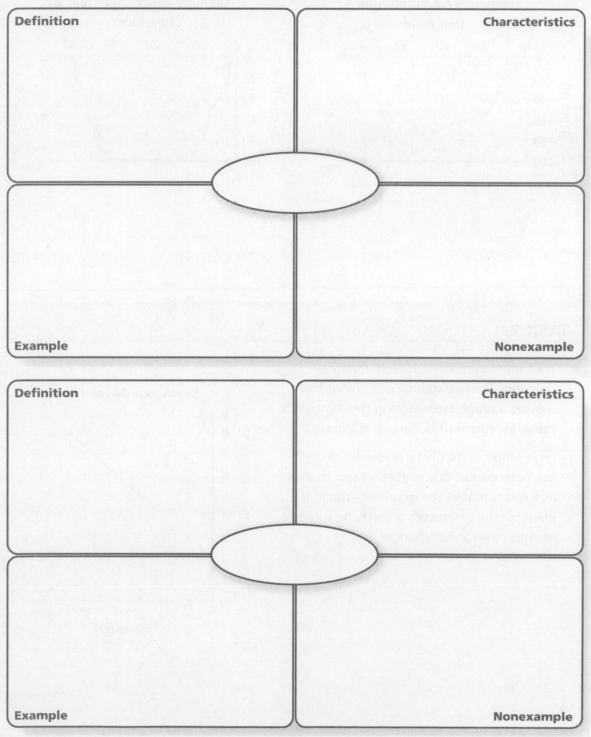

Definition

Characteristics

Example

Nonexample

Definition

Characteristics

Example

Nonexample

Pull It All Together

TASK 1

A submarine adventure tour company offers two 40-minute underwater tours.

Explain what is happening in each graph. Which graph would represent a more fun underwater tour for you, and why?

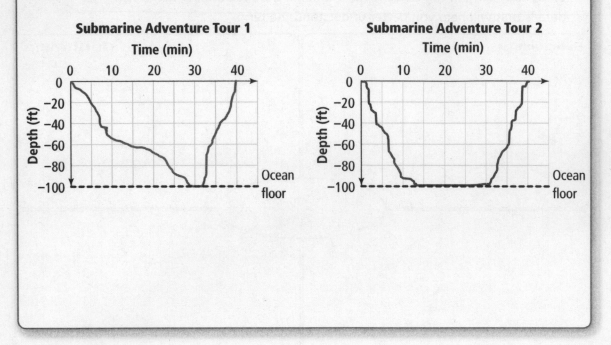

Submarine Adventure Tour 1

Time (min)

Depth (ft)

Ocean floor

Submarine Adventure Tour 2

Time (min)

Depth (ft)

Ocean floor

TASK 2

Your submarine adventure company is growing! The marketing coordinator has created a graph representing the company's value, in billions of dollars, over time.

He is supposed to give a presentation to the company owner, but he lost his report. Write an explanation of the graph describing the plans for the company's growth. Be sure to mention the rate of change!

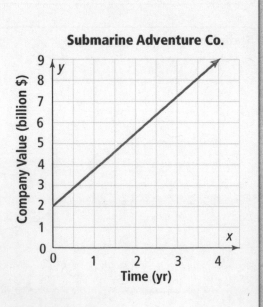

Submarine Adventure Co.

Company Value (billion $)

Time (yr)

Defining a Linear Function Rule

CCSS: 8.F.A.3: Interpret the equation $y = mx + b$ as defining a linear function, whose graph is a straight line .... **8.F.B.4:** Construct a function to model a linear relationship between two quantities .... Also, **8.F.A.1** and **8.F.B.5.**

Launch

MP2, MP4

Draw a line to the graph that could represent each situation.

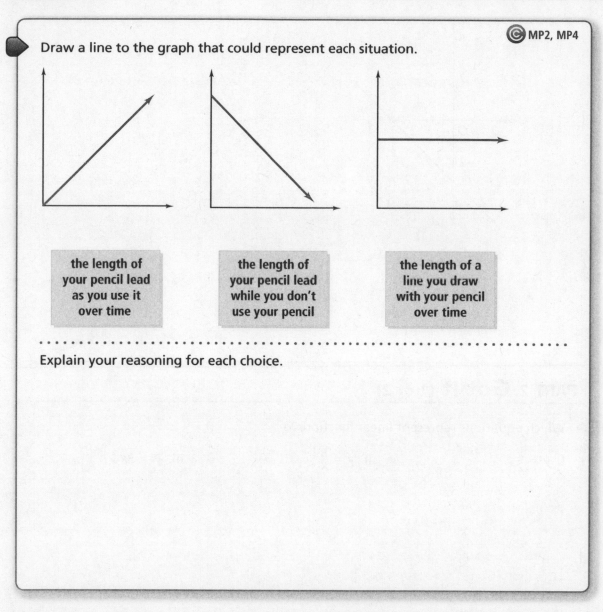

the length of your pencil lead as you use it over time

the length of your pencil lead while you don't use your pencil

the length of a line you draw with your pencil over time

Explain your reasoning for each choice.

Reflect Think of the graphs where the pencil lead is being used. Is the person using the pencil at a constant rate or stopping and starting a lot? Explain your thinking.

_____

_____

_____

_____

Got It?

PART 1 Got It

What is the function rule for the graph?

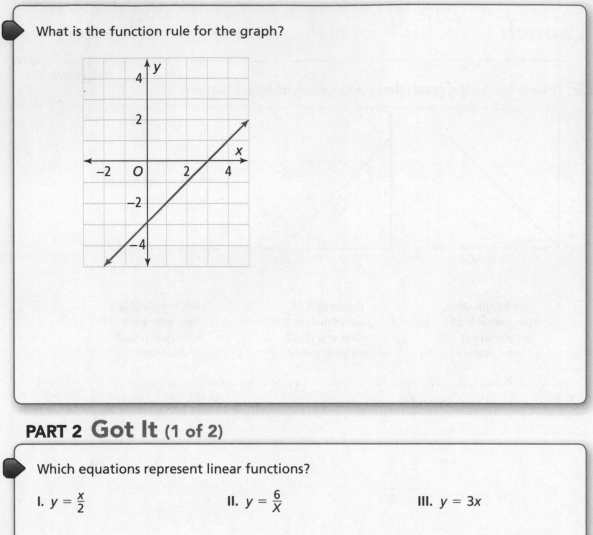

PART 2 Got It (1 of 2)

Which equations represent linear functions?

I. $y = \dfrac{x}{2}$
II. $y = \dfrac{6}{X}$
III. $y = 3x$

Got It?

The points $(-1, -1)$, $(0, 0)$, and $(1, 1)$ are on the graph of $y = x^3$. Your friend says that since you can draw a straight line through the three points, $y = x^3$ is a linear function. Do you agree? Why or why not?

PART 3 Got It

Matt is $3\frac{1}{2}$ years older than Sam.
What function rule describes Matt's age during any given year?

Close and Check

Focus Question

MP6, MP7

How can you define or describe a linear function?

_____

_____

_____

Do you know HOW?

1. What linear function rule describes the graph?

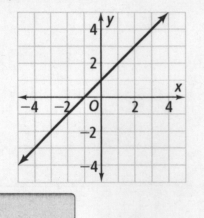

[   ]

2. Circle each linear function rule.

$y = 4x^2$

$y = x - 7$

$y = -\left(\dfrac{x}{9}\right)$

$y = 12 + \dfrac{2}{x}$

3. You earn an allowance of $5 each week. You earn additional money m for helping others in the neighborhood. Write a function rule to find the total income i you can earn in one week.

[   ]

Do you UNDERSTAND?

4. Error Analysis Your friend can jump rope 32 times in one minute. She writes a rule to predict how many times she can jump for other time periods.

$$j = 32 + m$$
$$j = \text{jumps} \quad m = \text{minutes}$$

Explain her error and write the correct equation.

_____

_____

_____

5. Reasoning A man in a 5K race runs 1 km and then walks 0.5 km. If the man continues this pattern for the entire race, is the graph of his distance over time linear? Explain.

_____

_____

_____

_____

Rate of Change

CCSS: 8.F.B.4: … Determine the rate of change and initial value of the function from a description of a relationship or from two (x, y) values … . Interpret the rate of change and initial value of a linear function in terms of the situation it models … . Also, **8.F.B.5.**

Launch

© MP2, MP3

Your friend walks from the bus stop to her favorite museum. She first walks one or more blocks along a street, then one or more blocks along an avenue. She continues this pattern until she reaches the museum, taking the shortest path possible.

Draw and describe her walking pattern.

| Drawing | Description |

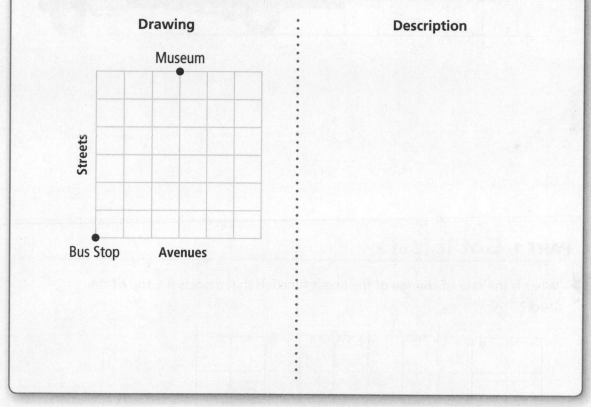

Reflect Suppose your friend could fly directly from the bus stop to the museum. How would the flight path compare with her walking path?

_____

_____

_____

_____

Got It?

What is the rate of change of the linear function that models the ramp's height above the road?

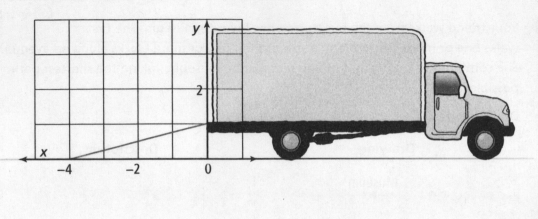

What is the rate of change of the linear function that models the top of the truck?

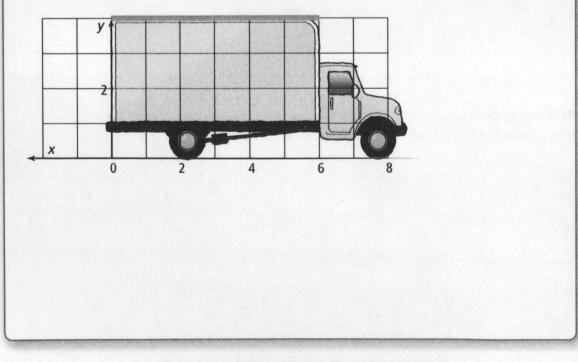

Got It?

PART 2 Got It

What is the rate of change of the linear function $y = \frac{3}{2}x - 2$?

PART 3 Got It

Use the values for a 1 oz candle and a 5 oz candle to find the rate of change for the data in the table. What does the rate of change mean in this situation?

Weight of Candle (ounces)	Burn Time (hours)
1	5.5
3	16.5
5	27.5

Close and Check

Focus Question

Each part of a linear function plays a role in how its graph looks. What role does the rate of change play?

_____

_____

_____

Do you know HOW?

1. A board is placed over the stairs of a store to allow wheelchair access. What is the rate of change of the linear function that models the height of the ramp?

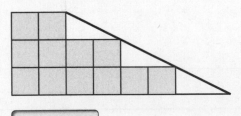

2. What is the rate of change of the linear function $y = -\frac{1}{7}x + 4$?

3. Find the rate of change for the data in the table as a unit rate.

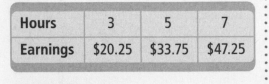

Hours	3	5	7
Earnings	$20.25	$33.75	$47.25

Do you UNDERSTAND?

4. **Reasoning** What does the rate of change mean in Exercise 3?

_____

_____

_____

_____

5. **Writing** Explain how to use the table to determine the rate of change.

Customers	CDs Sold
20	24
30	36
40	48

_____

_____

_____

_____

_____

_____

Initial Value

CCSS: **8.F.B.4:** ... Determine the rate of change and initial value of the function .... Interpret the rate of change and initial value of a linear function in terms of the situation it models .... Also, **8.F.A.3** and **8.F.B.5.**

Launch

© MP4, MP7, MP8

At a school craft fair, you sell T-shirts of your own design for $6 each. You bring money with you to make change. After selling 5 T-shirts, you have $44.

How much money did you bring to make change? Show your solution in a table or graph and explain your reasoning.

Reflect Why didn't you have $0 when you had not sold a T-shirt?

_____

_____

_____

_____

_____

Got It?

PART 1 Got It

Which linear function(s) have an initial value of −4?

I. $y = 4x + 5$ **II.** $y = -4 - 5x$ **III.** $y = -4x + 5$

PART 2 Got It

What is the rate of change and the initial value for the function in the graph?

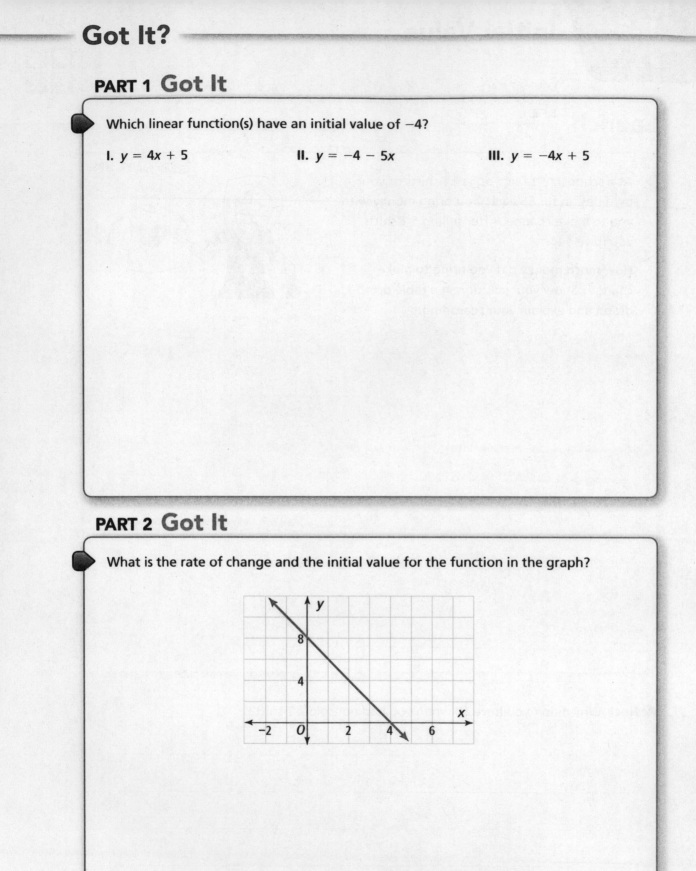

Got It?

PART 3 Got It

The function $d = 125 + 80n$ models the amount of money, in dollars, the zip line ticket cashier has in her cash register after selling n tickets.

How much money did the cashier have in the register before she sold any tickets?

Close and Check

Focus Question

Each part of a linear function plays a role in how its graph looks. What role does the initial value play?

_____

_____

_____

_____

Do you know HOW?

1. What is the initial value of the linear function $y = 5x - 6$?

2. The graph below shows the outside temperature for several hours in one day. Write each value and the equation of the linear function.

   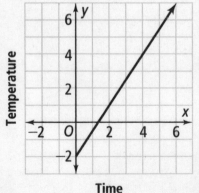

   Time

   rate of change:

   initial value: _____

   function rule: _____

Do you UNDERSTAND?

3. **Reasoning** Explain what the initial value and the rate of change mean in Exercise 2.

   _____

   _____

   _____

   _____

4. **Error Analysis** A student looks at the graph below and says that the rate of change is $\frac{2}{1}$ and the initial value is 2. Explain why this is incorrect.

   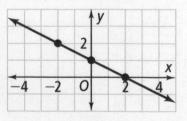

   _____

   _____

   _____

   _____

Comparing Two Linear Functions

Digital Resources

CCSS: 8.F.A.2: Compare properties of two functions each represented in a different way (algebraically, graphically, numerically in tables, or by verbal descriptions).

Launch

(C) MP1, MP7

The city's second-best scientist knew his Robot Blue was too slow to beat Robot Red in a 100-yard race. So, he rigged the race to make it end in a tie.

How did the scientist rig the race? How much faster than Robot Blue does Robot Red run?

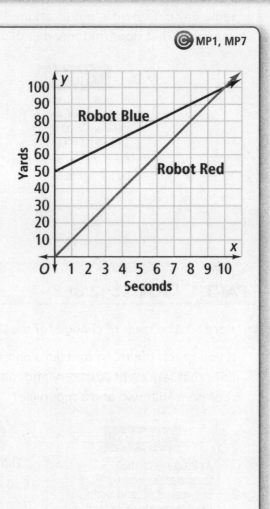

Reflect When you compare the linear functions of the two robots on the graph, what are you comparing?

_____

_____

_____

_____

_____

Got It?

PART 1 Got It (1 of 2)

The functions below describe the temperatures in degrees Fahrenheit on the same day in two different locations. Which function has the greater rate of change? What does that mean in this situation?

Funtown

At 4:00 P.M., the temperature was 70°F. Between 4:00 P.M. and 10:00 P.M., the temperature decreased by 2°F per hour.

Shoester

$t = 72 - 2h$, where t is the temperature and h is the number of hours since 4:00 P.M.

PART 1 Got It (2 of 2)

Here are the rates of change for the three temperature functions from the Example.

If you graph the three functions on the same set of axes, what will be true about the lines that represent Eastberry and Hilltown? What will be true about the lines that represent Hilltown and Topperville?

Eastberry

At 8:00 A.M., the temperature was 62°F. Between 8:00 and noon, the temperature increased by 3°F per hour.

In Eastberry, the rate of change is 3.

Hilltown

Time	Temp. (°F)
6:00 A.M.	58
7:00 A.M.	60
8:00 A.M.	62
9:00 A.M.	64
10:00 A.M.	66
11:00 A.M.	68
12 noon	70

In Hilltown, the rate of change is 2.

Topperville

$t = 54 + 2h$, where t is the temperature in degrees Fahrenheit and h is the number of hours since 8:00 A.M.

In Topperville, the rate of change is also 2.

Got It?

PART 2 Got It

 These functions describe the temperatures in degrees Fahrenheit on the same day in two different locations. Compare the initial values of the functions. What can you conclude in this situation?

Funtown	Shoester
At 4:00 P.M., the temperature was 70°F. Between 4:00 P.M. and 10:00 P.M., the temperature decreased by 2°F per hour.	$t = 72 - 2h$, where t is the temperature and h is the number of hours since 4:00 P.M.

Close and Check

Focus Question

How can you compare linear functions? Why would you want to?

_____

_____

_____

_____

Do you know HOW?

1. Circle the two linear functions of the lines that do not intersect.

$y = \frac{1}{4}x + 5$ $y = \frac{4}{1}x - 5$

$y = \frac{1}{4}x - 5$ $y = -\frac{4}{1}x + 5$

Use the graph below to answer Exercises 2 and 3.

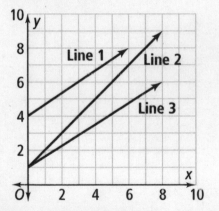

2. Which two lines have the same rate of change?

Lines 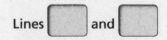 and

3. Which two lines have the same initial value?

Lines 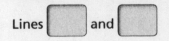 and

Do you UNDERSTAND?

4. **Reasoning** Two linear functions have the same rate of change and the same initial value. What do you know about the graph of the two lines? Explain.

_____

_____

_____

_____

_____

5. **Writing** You sell 7 tickets to the school play to your family. Your friend sells 4 tickets to her family. On Saturday, your friend sells twice as many tickets as you. Describe the graphs of these ticket sales.

_____

_____

_____

_____

_____

Constructing a Function to Model a Linear Relationship

Digital Resources

CCSS: 8.F.B.4: Construct a function to model a linear relationship between two quantities .... Interpret the rate of change and initial value of a linear function in terms of the situation it models, and in terms of its graph or a table of values.

Launch

© MP1, MP3

The equation, the table, and the graph each represent the same functional relationship. Make up a real-world situation that matches this function. Tell how it matches.

$$y = 2x + 10$$

Input	Output
0	10
2	14
4	18
6	22
8	26
10	30

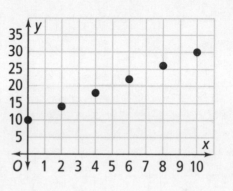

Reflect Which representation was most helpful in thinking of a situation—the equation, the table, or the graph? Explain.

_____

_____

_____

_____

Got It?

PART 1 Got It

A model train passes its model depot at time $t = 0$. After 3 minutes, the train has traveled a distance of 132 ft along the track.

Write a linear function rule that models the distance from the depot the train has traveled after any number of minutes.

PART 2 Got It

Another jewelry store sells similar charm bracelets and charms. A bracelet with three charms costs $8. A bracelet with four charms costs $9.

Write a function rule to model the cost of a bracelet with any number of charms.

Got It?

PART 3 Got It

The gardener used a hose to refill the tank when it reached 5 gallons. The hose filled the tank at a rate of 6 gallons per minute.

Write a function rule to model the amount of water in the tank as it was being refilled.

Close and Check

> **Focus Question**
>
> What do you need to know to write a linear function rule?
>
> _____
>
> _____
>
> _____

Do you know **HOW?**

1. A box office is selling concert tickets for $5 each.

   Write a function rule to model the price p for any number of tickets t.

   [ ]

2. The same box office offers buttons with pictures of the band with the purchase of any ticket. You pay $6 for a ticket and 1 button, while your friend pays $8 for a ticket and 3 buttons.

   Write a function rule to model the price *p* for a ticket and any number of buttons *b*.

   [ ]

3. The box office decides to charge a service fee of $1.75 for each transaction.

   Write a function rule to model the new price *p* for any number of tickets *t*.

   [ ]

Do you **UNDERSTAND?**

4. **Compare and Contrast** Tell what is the same and what is different about the graphs of the following function rules.

   $y = 3x + 5$ and $y = -3x + 5$

   _____

   _____

   _____

   _____

   _____

   _____

5. **Writing** Explain how it is possible to write the linear function rule for a line by using the point and the rate of change given below.

   $(0, -6); m = \frac{3}{4}$

   _____

   _____

   _____

   _____

Problem Solving

CCSS: 8.F.B.4: Construct a function to model a linear relationship between two quantities ... .
Interpret the rate of change and initial value of a linear function in terms of the situation it models, and
in terms of its graph or a table of values.

Launch

MP4, MP5

The city's second-best scientist makes 95 Robot Blues. He sells them
only in boxes of 4 robots each and waits for orders.

After how many orders will the scientist have to make more robots? Use a table,
graph, or equation to support your answer.

Reflect How does the graph, table, or equation help you solve the problem?

_____

_____

_____

_____

Got It?

PART 1 Got It

At time $t = 0$, a bicyclist begins riding at a constant speed. Ten minutes later the bicyclist has traveled 2.5 miles.

After 25 minutes, the bicyclist narrowly misses a pothole. How far has the bicyclist traveled?

PART 2 Got It

A jewelry store sells charm bracelets and charms. A bracelet with two charms costs $7.50. A bracelet with four charms costs $9.50.

Use a linear function to model the cost of a bracelet with c charms. Find the value of the function for $c = -2$. Explain the meaning of the associated point on the graph of the function, in terms of the situation.

Got It?

PART 3 Got It

After how many minutes is there no longer enough water in the tank to water the vegetable garden?

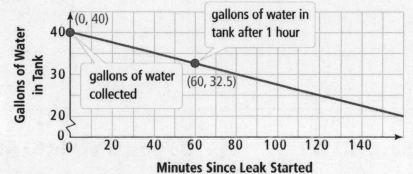

Close and Check

Focus Question

How are linear functions useful?

_____

_____

_____

_____

Do you know HOW?

1. At $t = 0$, a sudden downpour of rain begins to fall at a constant rate. After 15 minutes, 1.5 inches of rain has fallen. Later during the storm, you check the rain gauge. How long has it been raining when you check the gauge?

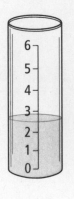

☐ minutes

2. The rain suddenly stops 30 minutes after it began. How much total rain has fallen?

☐ inches

Do you UNDERSTAND?

3. **Error Analysis** The data in the table was used to write the linear function rule $y = -x + 5$. Explain the error in the function rule.

Grade	Age
?	3
1	6
4	9
7	12

_____

_____

_____

4. **Writing** How can understanding the meaning of the parts of a linear function rule be helpful when evaluating the positive and negative solutions of a function?

_____

_____

_____

_____

_____

New Vocabulary: initial value, linear function rule
Review Vocabulary: linear function, rate of change, slope, *y*-intercept

Vocabulary Review

Identify two challenging vocabulary terms from this topic. Write one vocabulary term in the center oval, and fill in the surrounding boxes with details that will help you better understand the term.

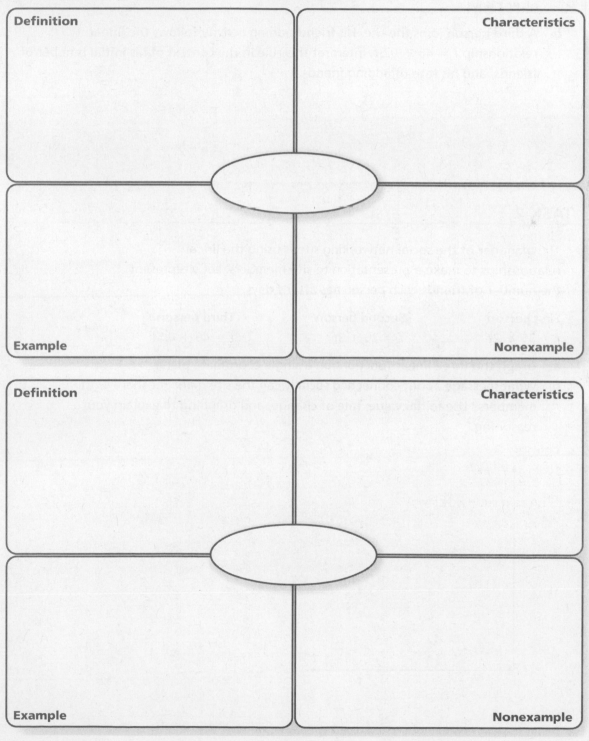

Definition

Characteristics

Example

Nonexample

Definition

Characteristics

Example

Nonexample

Pull It All Together

TASK 1

Two people join a social networking website. The first person adds 35 friends initially, and 2 friends each day. The second person adds 20 friends initially, and then 3 friends each day.

a. Write a linear function rule for the number of friends each person has on the site after t days.

b. A third person joins the site. His friend-adding activity follows the linear relationship $f = 40 + 0.5t$. Interpret this rule in the context of his initial number of friends, and his rate of adding friends.

TASK 2

The manager of the social networking site is using the linear relationships to make a presentation to site members. Let y represent the number of friends each person has after f days.

First person
$f = 35 + 2t$

Second person
$f = 20 + 3t$

Third person
$f = 40 + 0.5t$

a. Graph the three linear functions on a single coordinate plane.

b. What message about connecting socially can the site manager share with members? Use initial value, rate of change, and graphing to explain your reasoning.

Translations

Digital Resources

CCSS: **8.G.A.1:** Verify ... properties of ... translations: **8.G.A.1a:** Lines are taken to lines ... segments to ... segments .... **8.G.A.1b:** Angles ... to angles .... **8.G.A.1c:** Parallel lines ... to parallel lines. **8.G.A.3:** Describe the effect of dilations ... and reflections ... using coordinates.

Launch

Ⓒ MP3, MP5

Your friend begins building a figure out of shapes. He traces a trapezoid, slides it, traces one side, and then strangely stops.

Complete the tracing of the trapezoid to show your friend's slide. Explain why your tracing shows the slide.

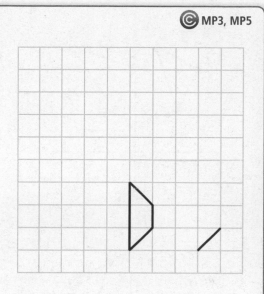

How my friend slid the trapezoid:

How my tracing shows the slide:

Reflect Were there parallel line segments in the trapezoid before the slide? What about after the slide? Tell how you know.

_____

_____

_____

_____

Got It?

PART 1 Got It

Which graph shows △DEF and △D′E′F′, its image after a translation?

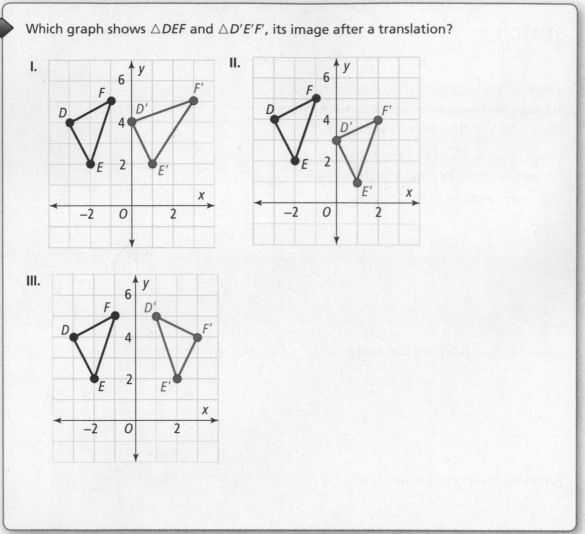

PART 2 Got It

The vertices of △JKL are J(−4, 1), K(−2, −2), and L(1, 2). If you translate △JKL 4 units right and 2 units up, what are the coordinates of K′?

Got It?

PART 3 Got It

PQRS is a parallelogram. Use arrow notation to write a rule that describes the translation of *PQRS* to *P'Q'R'S'*.

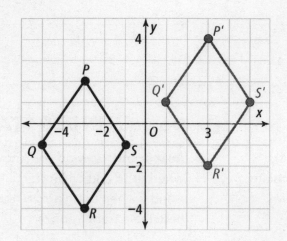

Close and Check

Focus Question

MP2, MP5

What effect does a slide have on a figure?

_____

_____

_____

Do you know HOW?

1. The vertices of △XYZ are X(−4, 1), Y(2, 2), and Z(−1, −1). If you translate △XYZ 3 units left and 1 unit down, what are the coordinates of Y'?

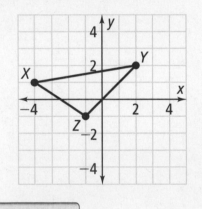

2. Use arrow notation to write a rule that describes the translation shown.

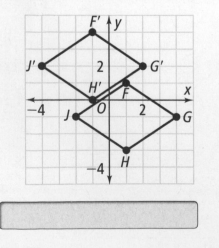

Do you UNDERSTAND?

3. Reasoning How do you know whether to add or subtract units from x and y when using arrow notation to describe a translation?

_____

_____

_____

_____

4. Error Analysis Explain the error in the translation below.

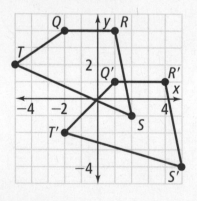

_____

_____

_____

_____

Reflections

CCSS: 8.G.A.1: Verify … properties of … reflections … : **8.G.A.1a:** Lines are taken to lines … segments to … segments … . **8.G.A.1b:** Angles … to angles … . **8.G.A.1c:** Parallel lines … to parallel lines. **8.G.A.3:** Describe the effect of dilations … and reflections … using coordinates.

Launch

Your friend continues the figure. He traces a triangle, flips it over his pencil, traces one side, and then suddenly ceases.
Complete the triangle tracing to show your friend's flip. Explain why your tracing shows the flip.

How my friend flipped the triangle:

How my tracing shows the flip:

Reflect Is there a right angle in the triangle before the flip? What about after the flip? Tell how you know.

_____

_____

_____

_____

Got It?

PART 1 Got It

Which graph shows a reflection of △DEF across the x-axis?

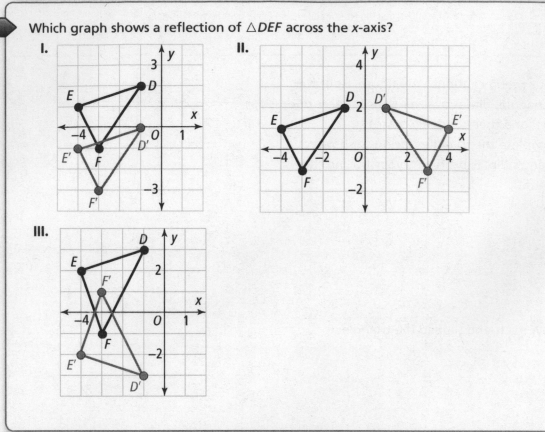

I.

II.

III.

PART 2 Got It

LMNP is a parallelogram. Describe in words how to map LMNP to its image L'M'N'P'.

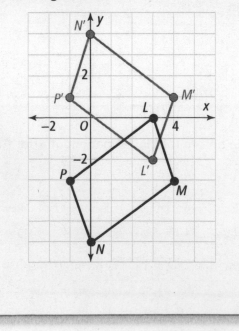

Got It?

If you reflect △*JKL* across the *y*-axis,, what are the coordinates of *J'*?

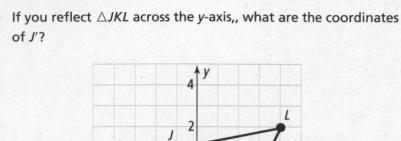

Discuss with a classmate

Circle the keyword *coordinates*.

Write a definition for this word, using the diagram from the problem as part of your definition.

Close and Check

Focus Question

What effect does a flip have on a figure?

_____

_____

_____

Do you know HOW?

1. The vertices of quadrilateral *QRST* are
   Q(−1, 3), *R*(2, 2), *S*(3, −2), *T*(1, −2).
   Graph quadrilateral *QRST* and
   quadrilateral *Q′R′S′T′*, its image after a
   reflection across the *x*-axis.

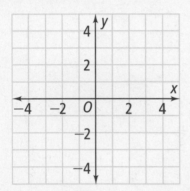

2. Use arrow notation to show how *QRST*
   maps to *Q′R′S′T′* from Exercise 1.

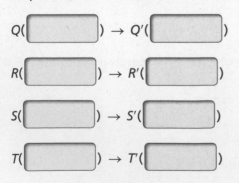

$Q(\qquad) \rightarrow Q'(\qquad)$

$R(\qquad) \rightarrow R'(\qquad)$

$S(\qquad) \rightarrow S'(\qquad)$

$T(\qquad) \rightarrow T'(\qquad)$

Do you UNDERSTAND?

3. **Compare and Contrast** How are
   translations and reflections the same
   and different?

   _____

   _____

   _____

   _____

4. **Error Analysis** A classmate says that
   the reflection across the *x*-axis
   of △*PQR* is △*P′Q′R′* where *P′*(−2, 1),
   Q′(−5, −2), and *R′*(2, −4). What error
   did he make? What should the
   vertices be?

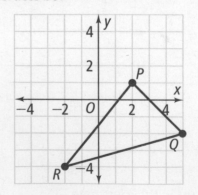

   _____

   _____

   _____

Rotations

CCSS: 8.G.A.1: Verify … properties of rotations … : **8.G.A.1a:** Lines are taken to lines … segments to … segments … . **8.G.A.1b:** Angles … to angles … . **8.G.A.1c:** Parallel lines … to parallel lines.
8.G.A.3: Describe the effect of dilations … and reflections … using coordinates.

Launch

MP1, MP5

Your friend nearly completes his figure. He traces a square, turns it, traces one side, and then curiously quits.

Complete the turn and tracing of the square. Explain why your tracing shows your friend's turn.

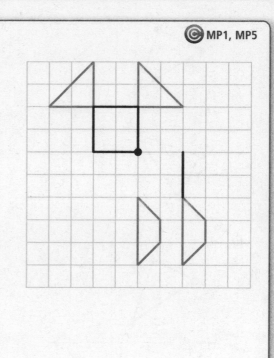

How my friend turned the square:

How my tracing shows the turn:

Reflect What other transformations could your friend have used to move the square to the same position?

_____

_____

_____

_____

_____

Got It?

PART 1 Got It

Which graph shows a rotation of △DEF about the origin?

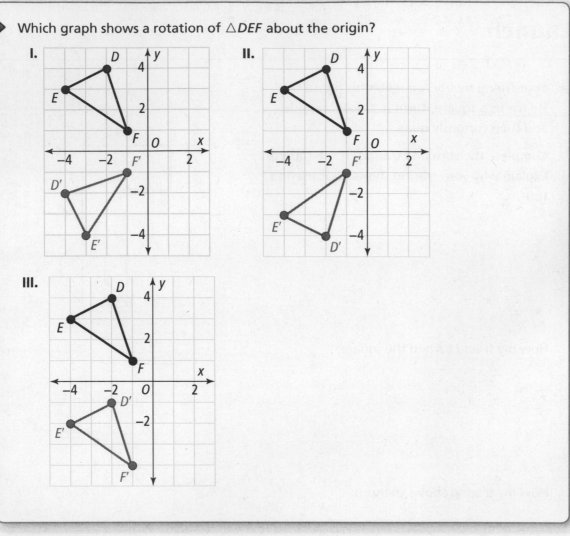

PART 2 Got It (1 of 2)

What is the angle of rotation about the origin that maps △JKO to △J'K'O'?

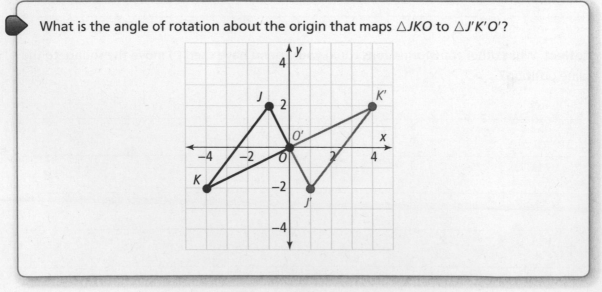

Got It?

PART 2 Got It (2 of 2)

$\triangle ABC$ maps to its image $\triangle A'B'C'$ so that $A = A'$, $B = B'$, and $C = C'$. What is the angle of rotation?

PART 3 Got It

Point P has coordinates $(3, 0)$. If you rotate P $270°$ about the origin, what are the coordinates of P'?

Close and Check

Focus Question

MP2, MP5

What effect does a turn have on a figure?

_____

_____

_____

_____

Do you know HOW?

1. Use arrow notation to show how △*JKL* maps to its image after a rotation 180° about the origin.

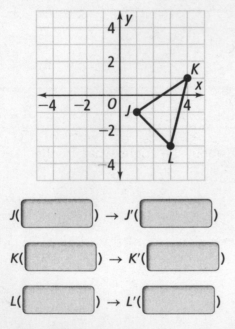

J(_____) → J'(_____)

K(_____) → K'(_____)

L(_____) → L'(_____)

2. The vertices of parallelogram *WXYZ* are *W*(−1, 1), *X*(3, 2), *Y*(3, −1), *Z*(−1, −2). The vertices of its image, parallelogram *W'X'Y'Z'*, are *W'*(−1, 1), *X'*(3, 2), *Y'*(3, −1), *Z'*(−1, −2). What is the angle of rotation?

_____

Do you UNDERSTAND?

3. Compare and Contrast How are reflections and rotations the same and different?

_____

_____

_____

_____

_____

4. Reasoning Would the relationship between the vertices of any figure rotated 360° and its image always be true regardless of the point of rotation? Explain.

_____

_____

_____

_____

_____

Congruent Figures

CCSS: 8.G.A.2: Understand that a two-dimensional figure is congruent to another if the second can be obtained from the first by a sequence of rotations, reflections, and translations; given two congruent figures, describe a sequence that exhibits the congruence ... .

Launch

Ⓒ MP5, MP6, MP8

Your neighbor drew three kites on the grid.
She said they were all exactly the same.
Do you agree? Explain how you know.

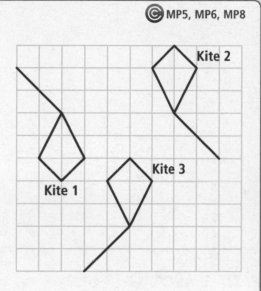

Reflect How can two shapes be exactly the same but look different?

_____

_____

_____

Got It?

PART 1 Got It (1 of 2)

Given $\triangle DEF \cong \triangle D'E'F'$, describe a sequence of rigid motions that maps $\triangle DEF$ to $\triangle D'E'F'$.

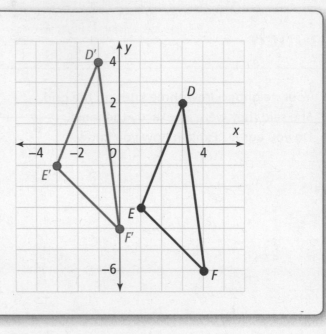

PART 1 Got It (2 of 2)

A translation followed by a translation is equivalent to which single rigid motion?

PART 2 Got It (1 of 2)

$JKLM$ is a square. Given $JKLM \cong J'K'L'M'$, describe a sequence of rigid motions that maps $JKLM$ to $J'K'L'M'$.

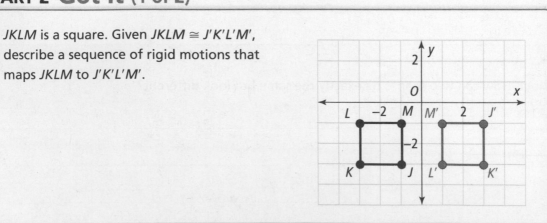

Got It?

A reflection followed by a reflection is equivalent to which single rigid motion?

PART 3 Got It

Which two triangles are congruent?

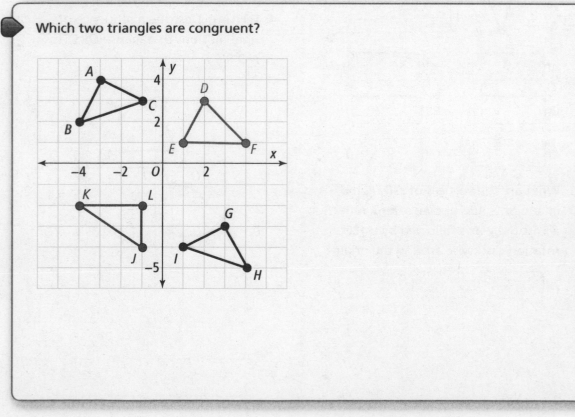

Close and Check

Focus Question

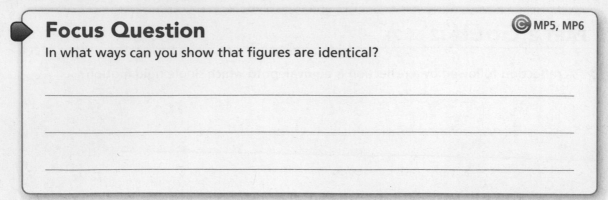

© MP5, MP6

In what ways can you show that figures are identical?

_____

_____

_____

Do you know HOW?

1. Use arrow notation to show how △ABC maps to its image after a reflection across the x-axis followed by a reflection across the y-axis.

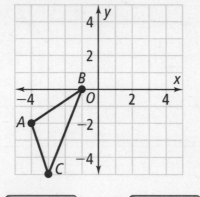

A(⬚) → A'(⬚)

B(⬚) → B'(⬚)

C(⬚) → C'(⬚)

2. What are the vertices of △DEF, the image of △ABC above, after a reflection across the y-axis followed by a 180° rotation clockwise around the origin?

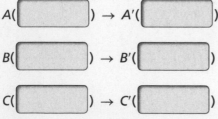

D(⬚)   E(⬚)   F(⬚)

Do you UNDERSTAND?

3. **Reasoning** Assume △ABC in Problem 1 is rotated 180° about point B. What other transformation(s) could you use to map △ABC to △A'B'C'?

_____

_____

_____

_____

4. **Writing** Describe a sequence of rigid motions that maps PQRST to P'Q'R'S'T'.

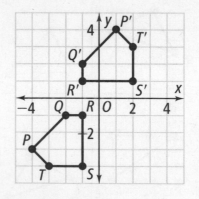

_____

_____

_____

_____

Problem Solving

CCSS: 8.G.A.2: Understand that a two-dimensional figure is congruent to another if the second can be obtained from the first by a sequence of rotations, reflections, and translations; given two congruent figures, describe a sequence that exhibits the congruence ... .

Launch

Ⓒ MP2, MP8

Draw and label three congruent figures. Each figure must be composed of more than one shape. Describe the moves needed to verify that the figures are congruent.

Reflect Besides in the last two lessons, explain how you have used or could use congruence in your life.

_____

_____

_____

_____

Got It?

PART 1 Got It

Given △GHI ≅ △JKL, describe a sequence of three different rigid motions that maps △GHI to △JKL.

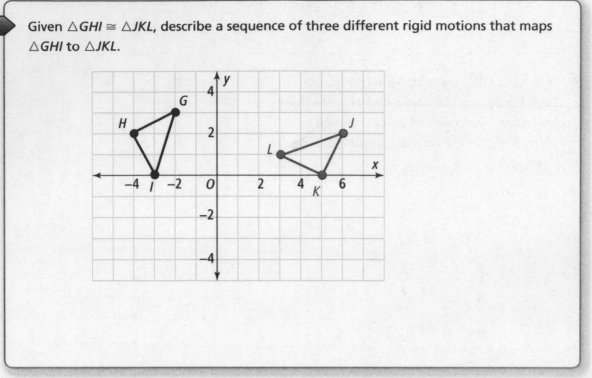

PART 2 Got It

Given that the triangle in Quadrant I is congruent to the triangle in Quadrant III, find possible coordinates for the third vertex of the triangle in Quadrant III.

I. (−1, −1)   **II.** (−1, −4)   **III.** (−5, −1)   **IV.** (−5, −4)

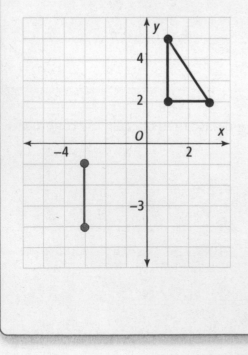

Discuss with a classmate

Define the key terms: quadrant, coordinates. Label all the quadrants and the coordinates of the given figures in the diagram at the left.

Close and Check

Focus Question

© MP1, MP4

How can you use what you know about transformations and congruence to solve problems?

_____

_____

_____

_____

 ## Do you know HOW?

1. Given figure *ABCDEF* ≅ *LMNPQR*, circle the sequence of rigid motions that maps *ABCDEF* to *LMNPQR*.

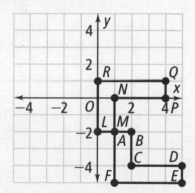

A. Reflection across *x*-axis, rotation 90° clockwise about point *B'*, translation 1 unit right

B. Rotation 180° counterclockwise about point *A'*, reflection across *y*-axis, translation 2 units left

C. Reflection across *y*-axis, rotation 180° clockwise about point *A'*, translation 1 unit right

D. Rotation 90° counterclockwise about point *C'*, translation 2 units left, reflection across *y* = 1

Do you UNDERSTAND?

2. Reasoning Given △*PQR* ≅ △*STU*, explain how to find a possible coordinate for point *T*.

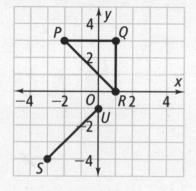

_____

_____

_____

3. Writing Explain why there are two possible coordinates for point *T*.

_____

_____

_____

_____

_____

This page intentionally left blank.

New Vocabulary: congruent figures, image, reflection, rigid motion, rotation, transformation, translation
Review Vocabulary: vertex of a polygon

Vocabulary Review

 Identify two challenging vocabulary terms from this topic. Write one vocabulary term in the center oval, and fill in the surrounding boxes with details that will help you better understand the term.

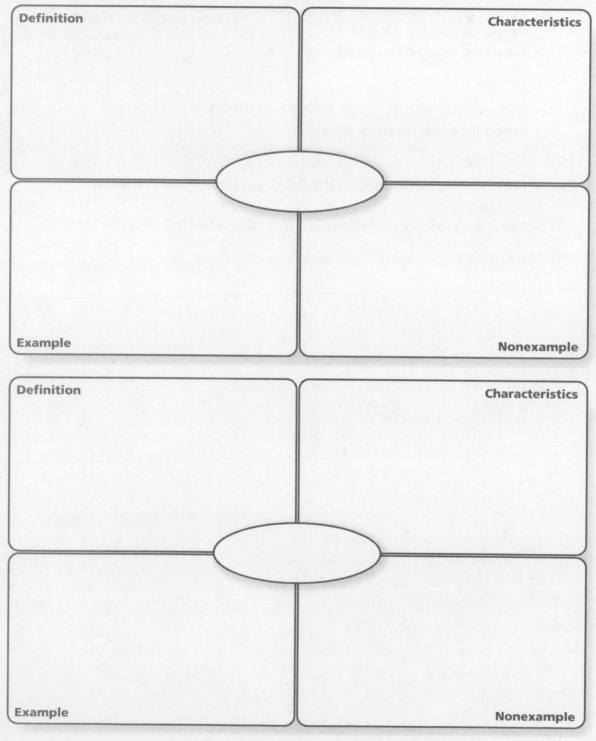

Definition	Characteristics
Example	Nonexample

Definition	Characteristics
Example	Nonexample

Pull It All Together

TASK 1

Complete all parts to solve the riddle at the right.

a. Letter One

- Start with a point at $(-2, 3)$. Translate the point 2 units left, 1 unit down, and 2 units right. Draw segments to show the translation path.
- Reflect the segments across the line $y = 2$.

> I come in all shapes and sizes. I am spelled the same forward and backward. I sound like one letter, but I really have three. What am I?

b. Letter Two

- Draw two segments: $(0, -1)$ to $(0, 0)$ and $(0, 0)$ to $(1, 1)$.
- Reflect the segments across the y-axis.

c. Letter Three

- Letter Three is congruent to Letter One. Draw Letter Three in the fourth quadrant.
- Describe a sequence of rigid motions that maps Letter One to Letter Three.

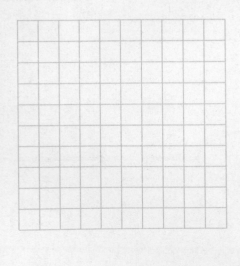

Dilations

Digital Resources

CCSS: 8.G.A.3: Describe the effect of dilations, translations, rotations, and reflections on two-dimensional figures using coordinates.

Launch

© MP2, MP6

A modern art painter used an inch-grid canvas for a figure painting.

Did the artist paint the figure to scale? Explain.

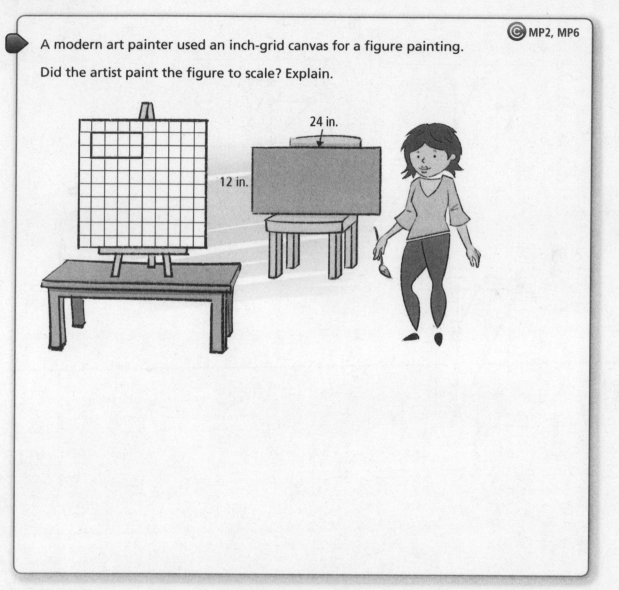

Reflect Why did the artist have to scale the painting?

_____

_____

_____

_____

Got It?

PART 1 Got It

Which graph shows a dilation?

I.

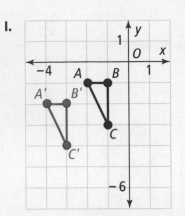

II.

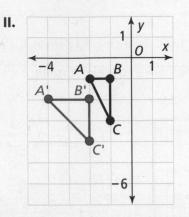

III.

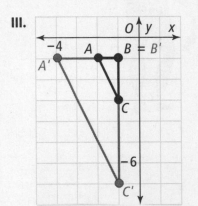

Got It?

PART 2 Got It

For the given dilation, find the scale factor. Then decide whether the dilation is an enlargement or a reduction.

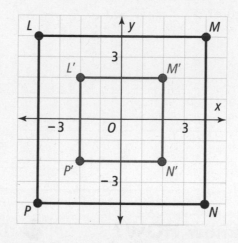

PART 3 Got It

$\triangle MNO$ has vertices $M(8, 4)$, $N(4, -4)$, and $O(0, 0)$. $\triangle M'N'O'$ is the image of $\triangle MNO$ after a dilation with center $(0, 0)$ and a scale factor of $\frac{3}{4}$. What are the coordinates of M'?

Close and Check

MP2, MP6

Focus Question

What effect does an enlargement have on a figure? What effect does a reduction have on a figure?

_____

_____

_____

_____

Do you know HOW?

1. Find the scale factor for the given dilation and tell whether the image is an enlargement or a reduction.

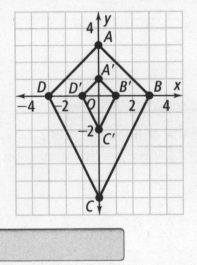

2. Parallelogram *QRST* has vertices at *Q*(−3, 1), *R*(2, 1), *S*(0, −2), and *T*(−5, −2). Find the coordinates of *Q′* after a dilation with the center at the origin and scale factor 5.

Do you UNDERSTAND?

3. **Writing** △*XYZ* has vertex *Y*(0, 0). The center of the dilation is at the origin. Describe the location of *Y′* after a dilation with scale factor $\frac{1}{5}$. Explain.

_____

_____

_____

_____

4. **Error Analysis** A classmate creates dilation *A″B″C″D″* for Exercise 1 with the origin at the center with scale factor 4. She says the coordinates are *A″*(0, 5), *B″*(5, 0), *C″*(0, −6), and *D″*(−5, 0). Explain her error.

_____

_____

_____

_____

10-2

Similar Figures

CCSS: 8.G.A.3: Describe the effect of dilations ... . **8.G.A.4:** Understand that a ... figure is similar to another if the second can be obtained from the first by a sequence of ... dilations; given two similar ... figures, describe a sequence that exhibits the similarity between them.

Launch

© MP3, MP5, MP6

The artist continues to paint the figure in different sizes on the inch-grid canvas. She stops and says, "One of these shapes clearly doesn't belong. I'd better start over."

Which shape does not belong? Explain your reasoning.

Reflect Do shapes have to be the same size to belong together? Explain.

_____

_____

_____

_____

Got It?

Given △ABC ~ △DEF, describe a sequence of a rigid motion followed by a dilation with center (0, 0) that maps △ABC to △DEF.

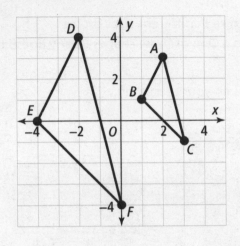

Does a given translation followed by a given dilation always map a figure to the same image as that same dilation followed by that same translation?

Got It?

JKLM and *PQRS* are squares. Given *JKLM* ~ *PQRS*, describe a sequence of a rigid motion followed by a dilation with center (0, 0) that maps square *JKLM* to square *PQRS*.

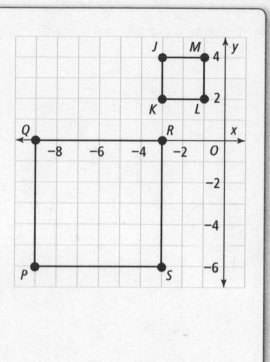

Does a given reflection followed by a given dilation always map a figure to the same image as that same dilation followed by that same reflection?

Got It?

PART 3 Got It

Which two triangles are similar?

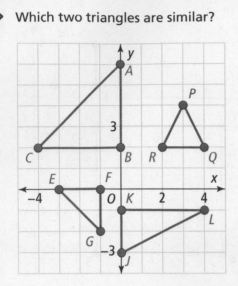

Close and Check

Focus Question

How can you show that figures are similar?

_____

_____

_____

_____

Do you know HOW?

1. Given trapezoid *QRST*, draw trapezoid *WXYZ* ~ *QRST* after a 90° clockwise rotation about the origin followed by a dilation with center (0, 0) and scale factor $\frac{1}{2}$.

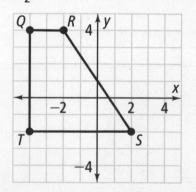

2. What would be the coordinates of *JKLM* ~ *QRST* after a reflection across the *y*-axis and a dilation with the center at the origin and scale factor 2?

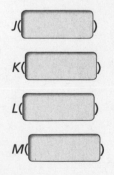

Do you UNDERSTAND?

3. **Writing** How would the figure in Exercise 1 change if trapezoid *QRST* were translated up 1 unit and right 3 units followed by a dilation with center (0, 0) and scale factor 1? Explain.

_____

_____

_____

_____

_____

4. **Compare and Contrast** How are a pair of congruent figures and a pair of similar figures alike? How are they different?

_____

_____

_____

_____

_____

This page intentionally left blank.

Relating Similar Triangles and Slope

CCSS: 8.G.A.3: Describe the effect of dilations … . **8.G.A.4:** Understand that a … figure is similar to another … . **8.EE.B.6:** Use similar triangles to explain why the slope m is the same between any two distinct points on a non-vertical line in the coordinate plane … .

Launch

Ⓒ MP3, MP8

A museum displays the artist's right triangle series. The series features right triangles painted in proportion on each painting. One painting is a fake. Which is it? Explain how you know.

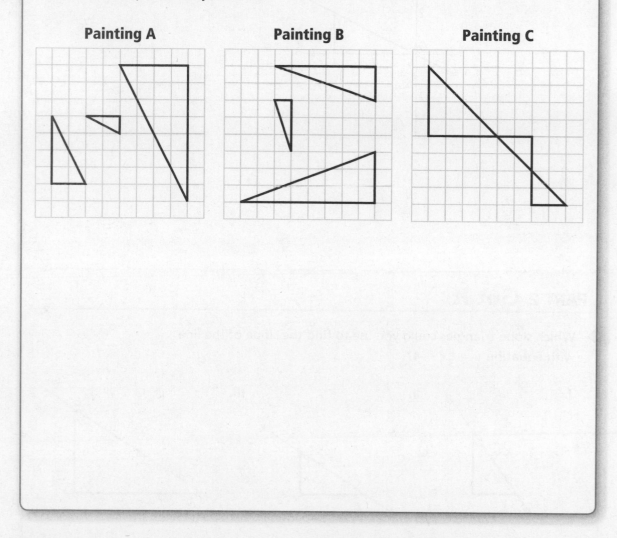

Painting A   Painting B   Painting C

Reflect For which painting was it easiest to find equivalent ratios? Explain.

_____

_____

_____

_____

Got It?

PART 1 Got It

Consider the image of the given triangle after a dilation with center (0, 0) and scale factor of $\frac{1}{2}$. What is the ratio of the rise to the run of the image triangle?

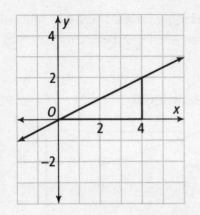

PART 2 Got It

Which slope triangles could you use to find the slope of the line with equation $y = \frac{2}{3}x - 4$?

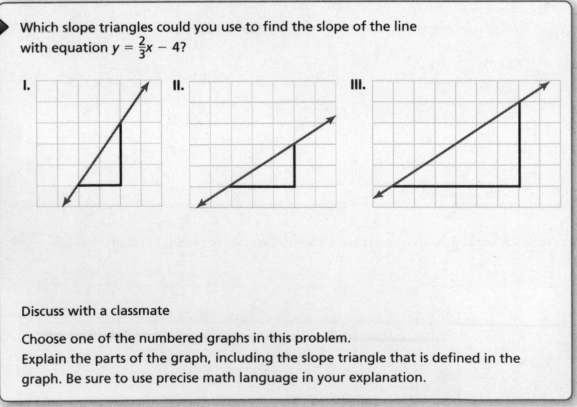

I. II. III.

Discuss with a classmate

Choose one of the numbered graphs in this problem.

Explain the parts of the graph, including the slope triangle that is defined in the graph. Be sure to use precise math language in your explanation.

Close and Check

▶ Focus Question

How are similar triangles and slope related?

_____

_____

_____

_____

▶ Do you know **HOW?**

1. Consider the image △XYZ after a dilation with center (0, 0) and scale factor 2. What is the ratio of the rise to the run of the image triangle?

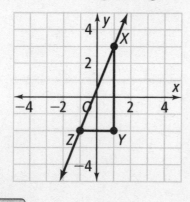

2. What is the slope of the image of △XYZ in Exercise 1 after a 180° rotation about point Y and a dilation with center (0, 0) and scale factor $\frac{1}{3}$?

▶ Do you **UNDERSTAND?**

3. **Writing** Explain how you can use slope to check the accuracy of a dilation.

_____

_____

_____

_____

4. **Error Analysis** Your friend uses the slope triangle below to write the equation of the line: $y = \frac{1}{3}x + 3$. Explain his error and write the correct equation.

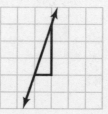

_____

_____

_____

_____

This page intentionally left blank.

Problem Solving

CCSS: 8.G.A.3: Describe the effect of dilations … . **8.G.A.4:** Understand that a … figure is similar to another if the second can be obtained from the first by a sequence of … dilations; given two similar … figures, describe a sequence that exhibits the similarity between them.

Launch

© MP1, MP5

Use the criteria to draw your own modern art figure painting on the grid. Give your painting a name.

Explain how your work of art meets the criteria.

Criteria

- Three of the figures are similar.
- Has at least one dilation.
- Has at least one translation, rotation, or reflection.

Title of Painting:

Reflect How did you choose your painting's name?

_____

_____

_____

_____

Got It?

PART 1 Got It

Given $\triangle JKL \sim \triangle PQR$, find possible coordinates for point R.

I. $\left(-\frac{1}{2}, 0\right)$ II. $(1, 0)$

III. $(5, 0)$ IV. $\left(7\frac{1}{2}, 0\right)$

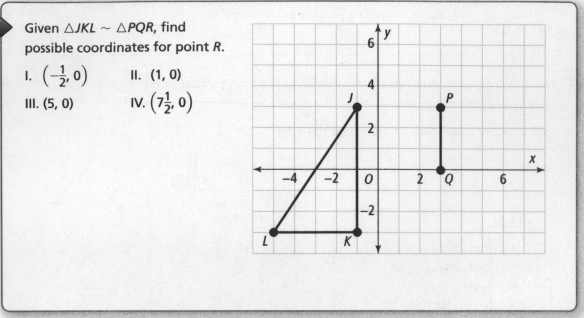

PART 2 Got It

You want to make a scale drawing of your bedroom. You decide on a scale of 3 in. = 4 ft. Your bedroom is a 12 ft-by-16 ft rectangle. What should be the dimensions of the bedroom in the scale drawing?

PART 3 Got It

A 4-ft vertical post casts a 3-ft shadow at the same time a nearby tree casts a 24-ft shadow. How tall is the tree?

Discuss with a classmate

Draw a diagram to model the problem situation.
Compare your diagrams. How are they alike? How are they different?
Is one diagram more accurate than the other? What makes it more accurate?

Close and Check

Focus Question

MP1, MP4

How can you use what you know about transformations and similarity to solve problems?

_____

_____

_____

_____

Do you know HOW?

1. Given $\triangle ABC \sim \triangle EFG$, circle the possible coordinate pair(s) for point G after a dilation only.

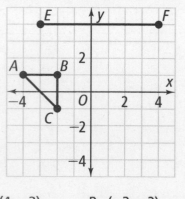

A. $(4, -3)$ B. $(-3, -3)$

C. $(-3, 11)$ D. $(4, 11)$

2. A landscaper makes a scale drawing of a triangular flowerbed. The side lengths of the drawing are 3 cm, 4 cm, and 5 cm. If the scale is 2 cm = 7 m, what are the dimensions of the actual flowerbed?

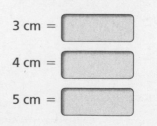

3 cm = [   ]

4 cm = [   ]

5 cm = [   ]

Do you UNDERSTAND?

3. **Reasoning** Explain how scale drawings and indirect measurements are similar. Give an example of how one is used in real life.

_____

_____

_____

_____

4. **Error Analysis** A friend is 5.5 ft tall and her shadow is 8 ft long. The shadow of a building is 160 ft long. Explain her error in calculating the height of the building. What is the actual height?

$$\frac{5.5}{160} = \frac{8}{x}; \, x = 27 \text{ ft}$$

_____

_____

_____

_____

This page intentionally left blank.

New Vocabulary: dilation, scale factor, similar figures
Review Vocabulary: rigid motion, slope, transformation

Vocabulary Review

 Identify two challenging vocabulary terms from this topic. Write one vocabulary term in the center oval, and fill in the surrounding boxes with details that will help you better understand the term.

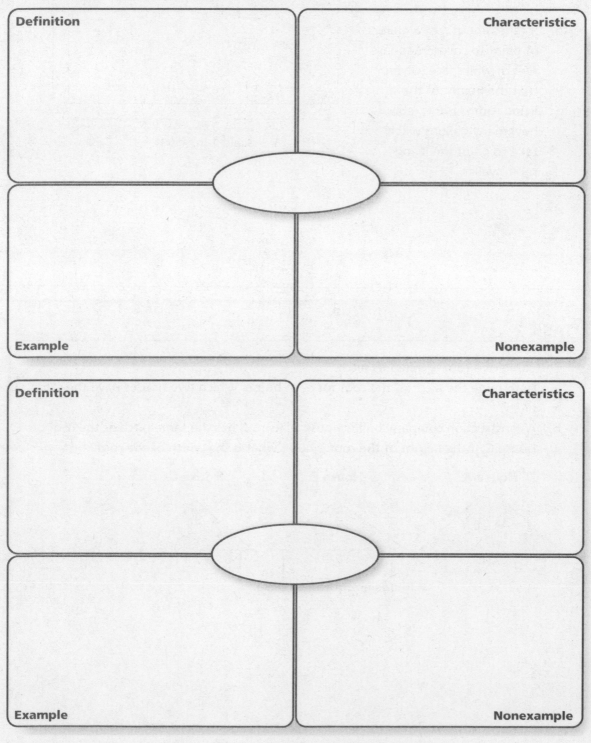

Definition

Characteristics

Example

Nonexample

Definition

Characteristics

Example

Nonexample

Pull It All Together

TASK 1

Use the scale drawing of a living room.

a. What are the length and the width of the actual living room?

b. It takes about $\frac{1}{5}$ of a gallon of paint to cover 90 square feet of wall space. Given that the height of the living room is 10 ft, about how many gallons will it take to paint the living room walls?

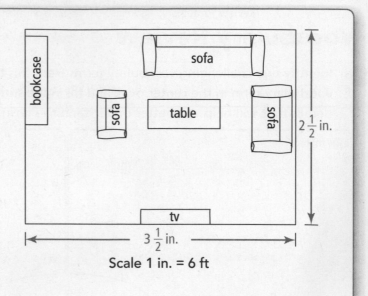

$2\frac{1}{2}$ in.

$3\frac{1}{2}$ in.

Scale 1 in. = 6 ft

TASK 2

The slope of a roof is called its pitch.

a. Determine the pitch of the roof for each house. Which two houses have the same pitch?

b. A construction company builds House D. Its roof has the same pitch as the roof of House C. If the height of the roof is 40 ft, what is the width of the roof?

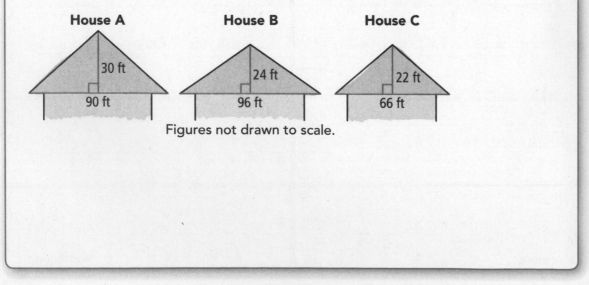

House A — 30 ft, 90 ft

House B — 24 ft, 96 ft

House C — 22 ft, 66 ft

Figures not drawn to scale.

Angles, Lines, and Transversals

Digital Resources

CCSS: 8.G.A.5: Use informal arguments to establish facts about the angle sum and exterior angle of triangles, about the angles created when parallel lines are cut by a transversal, and the angle-angle criterion for similarity of triangles …

Launch

Ⓒ MP5, MP6, MP8

Which angles have equal measures? Justify your reasoning.

Reflect Where have you seen angles like these in the real world? Explain.

_____

_____

_____

_____

_____

Got It?

PART 1 Got It

Which pairs of angles are corresponding angles?

I. $\angle 3$ and $\angle 7$

II. $\angle 1$ and $\angle 2$

III. $\angle 2$ and $\angle 6$

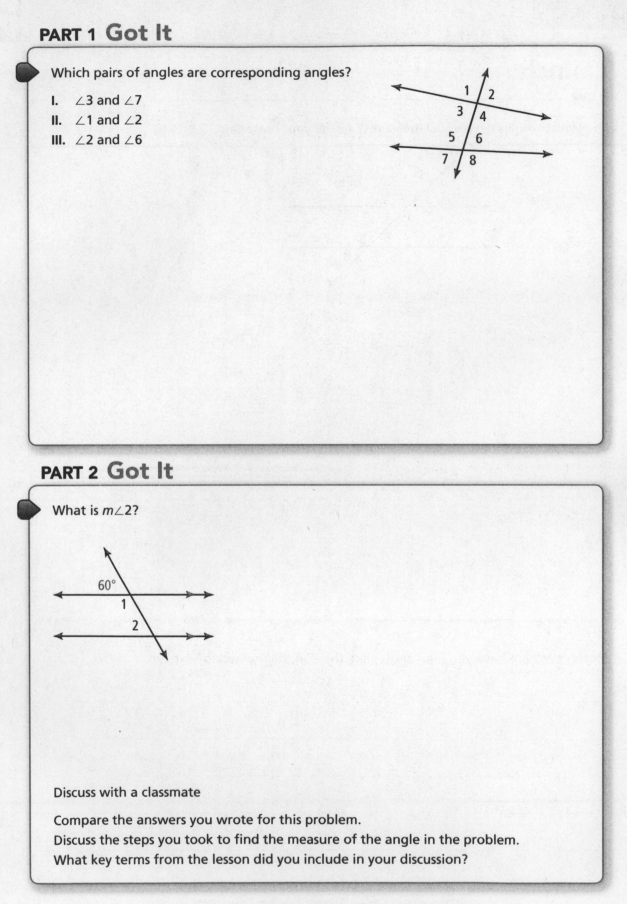

PART 2 Got It

What is $m\angle 2$?

Discuss with a classmate

Compare the answers you wrote for this problem.

Discuss the steps you took to find the measure of the angle in the problem.

What key terms from the lesson did you include in your discussion?

Got It?

PART 3 Got It (1 of 2)

What is $m\angle 1$?

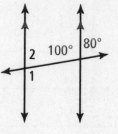

PART 3 Got It (2 of 2)

Make a conjecture about the relationship between $\angle 1$ and $\angle 4$. Justify your reasoning.

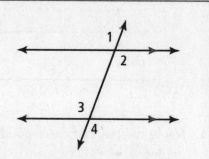

Close and Check

Focus Question

If a line intersects two parallel lines, what are the relationships among the angles formed by the lines?

_____

_____

_____

_____

Do you know HOW?

Use the diagram to complete Exercises 1–4.

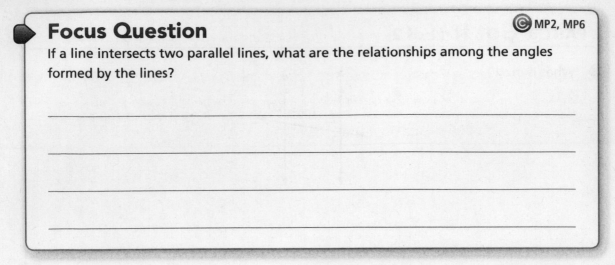

1. Name the pairs of corresponding angles.

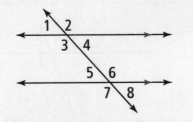

2. Name the pairs of alternate interior angles.

3. If $m\angle 4 = 50°$, what is $m\angle 8$?

4. If $m\angle 6 = 130°$, what is $m\angle 3$?

Do you UNDERSTAND?

5. **Reasoning** How many different angle measures are there in the diagram? Explain.

_____

_____

_____

_____

_____

Reasoning and Parallel Lines

Digital Resources

CCSS: 8.G.A.5: Use informal arguments to establish facts about the angle sum and exterior angle of triangles, about the angles created when parallel lines are cut by a transversal, and the angle-angle criterion for similarity of triangles ... .

Launch

© MP3, MP5, MP7

Decide whether $\overline{AB}$ and $\overline{CD}$ are parallel. Justify your reasoning.

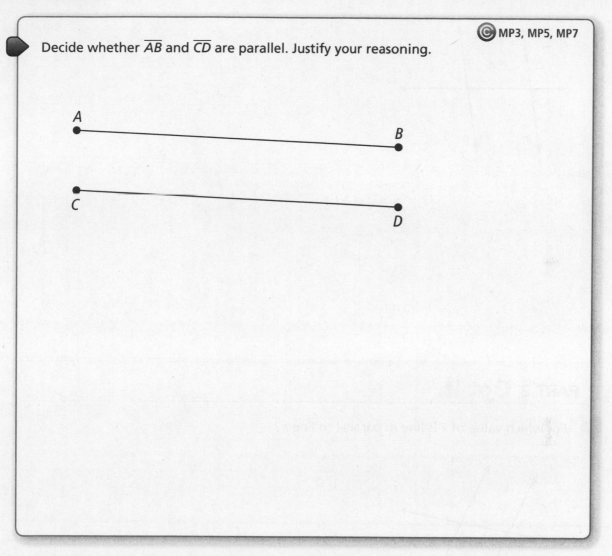

Reflect What tools or materials did you use to solve the problem? Explain your choice.

_____

_____

_____

_____

_____

Got It?

PART 1 Got It

For which value of *x* is line *m* parallel to line *n*?

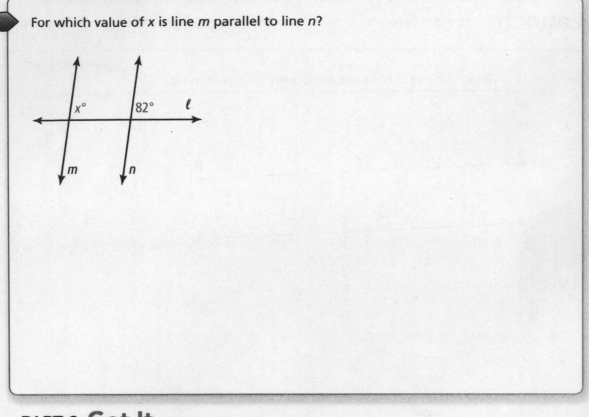

PART 2 Got It

For which value of *x* is line *m* parallel to line *n*?

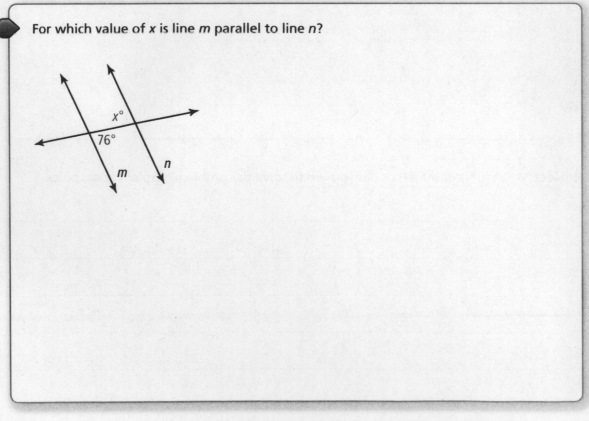

Got It?

PART 3 Got It

Which lines, if any, are parallel?

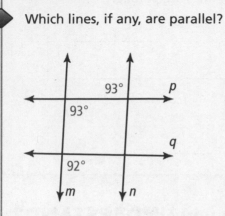

Close and Check

Focus Question

How can you use congruent angles to decide whether lines are parallel?

_____

_____

_____

_____

Do you know HOW?

Use the diagram to complete Exercises 1–3.

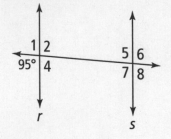

1. For what value of $m\angle 7$ is $r \parallel s$?

[ ]

2. Write **T** if the statement is true and **F** if the statement is false.

   [ ] If $m\angle 8 = 95°$, then $r \parallel s$.

   [ ] If $m\angle 5 = 85°$, then $r \parallel s$.

   [ ] If $m\angle 6 = 95°$, then $r \parallel s$.

3. If $\angle 7 \cong \angle 2$, then $r \parallel s$ because if

   [_____] angles are

   congruent, then lines are

   [_____].

Do you UNDERSTAND?

4. **Vocabulary** Explain how deductive reasoning is used to prove an argument.

   _____

   _____

   _____

   _____

   _____

5. **Reasoning** Explain why two lines cannot be assumed to be parallel just because they look parallel.

   _____

   _____

   _____

   _____

   _____

   _____

Interior Angles of Triangles

Digital Resources

CCSS: 8.G.A.5: Use informal arguments to establish facts about the angle sum and exterior angle of triangles, about the angles created when parallel lines are cut by a transversal, and the angle-angle criterion for similarity of triangles … .

Launch

© MP5, MP6

Which is greater—the measure of a straight angle or the sum of the measures of the angles of a triangle?

Use copies of the triangle to justify your reasoning. You cannot use a protractor.

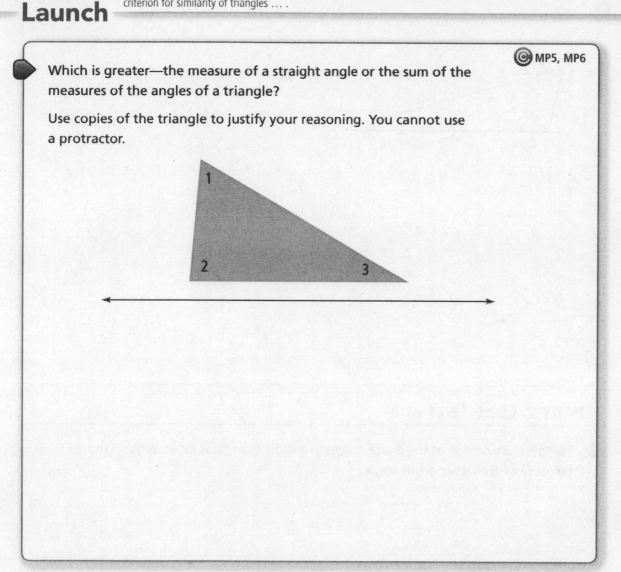

Reflect Do the angle measures of the triangle you use to compare to the straight angle matter? Explain how you could determine the answer.

_____

_____

_____

_____

Got It?

PART 1 Got It

What is $m\angle F$?

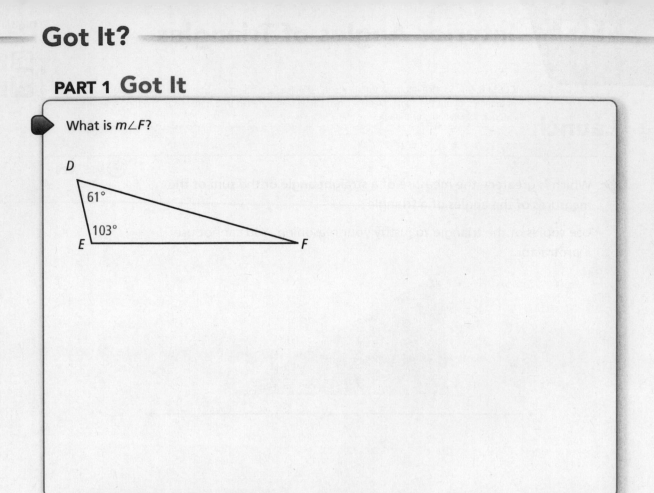

PART 2 Got It (1 of 2)

The measure of one of the acute angles in a right triangle is 42.4°. What is the measure of the other acute angle?

Discuss with a classmate

Draw a diagram to model the triangle being described in the problem.
Then, use your model to discuss how you solved the problem.
How can you check that your answer to the problem is reasonable?
Show at least one way to check your answer.

Got It?

> Make a conjecture about the sum of the measures of the acute angles in a right triangle. Justify your reasoning.

PART 3 Got It

> What is $m\angle F$?

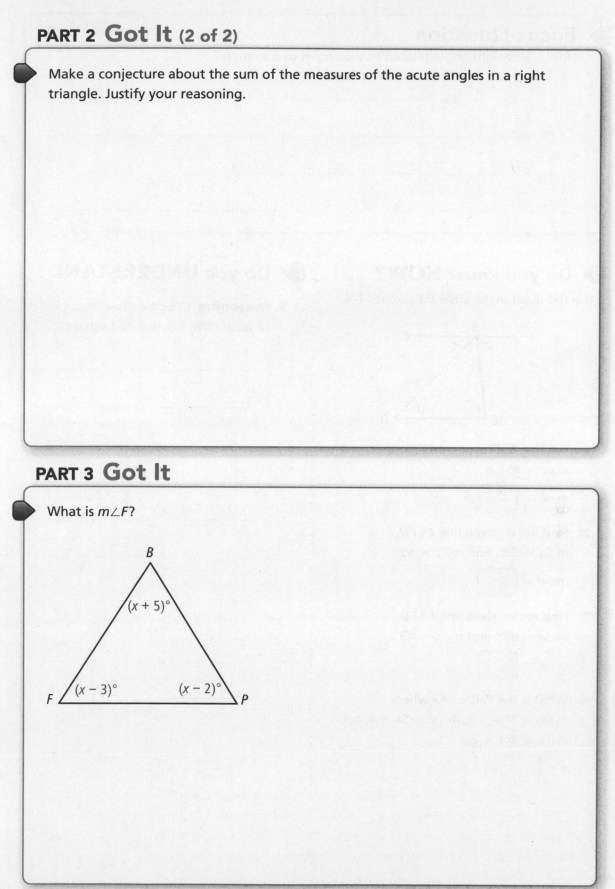

Close and Check

© MP3, MP8

Focus Question

How is a straight angle related to the angles of a triangle?

_____

_____

_____

_____

Do you know HOW?

Use the diagram to answer Exercises 1–4.

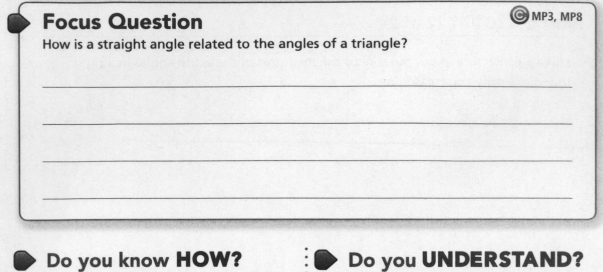

1. Find $m\angle b$, if $m\angle a = 83°$, and $m\angle c = 45°$.

   $m\angle b =$

2. Find $m\angle d$, given line $\ell \parallel \overline{ED}$, $m\angle a = 83°$, and $m\angle c = 45°$.

   $m\angle d =$

3. Find $m\angle e$, given line $\ell \parallel \overline{ED}$, $m\angle a = 83°$, and $m\angle c = 45°$.

   $m\angle e =$

4. What is the value of x when $m\angle b = 10x - 3$, $m\angle d = 5x + 6$, and $m\angle e = 8(x + 2)$?

   $x =$

Do you UNDERSTAND?

5. **Reasoning** Use deductive reasoning to justify the solution to Exercise 2.

   _____

   _____

   _____

   _____

   _____

   _____

Exterior Angles of Triangles

CCSS: 8.G.A.5: Use informal arguments to establish facts about the angle sum and exterior angle of triangles, about the angles created when parallel lines are cut by a transversal, and the angle-angle criterion for similarity of triangles ... .

Launch

ⓒ MP3, MP5

State how the sum of the measures of angles 1, 2, and 3 compares to the sum of the measures of angles 4, 5, and 6. You cannot use a protractor. Justify your reasoning.

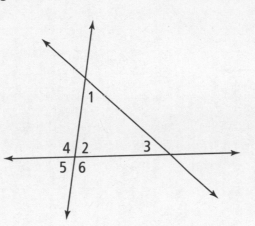

Reflect Would using a protractor make this problem easier? Explain.

_____

_____

_____

_____

_____

Got It?

PART 1 Got It

Which are the two remote interior angles of ∠6?

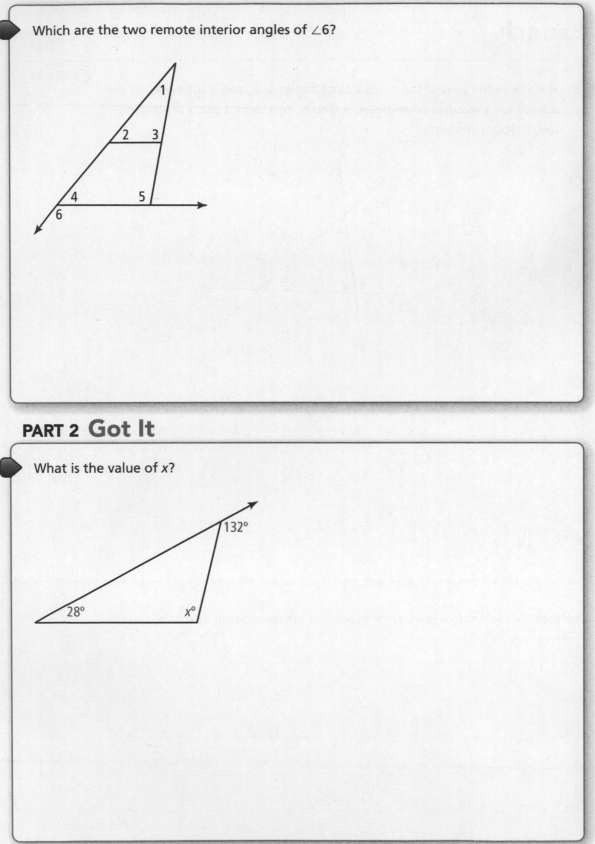

PART 2 Got It

What is the value of x?

Got It?

Given $m\angle 1 = (5x - 18)°$ and $m\angle 2 = (3x - 40)°$, what is $m\angle 1$?

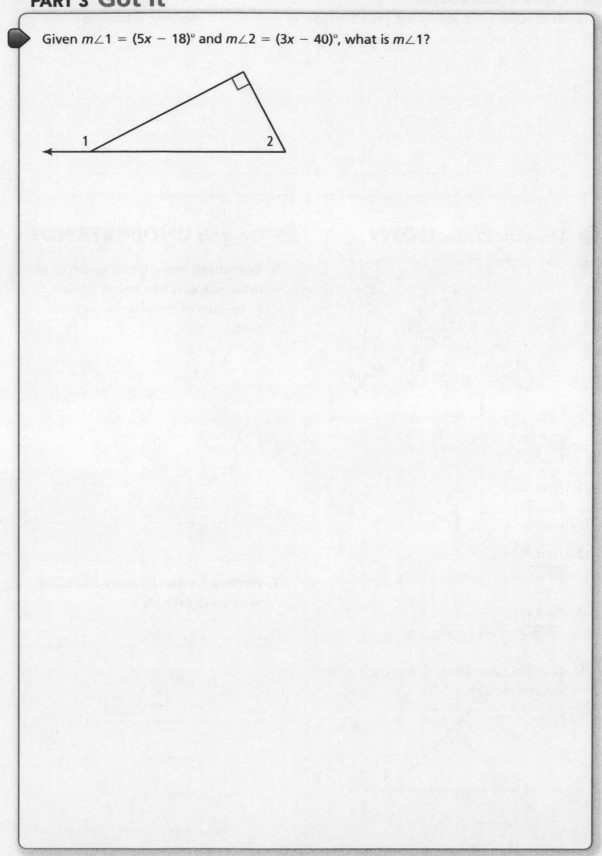

Close and Check

> ## Focus Question
>
> © MP2, MP8
>
> What is the relationship between the exterior and interior angles of a triangle?
>
> _____
>
> _____
>
> _____
>
> _____

▶ Do you know HOW?

Use the diagram to solve Exercises 1–4.

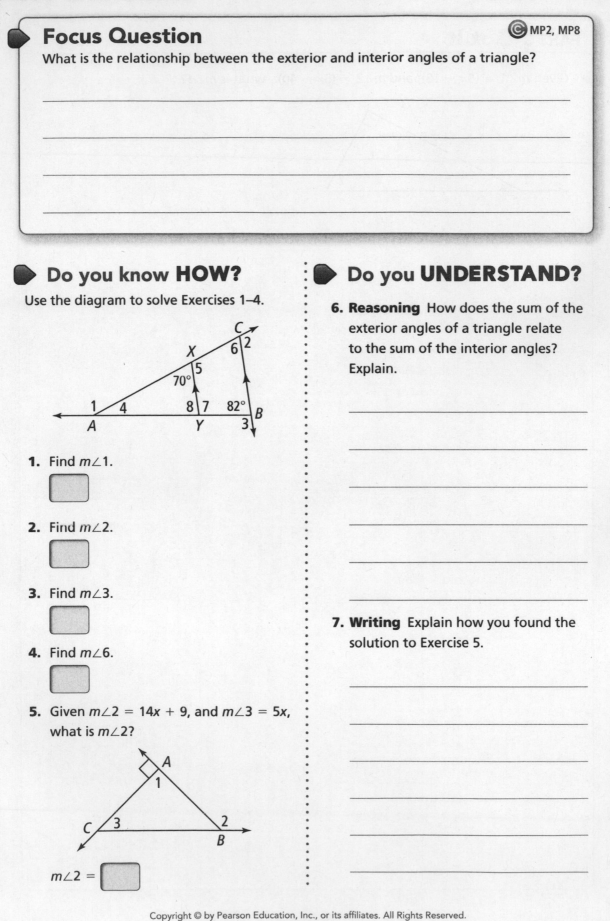

1. Find $m\angle 1$.

☐

2. Find $m\angle 2$.

☐

3. Find $m\angle 3$.

☐

4. Find $m\angle 6$.

☐

5. Given $m\angle 2 = 14x + 9$, and $m\angle 3 = 5x$, what is $m\angle 2$?

$m\angle 2 = $ ☐

▶ Do you UNDERSTAND?

6. Reasoning How does the sum of the exterior angles of a triangle relate to the sum of the interior angles? Explain.

_____

_____

_____

_____

_____

_____

7. Writing Explain how you found the solution to Exercise 5.

_____

_____

_____

_____

_____

_____

CCSS: **8.G.A.4:** Understand that … figure is similar to another if the second can be obtained from the first by … dilations … . **8.G.A.5:** Use informal arguments to establish facts about … the angle-angle criterion for similarity of triangles … . Also, **8.G.A.3.**

Launch

© MP5, MP6

Is there a relationship between the triangles? Explain. You can use a protractor, a ruler, and copies of the triangles.

Triangle 1   **Triangle 2**

Reflect Could you make another triangle related to either triangle? Explain.

_____

_____

_____

_____

_____

Got It?

PART 1 Got It

Is △GHI ~ △JKL? Justify your reasoning.

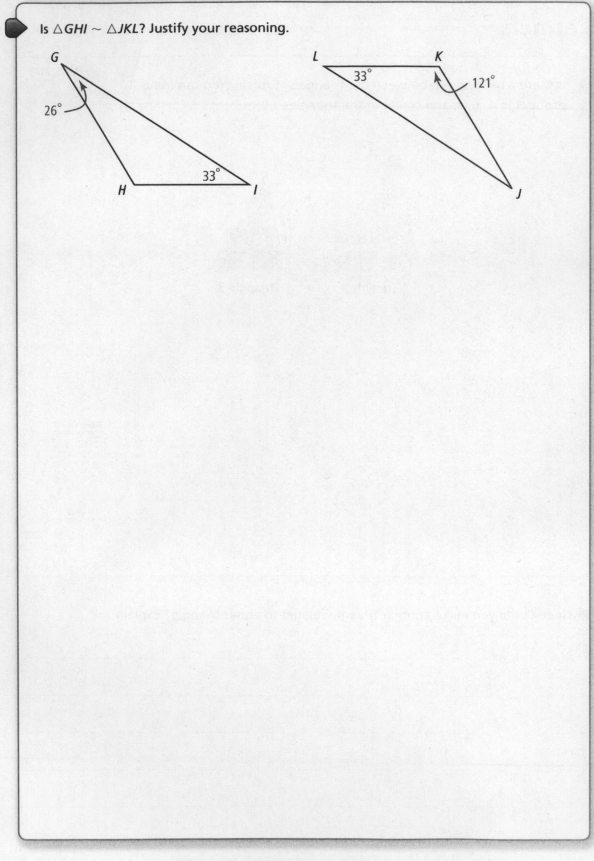

Got It?

Can you conclude that
△FGH ~ △JIH?
Justify your reasoning.

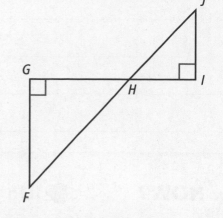

Which statements must be true?

I. △AZR ~ △AKL

II. △ZGL ~ △KGR

III. △AKL ~ △GKR

Close and Check

Focus Question

How can you use angle relationships to decide whether two triangles are similar?

Do you know HOW?

1. Which pair of triangles are similar?

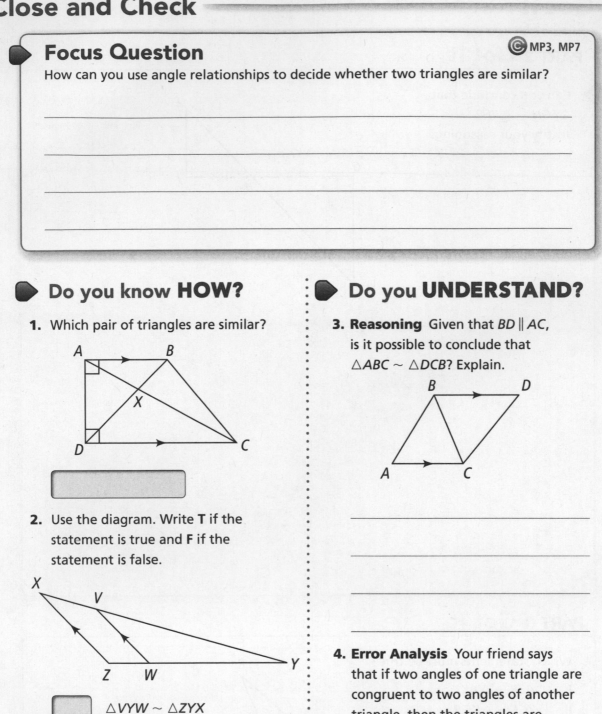

2. Use the diagram. Write **T** if the statement is true and **F** if the statement is false.

[ ] △VYW ~ △ZYX

[ ] △ZXY ~ △WVY

[ ] △VWY ~ △XZY

Do you UNDERSTAND?

3. Reasoning Given that $BD \parallel AC$, is it possible to conclude that △ABC ~ △DCB? Explain.

4. Error Analysis Your friend says that if two angles of one triangle are congruent to two angles of another triangle, then the triangles are congruent. Do you agree? Explain.

Problem Solving

CCSS: 8.G.A.5: Use informal arguments to establish facts about the angle sum and exterior angle of triangles, about the angles created when parallel lines are cut by a transversal, and the angle-angle criterion for similarity of triangles … .

Launch

© MP1, MP5

Lines 1 and 2 are parallel horizontal lines. Draw a transversal *p* that passes through point *A* and makes the greatest number of angles with equal angle measure. Justify your reasoning.

Line 1 ←———————•———————→
                          A

Line 2 ←———————————————→

Reflect How many correct answers does this problem have? Why?

_____

_____

_____

_____

_____

Got It?

PART 1 Got It

In the diagram, $m \parallel n$ and $p \parallel q$. What is $m\angle 3$?

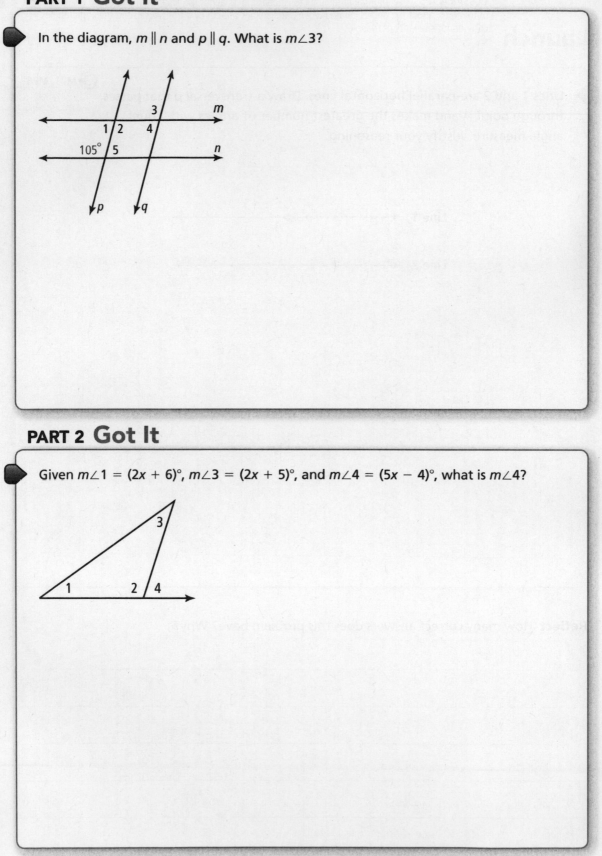

PART 2 Got It

Given $m\angle 1 = (2x + 6)°$, $m\angle 3 = (2x + 5)°$, and $m\angle 4 = (5x - 4)°$, what is $m\angle 4$?

Got It?

PART 3 Got It

Which triangles are similar?

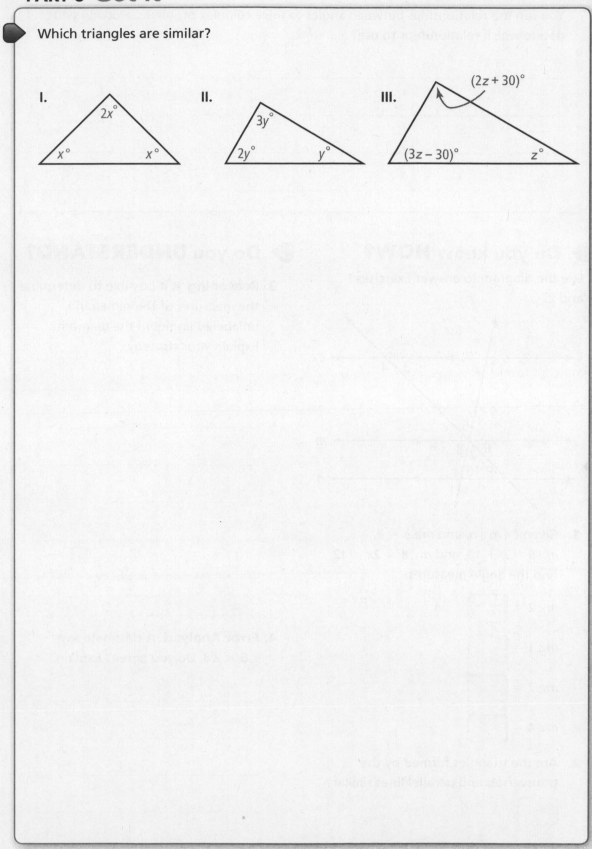

I.

$2x°$

$x°$ $x°$

II.

$3y°$

$2y°$ $y°$

III.

$(2z + 30)°$

$(3z − 30)°$ $z°$

Close and Check

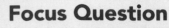

Focus Question

MP3, MP4

You can use relationships between angles to solve complex problems. How do you decide which relationships to use?

_____

_____

_____

_____

Do you know **HOW?**

Use the diagram to answer Exercises 1 and 2.

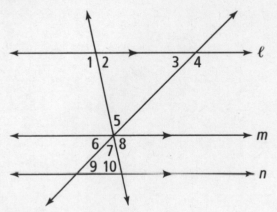

1. Given $\ell \parallel m \parallel n$, and $m\angle 3 = x$, $m\angle 5 = x + 12$, and $m\angle 8 = 2x - 12$, find the angle measures.

   $m\angle 2 = \boxed{}$

   $m\angle 1 = \boxed{}$

   $m\angle 7 = \boxed{}$

   $m\angle 4 = \boxed{}$

2. Are the triangles formed by the transversals and parallel lines similar?

   $\boxed{}$

Do you **UNDERSTAND?**

3. **Reasoning** Is it possible to determine the measures of the remaining unlabeled angles in the diagram? Explain your strategy.

   _____

   _____

   _____

   _____

   _____

   _____

   _____

4. **Error Analysis** A classmate says $\angle 6 \cong \angle 8$. Do you agree? Explain.

   _____

   _____

   _____

   _____

   _____

   _____

Topic Review

New Vocabulary: alternate interior angles, corresponding angles, deductive reasoning, exterior angle of a triangle, remote interior angles, transversal
Review Vocabulary: angle, congruent, parallel lines, straight angle

Vocabulary Review

Identify two challenging vocabulary terms from this topic. Write one vocabulary term in the center oval, and fill in the surrounding boxes with details that will help you better understand the term.

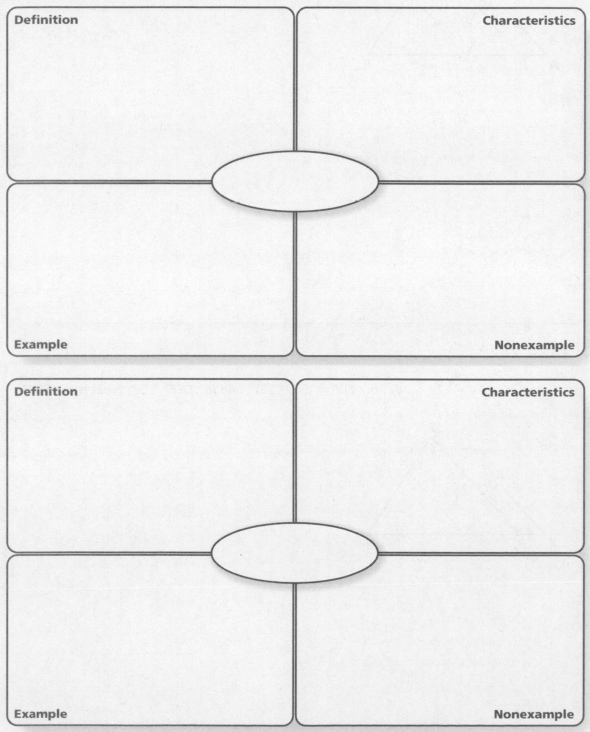

Definition

Characteristics

Example

Nonexample

Definition

Characteristics

Example

Nonexample

Pull It All Together

TASK 1

Name two pairs of similar triangles. Justify your reasoning.

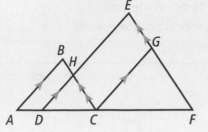

TASK 2

Given $m\angle BAC = (2x + 10)°$, $m\angle EDF = (5x - 35)°$, and $m\angle DEF = 7x°$, what is $m\angle EFD$?

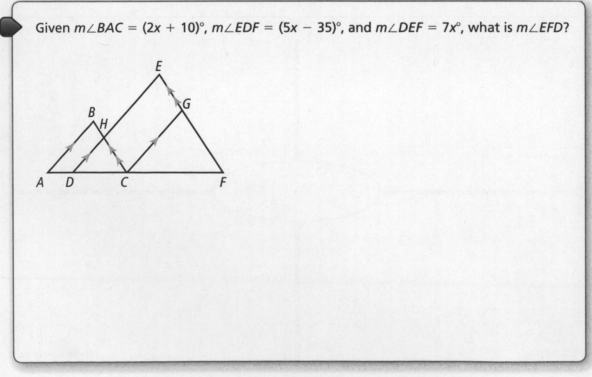

CCSS: 8.G.B.6: Explain a proof of the Pythagorean Theorem and its converse.

Launch

© MP1, MP3

No one believes the next math genius in line. He claims to know the exact coordinates of the squares that can be formed with the vertices shown, but he can't say why.

Do you believe the next math genius? Justify your reasoning.

Reflect Why is it important to justify your reasoning when showing the solution to a problem? Explain.

_____

_____

_____

_____

Got It?

PART 1 Got It

Given $\frac{x}{2} - 12 = 37$, prove $x = 98$. Complete the proof by giving the reason that justifies the second statement.

Statements	Reasons
1. $\frac{x}{2} - 12 = 37$	1. Given
2. $\frac{x}{2} = 49$	2.
3. $x = 98$	3. Multiplication Property of Equality

PART 2 Got It

It is given that $\angle A$ and $\angle B$ are the right angles. Write the missing statements and reasons in this proof that $\angle A \cong \angle B$.

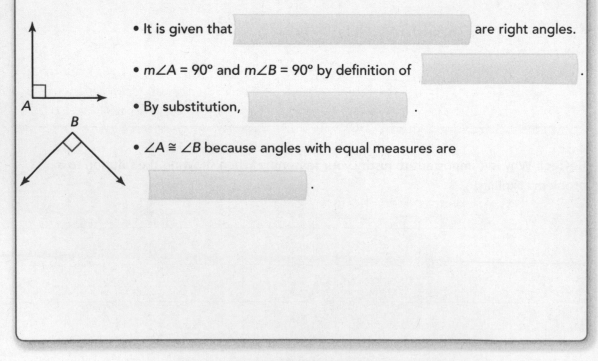

- It is given that [_____] are right angles.

- $m\angle A = 90°$ and $m\angle B = 90°$ by definition of [_____].

- By substitution, [_____].

- $\angle A \cong \angle B$ because angles with equal measures are

[_____].

Close and Check

Focus Question

© MP3, MP6

How can you use deductive reasoning to present a formal mathematical argument?

_____

_____

_____

_____

Do you know HOW?

1. Write the letters of the statements to complete the proof.

Given $5(2y + 4) = 50$, prove $y = 3$.

Statements

A. $10y + 20 = 50$ B. $5(2y + 4) = 50$

C. $y = 3$ D. $10y = 30$

[ ] Given

[ ] Distributive Property

[ ] Subtraction Property of Equality

[ ] Division Property of Equality

2. Line x intersects line y. Complete the proof that $m\angle 1 = m\angle 3$.

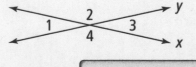

It is given that [   ].

$\angle 1 \cong \angle 3$ because $\angle 1$ and $\angle 3$ are

[   ] angles.

$m\angle 1 = m\angle 3$ because [   ]

angles have equal angle measures.

Do you UNDERSTAND?

3. Reasoning Given 1 nickel = 5 pennies and 1 dime = 10 pennies, prove 1 dime = 2 nickels.

_____

_____

_____

_____

_____

_____

_____

4. Writing How can justifying each step of a solution prevent you from making a mistake?

_____

_____

_____

_____

_____

This page intentionally left blank.

The Pythagorean Theorem

CCSS: 8.G.B.6: Explain a proof of the Pythagorean Theorem and its converse. **8.G.B.7:** Apply the Pythagorean Theorem to determine unknown side lengths in right triangles in real-world and mathematical problems in two and three dimensions.

Digital Resources

Launch

© MP1, MP3

The squares in Group 1 have a relationship. The squares in Group 2 have the same relationship.

Describe a possible relationship between the squares in each group.

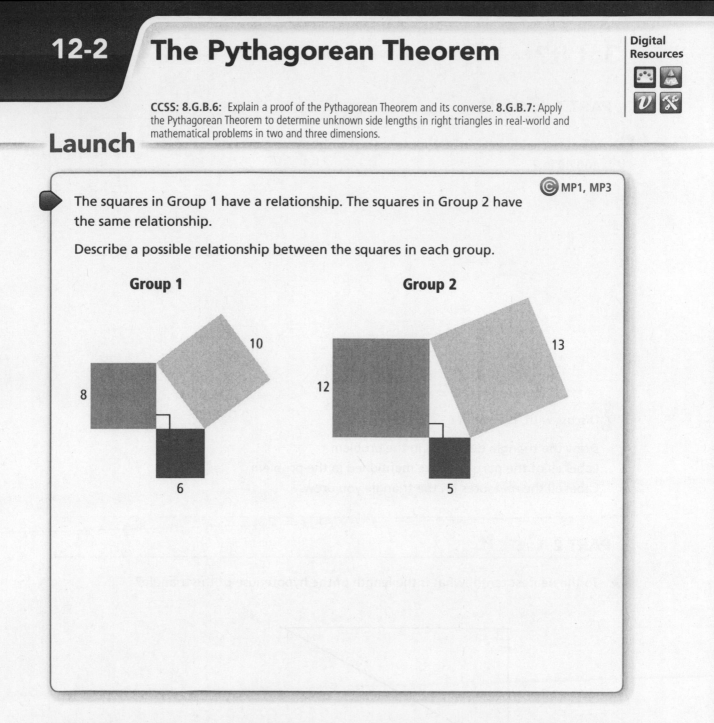

Group 1

10

8

6

Group 2

13

12

5

Reflect Do you think any group of three squares would have this relationship? Explain.

_____

_____

_____

_____

_____

Got It?

PART 1 Got It

What is the length of the hypotenuse of a right triangle with legs of lengths 9 in. and 40 in.?

Discuss with a classmate

Draw the triangle described in the problem.

Label all of the parts that are mentioned in the problem.

Label all the measures on the triangle you drew.

PART 2 Got It

To the nearest tenth, what is the length of the hypotenuse of the triangle?

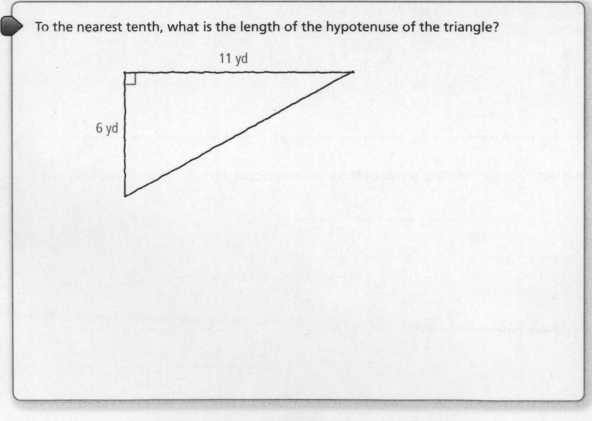

11 yd

6 yd

Got It?

PART 3 Got It

To the nearest tenth, what is the slant height of the square pyramid?

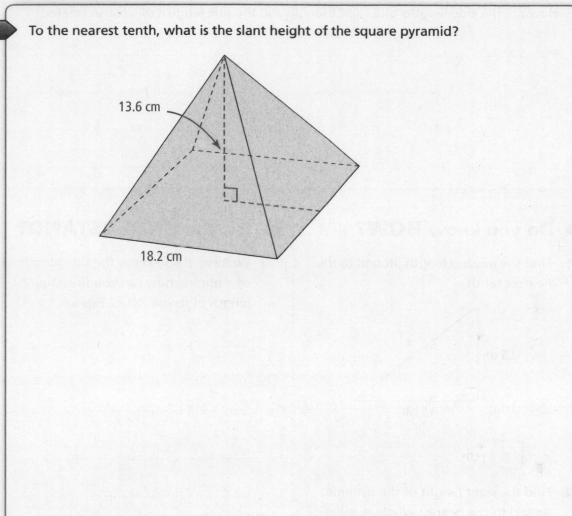

13.6 cm

18.2 cm

Close and Check

MP2, MP8

Focus Question

How are the side lengths of a right triangle and the side lengths of squares related?

_____

_____

_____

_____

Do you know HOW?

1. Find the missing length. Round to the nearest tenth.

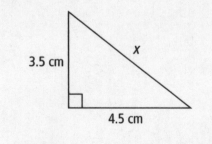

3.5 cm

x

4.5 cm

$x = $ [____] cm

2. Find the slant height of the pyramid. Round to the nearest whole number.

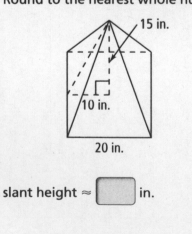

15 in.

10 in.

20 in.

slant height ≈ [____] in.

Do you UNDERSTAND?

3. **Writing** If you know the side length of a square, how can you find the length of its diagonal? Explain.

_____

_____

_____

_____

_____

4. **Error Analysis** Your friend knows that a triangle with side lengths 3, 4, and 5 is a right triangle. She says that the side lengths 5, 6, and 7 must also form a right triangle. Describe her error.

_____

_____

_____

_____

_____

_____

Finding Unknown Leg Lengths

CCSS: 8.G.B.7: Apply the Pythagorean Theorem to determine unknown side lengths in right triangles in real-world and mathematical problems in two and three dimensions.

Launch

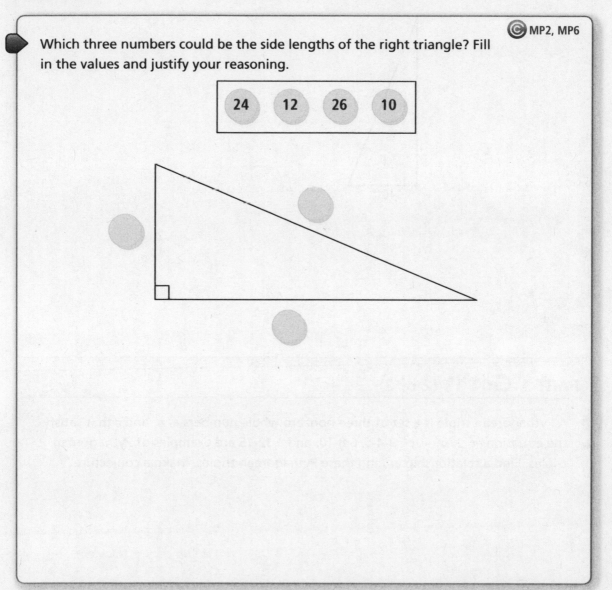

© MP2, MP6

Which three numbers could be the side lengths of the right triangle? Fill in the values and justify your reasoning.

24   12   26   10

Reflect Did you try the side lengths or the hypotenuse first when solving the problem? Does it matter? Explain.

_____

_____

_____

Got It?

What is the length of the unknown leg of the right triangle?

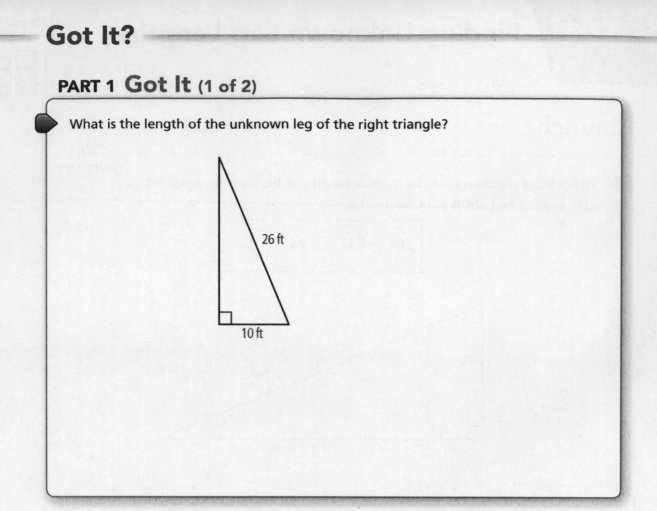

26 ft

10 ft

A Pythagorean triple is a set of three nonzero whole numbers a, b, and c that satisfy the equation $a^2 + b^2 = c^2$. 3-4-5, 6-8-10, and 9-12-15 are examples of Pythagorean triples. Find a relationship among these Pythagorean triples. Make a conjecture.

Got It?

PART 2 Got It

To the nearest tenth, what is the length of the unknown leg of the right triangle?

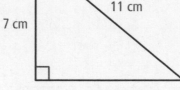

7 cm

11 cm

PART 3 Got It

To the nearest tenth, what is the height of the square pyramid?

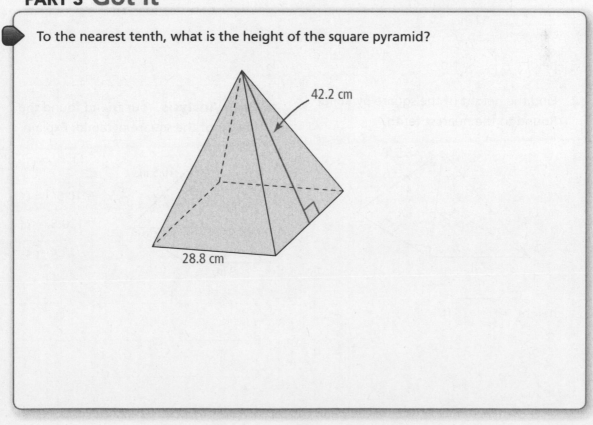

42.2 cm

28.8 cm

Close and Check

◆ Focus Question

When you know the lengths of two sides of a right triangle, how do you find the third?

_____

_____

_____

_____

◆ Do you know HOW?

1. Find the height of the sheet of paper. Round to the nearest whole number.

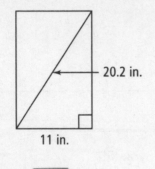

20.2 in.

11 in.

height = ☐ in.

2. Find the height of the square pyramid. Round to the nearest tenth.

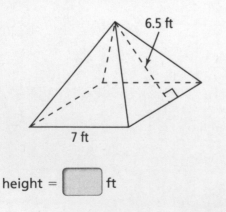

6.5 ft

7 ft

height = ☐ ft

◆ Do you UNDERSTAND?

3. **Reasoning** A square has a diagonal of $\sqrt{50}$. How can you find the side length of the square?

_____

_____

_____

_____

_____

4. **Error Analysis** Your friend found the height of the square pyramid. Explain her error.

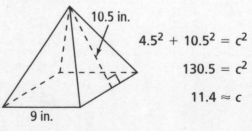

10.5 in.

$$4.5^2 + 10.5^2 = c^2$$

$$130.5 = c^2$$

$$11.4 \approx c$$

9 in.

_____

_____

_____

_____

The Converse of the Pythagorean Theorem

CCSS: 8.G.B.6: Explain a proof of the Pythagorean Theorem and its converse.

Launch

© MP3, MP5

The triangle formed by the squares is a right triangle. The squares have side lengths of 6, 8, and 10 units.

Can you use the vertices of squares with these side lengths to make a triangle other than a right triangle? Show and explain your response.

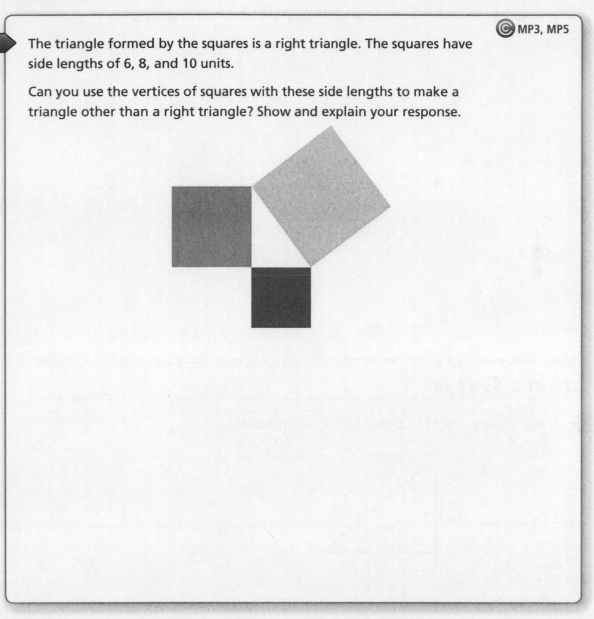

Reflect What would you need to change to get a different result from your work? Explain.

_____

_____

_____

_____

Got It?

PART 1 Got It

Which lengths represent the side lengths of a right triangle?

I. 9, 12, 15   **II.** 10, 15, 20   **III.** 3.5, 12, 12.5

PART 2 Got It

Is the triangle a right triangle? Justify your reasoning.

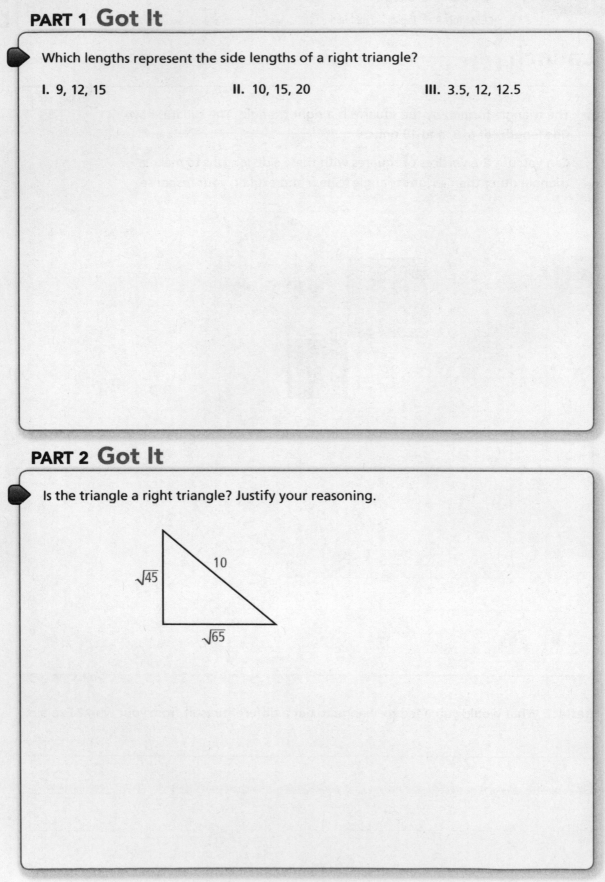

Close and Check

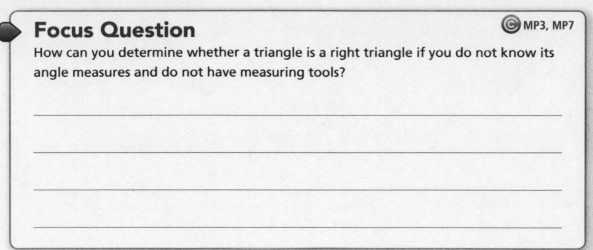

Focus Question

MP3, MP7

How can you determine whether a triangle is a right triangle if you do not know its angle measures and do not have measuring tools?

_____

_____

_____

_____

▶ Do you know HOW?

1. Which triangles are right triangles?

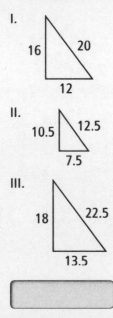

I.
16 20
12

II.
10.5 12.5
7.5

III.
18 22.5
13.5

[   ]

2. Write an R in the box to the right of the side lengths that form a right triangle.

   A. 30, 40, 50 [   ]

   B. 10, 15, 20 [   ]

   C. 18, 24, 30 [   ]

   D. 2, 2, 2.8 [   ]

▶ Do you UNDERSTAND?

3. **Reasoning** Your friend says that since the lengths 3, 4, and 5 form a right triangle, then the lengths 6, 8, and 10 must also form a right triangle. Explain why this works.

   _____

   _____

   _____

   _____

   _____

4. **Writing** If you have two 1-inch segments, how can you choose a third segment to make a right triangle? Is there more than one choice you can make? Explain.

   _____

   _____

   _____

   _____

   _____

This page intentionally left blank.

Distance in the Coordinate Plane

Digital Resources

CCSS: 8.G.B.8: Apply the Pythagorean Theorem to find the distance between two points in a coordinate system.

Launch

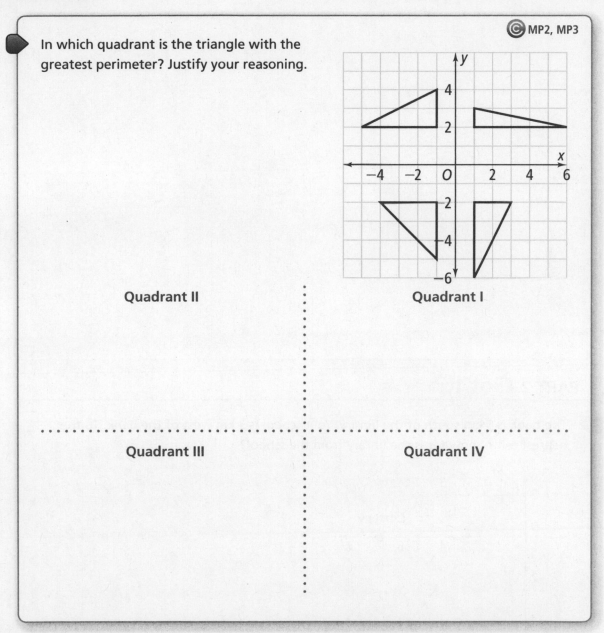

In which quadrant is the triangle with the greatest perimeter? Justify your reasoning.

MP2, MP3

Quadrant II

Quadrant I

Quadrant III

Quadrant IV

Reflect Which side of the triangle was the key to determining the triangle with the greatest perimeter? Why?

_____

_____

_____

Got It?

PART 1 Got It

What is the distance between $A(-6, -2)$ and $B(6, 3)$?

PART 2 Got It

The bank is 5 km south of the library. Your school is 3 km west of the bank. To the nearest tenth, how far is the library from the school?

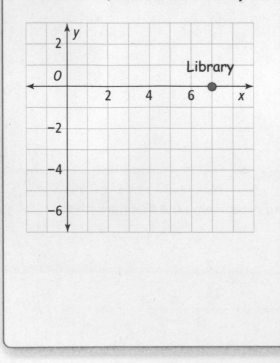

Got It?

PART 3 Got It

Classify $\triangle LMN$ by its side lengths.

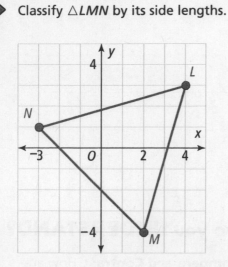

Discuss with a classmate

What does it mean to classify a triangle?

What math terms do you use to classify a triangle by its sides?

Review the list of terms you wrote.

Give a definition for each of the terms.

Close and Check

Focus Question

©MP3, MP8

How can you use the Pythagorean Theorem to find the distance between two points?

_____

_____

_____

_____

Do you know HOW?

1. What is the distance between $A(4, 3)$ and $B(-2, 6)$? Round to the nearest tenth.

   $c \approx$

2. Classify $\triangle ABC$ by its side lengths. Circle all that apply.

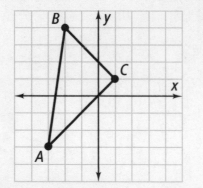

   scalene
   equilateral
   isosceles
   right

Do you UNDERSTAND?

3. **Compare and Contrast** How are finding the distance between two points on a number line and on a coordinate grid alike and different?

   _____

   _____

   _____

   _____

   _____

4. **Writing** You walk 3 blocks south and 2 blocks west to the museum. You find the length of the side that forms a right triangle with your path. What actual distance did you find? Is this useful? Explain.

   _____

   _____

   _____

   _____

   _____

Problem Solving

CCSS: 8.G.B.7: Apply the Pythagorean Theorem to determine unknown side lengths in right triangles in real-world and mathematical problems in two and three dimensions. **8.G.B.8:** Apply the Pythagorean Theorem to find the distance between two points in a coordinate system.

Launch

© MP2, MP3

What is the perimeter of a right triangle with an area of 60 in.² and a height of 8 in.?

Provide a picture and justify your response.

Picture	Reasoning

Reflect Did you draw the picture or do the reasoning first? Explain.

_____

_____

_____

Got It?

PART 1 Got It

Point A has coordinates $(1, -2)$. The x-coordinate of point B is 4. The distance between point A and point B is 5 units. What are the possible coordinates of point B?

I. $(1, 3)$

II. $(6, -2)$

III. $(4, 2)$

IV. $(4, -6)$

PART 2 Got It

The base of a square pyramid has a side length of 48 cm. The slant height of the pyramid is 25 cm. What is the volume of the pyramid?

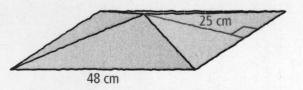

25 cm

48 cm

Got It?

PART 3 Got It

To the nearest tenth, what is the distance from vertex *B* to vertex *H* in the right rectangular prism?

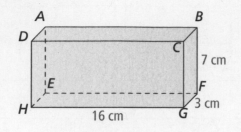

Close and Check

> ## Focus Question
> MP1, MP4
>
> How can you use the Pythagorean Theorem to help you solve real-world and mathematical problems?
>
> _____
>
> _____
>
> _____
>
> _____

Do you know HOW?

1. Find the surface area of the square pyramid. Round to the nearest whole number.

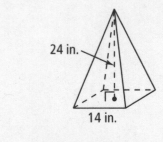

24 in.

14 in.

S.A. ≈ [   ]

2. What is the distance from vertex A to vertex G in the rectangular prism? Round to the nearest tenth.

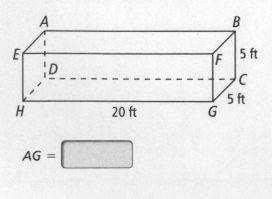

5 ft

5 ft

20 ft

AG = [   ]

Do you UNDERSTAND?

3. **Error Analysis** Your classmate says that the distance from vertex B to vertex H is about 13.4 cm. Explain his error.

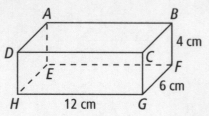

4 cm

6 cm

12 cm

_____

_____

_____

_____

4. **Reasoning** Can a 39.5-in. golf club fit in a 39 in. by 6 in. by 6 in. packing box? Explain.

_____

_____

_____

_____

Topic Review

New Vocabulary: Converse of the Pythagorean Theorem, hypotenuse, leg of a right triangle, proof, Pythagorean Theorem, theorem
Review Vocabulary: conjecture, pyramid, slant height

Vocabulary Review

 Identify two challenging vocabulary terms from this topic. Write one vocabulary term in the center oval, and fill in the surrounding boxes with details that will help you better understand the term.

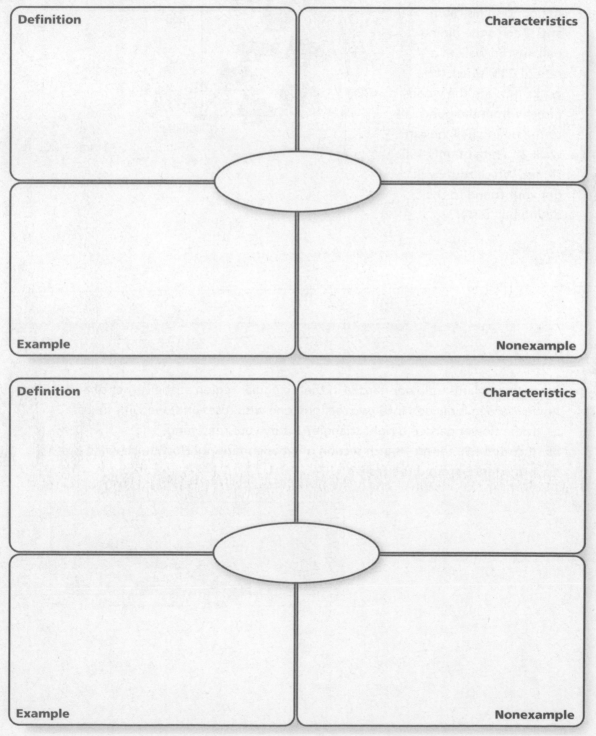

Definition	Characteristics
Example	**Nonexample**

Definition	Characteristics
Example	**Nonexample**

Pull It All Together

TASK 1

Your friend is at summer camp. He wants to get from the pond to the dining hall. If your friend walks on the paths from the pond to his cabin and then to the dining hall, he can walk at a rate of 250 ft/min. If he walks through the woods directly from the pond to the dining hall, he can walk at a rate of only 190 ft/min. Which route will get your friend to the dining hall faster?

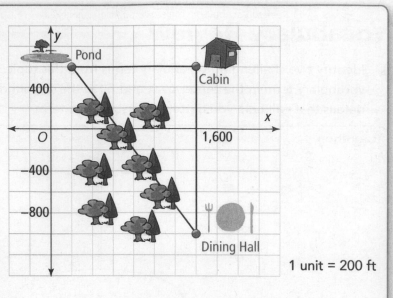

1 unit = 200 ft

TASK 2

A gardener plants a flower garden in the triangular region at the corner of a yard. The flower garden is divided into two sections: one with roses and one with tulips.

a. Is the flower garden a right triangle? Justify your reasoning.

b. It costs $4.59 for an 18-inch section of wooden fencing. How much will it cost to put a fence around the roses?

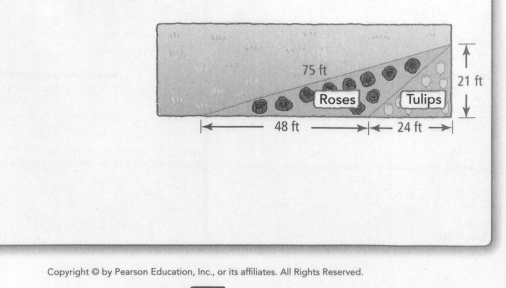

Surface Areas of Cylinders

Digital Resources

CCSS: 8.G.C.9: Know the formulas for the volumes of cones, cylinders, and spheres and use them to solve real-world and mathematical problems.

Launch

MP2, MP7

Your friend invents a new pop-up snake can. She says the height is 5 in. and traces the top of the can on an inch grid.

Draw a label that will cover the whole can except for the top and bottom. Estimate its approximate area. Explain your reasoning.

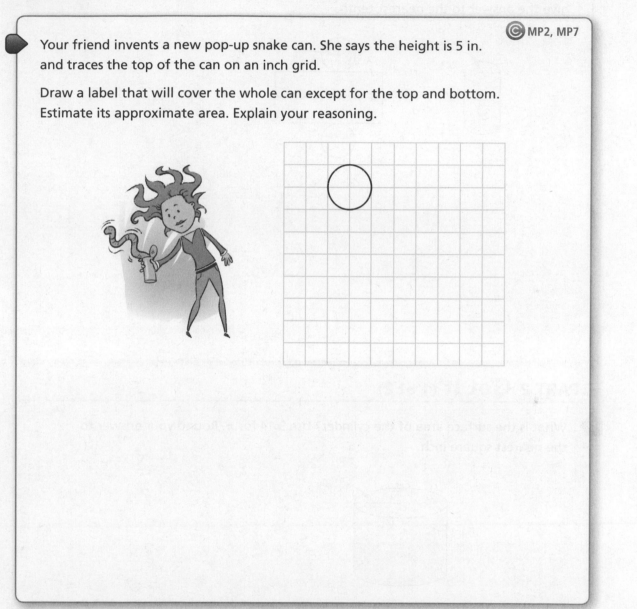

Reflect What previous mathematical knowledge did you need to solve the problem? Explain.

_____

_____

_____

Got It?

PART 1 Got It

Use the net to find the surface area of the cylindrical can. Use 3.14 for π and give the answer to the nearest tenth.

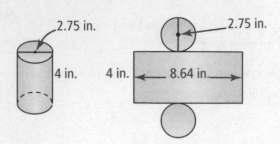

PART 2 Got It (1 of 2)

What is the surface area of the cylinder? Use 3.14 for π. Round your answer to the nearest square inch.

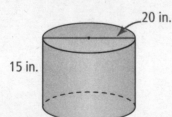

Discuss with a classmate

What is meant by a surface? Describe some familiar surfaces in your classroom. What other geometric surface areas are you familiar with?

Got It?

Use the Distributive Property to rewrite the formula for the surface area of a cylinder as a product rather than a sum. What are some advantages and disadvantages of your formula?

PART 3 Got It

You plan to stain the outside of a cylindrical wooden table. You do not plan to stain the bottom. To the nearest square inch, find the area that needs staining.

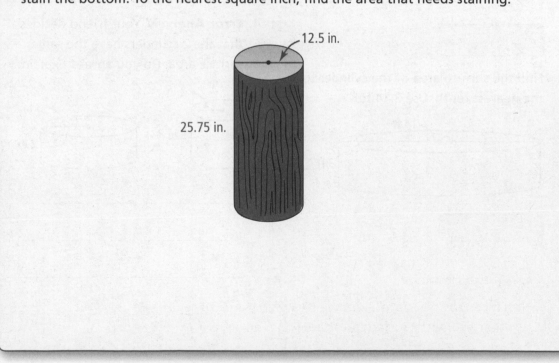

12.5 in.

25.75 in.

Close and Check

Focus Question

MP4, MP6

What types of things can you model with a cylinder? Why might you want to find the surface area of a cylinder?

_____

_____

_____

_____

Do you know HOW?

1. Use the net to find the surface area of the cylindrical can to the nearest tenth. Use 3.14 for π.

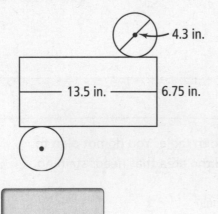

4.3 in.

13.5 in. — 6.75 in.

[ ]

2. Find the surface area of the cylinder to the nearest tenth. Use 3.14 for π.

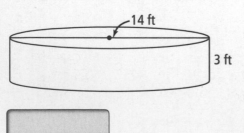

14 ft

3 ft

[ ]

Do you UNDERSTAND?

3. **Writing** Explain how using the calculator key for π rather than 3.14 affects the solution to a surface area problem.

_____

_____

_____

_____

4. **Error Analysis** Your friend decides that the 2 cylinders have the same surface area. Do you agree? Explain.

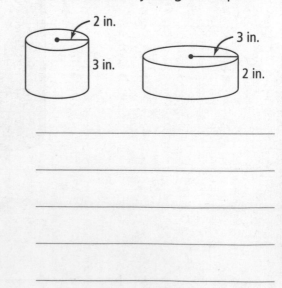

2 in.

3 in.

3 in.

2 in.

_____

_____

_____

_____

_____

_____

Volumes of Cylinders

CCSS: 8.G.C.9: Know the formulas for the volumes of cones, cylinders, and spheres and use them to solve real-world and mathematical problems.

Launch

MP4, MP6

Your friend claims that 20 in.^{3} of stuffed snake will fit in her new can. Her assistant says, "She better use the box."

Will the can work? Why did the assistant say she should use the box? Explain.

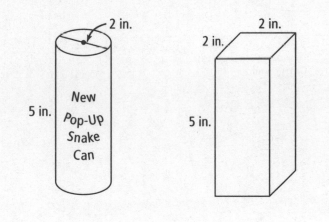

Reflect How much snake do you think the can would hold? Explain your reasoning.

_____

_____

_____

_____

Got It?

PART 1 Got It (1 of 2)

Find the volume. Leave the answer in terms of π.

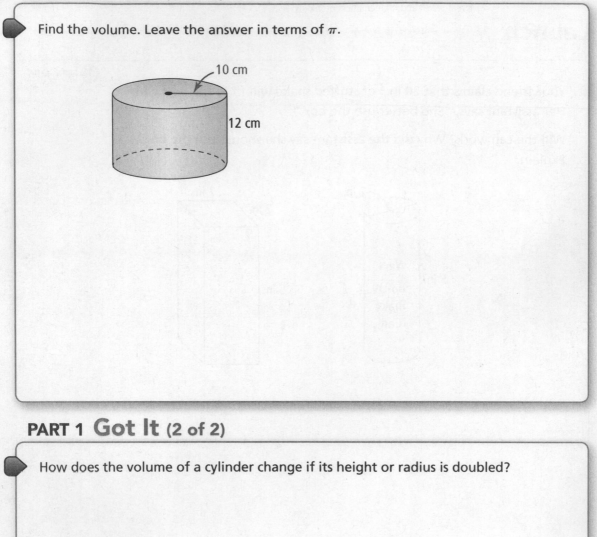

10 cm

12 cm

PART 1 Got It (2 of 2)

How does the volume of a cylinder change if its height or radius is doubled?

Got It?

PART 2 Got It

You are preparing juice from a can of liquid juice concentrate. The directions say to add three cans of water to the concentrate, and then stir. To the nearest cubic inch, how much juice will you have?

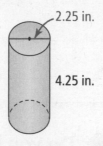

2.25 in.

4.25 in.

PART 3 Got It

What is the radius of a cylinder that has a volume of 192π cubic feet and a height of 12 feet?

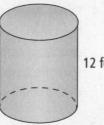

12 feet

Close and Check

Focus Question

Why might you want to find the volume of a cylinder?

_____

_____

_____

_____

Do you know HOW?

1. Find the volume. Leave the answer in terms of π.

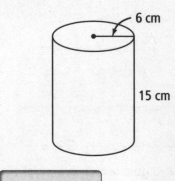
6 cm

15 cm

[ ]

2. The volume of a can of tuna is 562.76 cm³. Find the radius of the can to the nearest tenth. Use 3.14 for π.

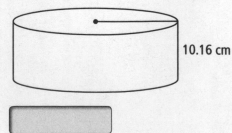
10.16 cm

[ ]

Do you UNDERSTAND?

3. **Reasoning** A pitcher holds 1,614.7 in.³ of liquid. Each can of punch is 15 in. tall with a diameter of 8 in. How many full cans will the pitcher hold? Explain.

_____

_____

_____

_____

4. **Error Analysis** A large can of beans has twice the radius and height of a small can of beans. Your friend says that the large can has twice the volume of the small can. Is he correct? Explain.

_____

_____

_____

_____

_____

_____

Surface Areas of Cones

Digital Resources

CCSS: 8.G.C.9: Know the formulas for the volumes of cones, cylinders, and spheres and use them to solve real-world and mathematical problems.

Launch

MP4, MP7

Your friend follows with a plan for a cone-shaped party hat. She says it is 5 in. tall and traces the bottom on the inch grid.

Draw the hat and estimate its surface area. Explain your reasoning.

Reflect Do you think drawing a net of a cone will give you a precise area? Explain.

_____

_____

_____

Got It?

PART 1 Got It (1 of 2)

Use the net to find the surface area of the cone to the nearest square centimeter. Use 3.14 for π.

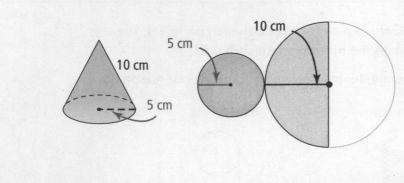

PART 1 Got It (2 of 2)

Make a conjecture that compares the area of the base with the lateral surface area. Justify your reasoning.

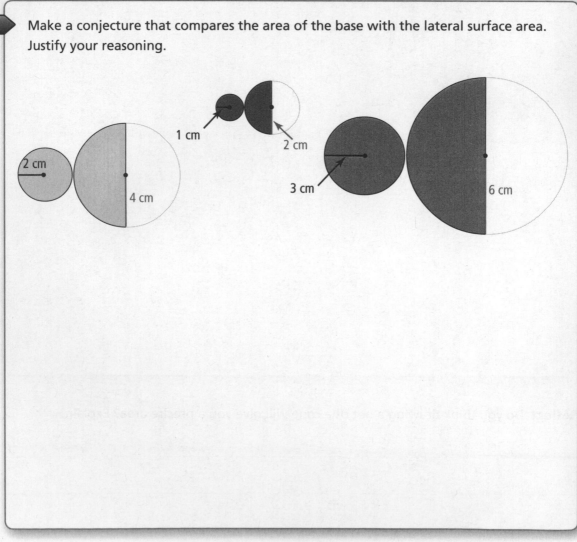

Got It?

PART 2 Got It

Find the surface area of the model volcano to the nearest square inch. Include the base since all surfaces will be painted. Use 3.14 for π.

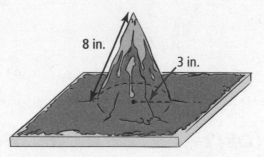

PART 3 Got It

To the nearest square inch, how much cardboard is needed to make the package for the hanging decoration?

Close and Check

Focus Question

© MP4, MP6

What types of things can you model with a cone? Why might you want to find the surface area of a cone?

_____

_____

_____

Do you know **HOW?**

1. Use the net to find the surface area of the cone to the nearest square meter. Use 3.14 for π.

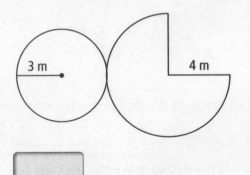

3 m   4 m

[   ]

2. Spiced pecans are sold in cone-shaped containers that include a circular lid. Find the surface area of the container to the nearest square inch. Use 3.14 for π.

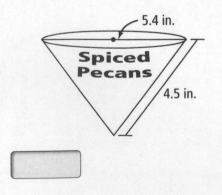

5.4 in.

Spiced Pecans

4.5 in.

[   ]

Do you **UNDERSTAND?**

3. **Compare and Contrast** Explain the difference between the height of a cone and the slant height of a cone. How do the measures compare?

_____

_____

_____

_____

_____

_____

_____

4. **Reasoning** Explain the differences between the surface areas of a cylinder and a cone with the same diameter.

_____

_____

_____

_____

CCSS: 8.G.C.9: Know the formulas for the volumes of cones, cylinders, and spheres and use them to solve real-world and mathematical problems.

Launch

© MP6, MP8

Look for a pattern in the volumes of the cylinder and cone pairs in terms of π. Then find the volume of the fourth cone in terms of π. Explain your reasoning.

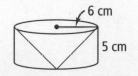

Cone volume: 60π cm³

Cylinder volume:

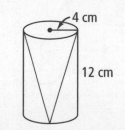

Cone volume: 64π cm³

Cylinder volume:

Cone volume: 24π cm³

Cylinder volume:

Cone volume:

Cylinder volume:

Reflect Describe another situation where you can use a pattern to figure out something you don't know.

_____

_____

_____

_____

Got It?

Find the approximate volume of the cone in terms of π.

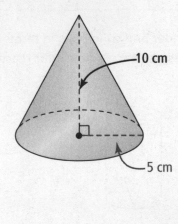

10 cm

5 cm

PART 1 Got It (2 of 2)

What happens to the volume of a cone when you double the radius?

Got It?

PART 2 Got It

Find the volume of sand in the bottom of the hourglass to the nearest cubic inch. Use 3.14 for π.

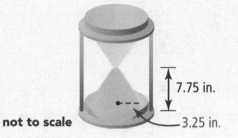

7.75 in.

not to scale

3.25 in.

PART 3 Got It

The volume of the tepee is 471 ft³. To the nearest foot, what is the radius? Use 3.14 for π.

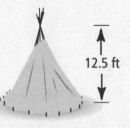

12.5 ft

Close and Check

Focus Question

Why might you want to find the volume of a cone?

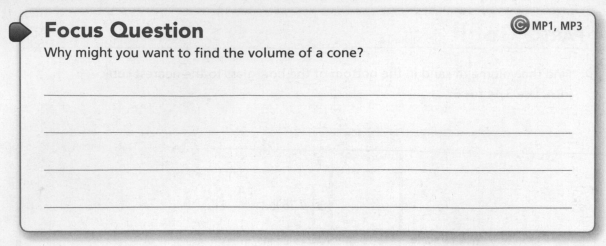

Do you know HOW?

1. Number the cones from 1 to 3 in order from least to greatest volume.

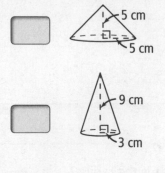

2. Find the volume of the funnel to the nearest cubic centimeter. Use 3.14 for π.

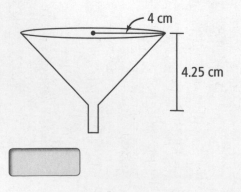

Do you UNDERSTAND?

3. Reasoning A juice company repackages individual juice cans in cone-shaped containers with the same volume. The can is 3 in. tall with a diameter of 2 in. What could be the dimensions of the cone container? Explain.

4. Writing A baker pours sugar into a cylindrical jar using the funnel from Exercise 2. If the jar holds 850 cm³, about how many times will he have to fill the funnel before the jar is full? Explain.

Surface Areas of Spheres

CCSS: 8.G.C.9: Know the formulas for the volumes of cones, cylinders, and spheres and use them to solve real-world and mathematical problems.

Launch

Ⓒ MP3, MP4

Which two-dimensional world map, Map #1 or Map #2, would you use to more accurately calculate the surface area of Earth? Explain your reasoning.

Map #1   **Map #2**

Reflect Which type of two-dimensional world map do you use and see more often? Why?

_____

_____

_____

_____

Got It?

PART 1 Got It

To the nearest tenth of a square inch, what is the surface area of the sphere? Use 3.14 for π.

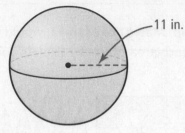

11 in.

PART 2 Got It

The new physical education instructor is 6 ft tall and his arm span is about the same as his height. When he puts his arms around the widest part of the exercise ball, his fingertips touch. What is the surface area of the exercise ball to the nearest square foot?

PART 3 Got It

The surface area of the sphere is 615.44 ft². What is the radius to the nearest foot?

Close and Check

What types of things can you model with a sphere? Why might you want to find the surface area of a sphere?

_____

_____

_____

_____

Do you know HOW?

1. Find the surface area of the sphere to the nearest tenth of a square centimeter. Use 3.14 for π.

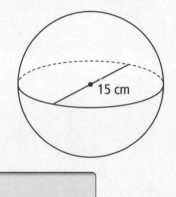

15 cm

[ ]

2. The circumference of a giant beach ball is 383.08 cm. Find the surface area of the beach ball to the nearest tenth of a square centimeter. Use 3.14 for π.

[ ]

3. The surface area of a sphere is 651 ft². Find the radius of the sphere to the nearest tenth of a square foot. Use 3.14 for π.

[ ]

Do you UNDERSTAND?

4. Writing Explain how to use the circumference to find the surface area of a sphere.

_____

_____

_____

_____

5. Error Analysis A classmate says it is impossible to find an exact solution for the surface area of a sphere because π is an irrational number. Do you agree? Explain.

_____

_____

_____

_____

_____

This page intentionally left blank.

CCSS: 8.G.C.9: Know the formulas for the volumes of cones, cylinders, and spheres and use them to solve real-world and mathematical problems.

Launch

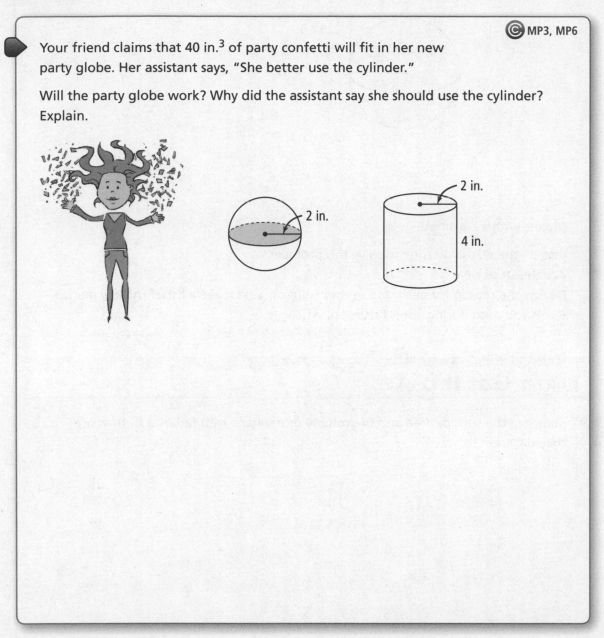

© MP3, MP6

Your friend claims that 40 in.³ of party confetti will fit in her new party globe. Her assistant says, "She better use the cylinder."

Will the party globe work? Why did the assistant say she should use the cylinder? Explain.

Reflect If you had to identify the height and width of a sphere with a radius of 2 inches what would it be?

_____

_____

_____

Got It?

PART 1 Got It (1 of 2)

Find the volume of the sphere to the nearest cubic inch. Use 3.14 for π.

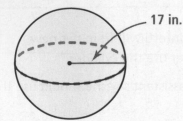

17 in.

Discuss with a classmate

Review the steps you took to solve this problem.
Are the steps clear?
Discuss the reason for each step in your solution, and make a list of the key math terms you used during your discussion.

PART 1 Got It (2 of 2)

Compare the surface area and the volume of a sphere with radius 3 ft. How are they different?

Got It?

PART 2 Got It

To the nearest tenth of a cubic millimeter, what is the volume of the sphere that appears when a nickel is spinning? Use 3.14 for π.

21.21 mm

PART 3 Got It

To the nearest foot, what is the radius of a sphere that has a volume of 523 ft³? Use 3.14 for π.

Close and Check

Focus Question

Why might you want to find the volume of a sphere?

Do you know HOW?

1. To the nearest cubic inch, how much space is there inside the ball for the hamster? Use 3.14 for π.

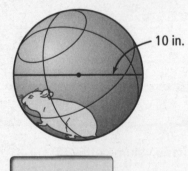

10 in.

2. A gazing ball in the center of a garden has a volume of 904.3 cm³. To the nearest centimeter, find the diameter of the gazing ball.

3. To the nearest tenth of a cubic foot, find the volume of a 9 ft diameter inflatable ball.

Do you UNDERSTAND?

4. **Writing** The height and diameter of a cylinder is equal to the diameter of a sphere. Explain the relationship between the volume of the sphere and the volume of the cylinder.

5. **Reasoning** A ball of twine has a diameter of 3.4 m. More twine is added until the diameter is 12 m. A classmate subtracts the diameters and uses the result to find the change in volume of the sphere. Is he correct? Explain.

Problem Solving

CCSS: 8.G.C.9: Know the formulas for the volumes of cones, cylinders, and spheres and use them to solve real-world and mathematical problems.

Launch

© MP1, MP6

The cylinder, cone, and sphere all have the same radius and height (or diameter). Describe how the volumes compare given these dimensions. State the volumes in terms of π.

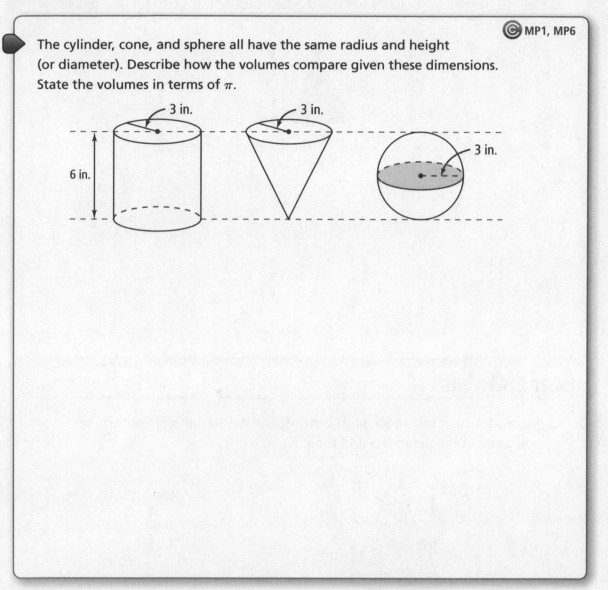

Reflect How could you use what you know about the relationships between the volumes of the shapes to make solving problems easier? Explain.

_____

_____

_____

_____

Got It?

PART 1 Got It

You are making a teepee for your little brother. The fabric will cover only the lateral surface. To the nearest dollar, what will the fabric cost if it is $1.30 for one square foot?

6 ft

4 ft

PART 2 Got It

To the nearest cubic inch, how much water does the watering can hold? Do not include water in the spout. Use 3.14 for π.

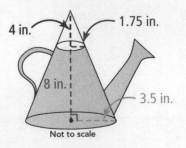

4 in.

1.75 in.

8 in.

3.5 in.

Not to scale

Close and Check

Focus Question

© MP1, MP3

How can you apply what you know about surface areas and volumes of cylinders, cones, and spheres to solve problems?

_____

_____

_____

_____

Do you know HOW?

1. A greenhouse is built in the shape of half of a sphere. To the nearest tenth of a cubic foot, find the volume of the greenhouse. Use 3.14 for π.

12.5 ft

25 ft

[_____]

2. Find the surface area of the serving dish to the nearest tenth of a square inch. Use 3.14 for π.

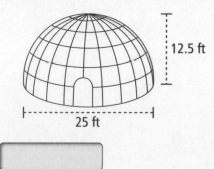
6 in.

5 in.

3 in.

5 in.

[_____]

Do you UNDERSTAND?

3. **Writing** Explain how to find the total volume of the silo.

_____

_____

_____

_____

_____

4. **Reasoning** You want the container with the largest volume. If the height and diameter of each container are equal, should you choose a sphere, cylinder, or cone? Explain.

_____

_____

_____

_____

_____

This page intentionally left blank.

New Vocabulary: cone, cylinder, lateral area, sphere, surface area, volume
Review Vocabulary: net

Vocabulary Review

 Identify two challenging vocabulary terms from this topic. Write one vocabulary term in the center oval, and fill in the surrounding boxes with details that will help you better understand the term.

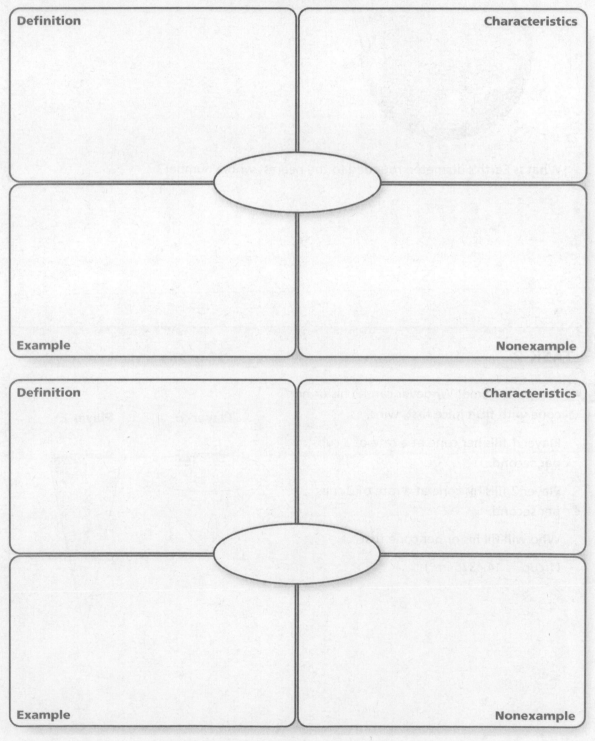

Definition

Characteristics

Example

Nonexample

Definition

Characteristics

Example

Nonexample

Pull It All Together

TASK 1

You can model Earth's shape with a sphere.

Planet Earth: 29.2%, or 57.5 million square miles of surface covered in land.

What is Earth's diameter, rounded to the nearest whole number?

TASK 2

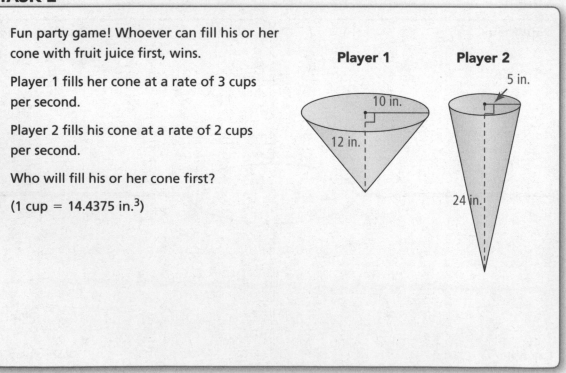

Fun party game! Whoever can fill his or her cone with fruit juice first, wins.

Player 1 fills her cone at a rate of 3 cups per second.

Player 2 fills his cone at a rate of 2 cups per second.

Who will fill his or her cone first?

(1 cup = 14.4375 in.³)

Player 1

10 in.

12 in.

Player 2

5 in.

24 in.

CCSS: 8.SP.A.1: Construct and interpret scatter plots for bivariate measurement data to investigate patterns of association between two quantities ... .

Launch

© MP5, MP7

Your very precise friend says there's nothing to be learned about the book data because the points don't line up with any exact page or width coordinates. Do you agree? If not, state something you know about at least two of the five books.

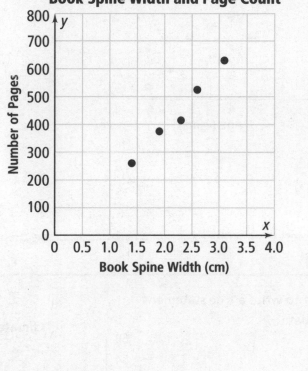

Book Spine Width and Page Count

Reflect Why don't the book dots hit any intersecting lines on the grid? Explain.

_____

_____

_____

Got It?

PART 1 Got It

What does the circled point on the scatter plot represent?

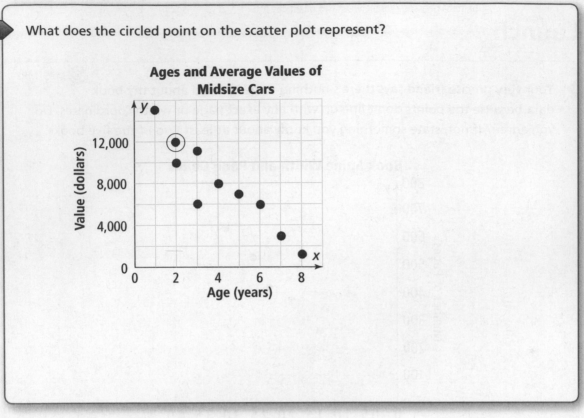

Ages and Average Values of Midsize Cars

PART 2 Got It

Use the scatter plot to write a true statement about the climate data.

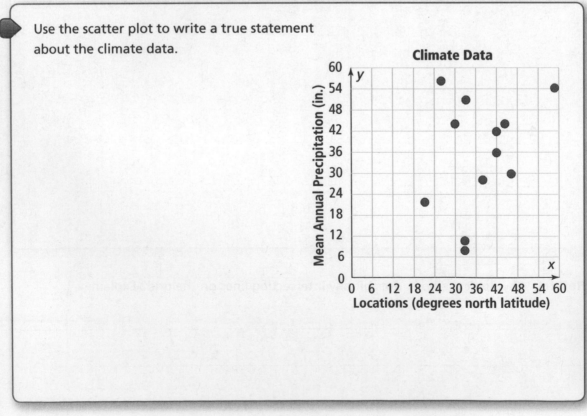

Climate Data

Close and Check

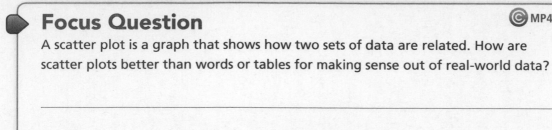

Focus Question

© MP4, MP5

A scatter plot is a graph that shows how two sets of data are related. How are scatter plots better than words or tables for making sense out of real-world data?

_____

_____

_____

_____

Do you know **HOW?**

Use the scatter plot to answer Exercises 1 and 2.

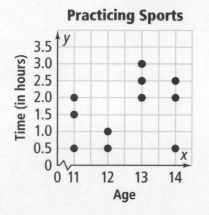

Practicing Sports

1. What does point (13, 2.5) represent?

2. Write **T** if the statement is true and **F** if the statement is false.

 Everyone in the group practices at least half an hour.

Six children practice more than 2 hours each day.

Do you **UNDERSTAND?**

3. **Writing** What information could you find more quickly in a scatter plot than in a table? Explain.

_____

_____

_____

_____

4. **Error Analysis** A classmate says the scatter plot shows that 11 children practice for 2 hours. Do you agree? Explain.

_____

_____

_____

_____

_____

_____

This page intentionally left blank.

Constructing a Scatter Plot

CCSS: 8.SP.A.1: Construct and interpret scatter plots for bivariate measurement data to investigate patterns of association between two quantities ... .

Launch

© MP3, MP4

Conduct your own study of spine widths and page counts. Graph the results for five books. Show your data in another way so you know your scatter plot is correct.

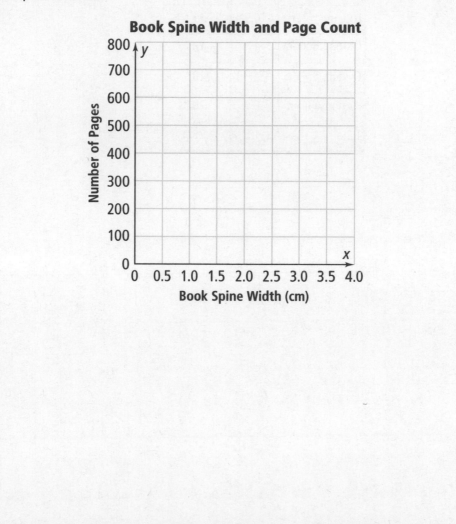

Book Spine Width and Page Count

Reflect Do you think the scatter plot or your other method displays the data in a better way? Explain.

Got It?

PART 1 Got It

The table shows several nutritional values per serving for various seafood items. A serving is approximately 5 ounces. Make a scatter plot of the data.

Seafood	Fat (g)	Protein (g)
Catfish	6	17
Lobster	0.5	17
Orange Roughy	1	16
Oysters	4	10
Rainbow Trout	6	20
Tuna	1.5	26

Got It?

PART 2 Got It

The table shows the worldwide ticket revenues (in billions of dollars) of the top-grossing movie for several years. Make a scatter plot to represent the data.

Year	Total Revenue (Billions of $)
2003	9.2
2004	9.4
2005	8.8
2006	9.2
2007	9.7
2008	9.6
2009	10.6
2010	10.6

Discuss with a classmate

Compare the scatter plots you made for this problem.

Which variable did you represent on the horizontal axis?

How did you decide the scale for the values on the horizontal axis?

Which variable did you represent on the vertical axis?

How did you decide the scale for the values on the vertical axis?

Where did you place labels for the scatter plot?

Got It?

PART 3 Got It

The table shows the year opened and the weekday ridership per mile for several major U.S. subway systems. Make a scatter plot to represent the data.

Year Opened	Ridership Per Mile
1860	1,014
1893	6,513
1972	3,447
1993	8,678
1984	2,645
1955	979

Close and Check

Focus Question

What characteristics of a data set should you consider in making a scatter plot?

_____

_____

_____

_____

Do you know HOW?

1. The table shows the relationship between hours of sleep each night and the average GPA in your friend's class. Make a scatter plot to represent the data.

The Effect of Sleep on Grades						
Sleep (h)	6	6.5	7	7.5	8	8.5	9
GPA	2.8	3	3.5	3.5	3.7	3.8	3.6

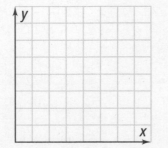

Do you UNDERSTAND?

2. **Reasoning** You collect data on the height of a group of plants and the amount of sunlight they get daily. Which set of data would you use for the x-values and which would you use for the y-values? Explain.

_____

_____

_____

_____

3. **Writing** Explain how to determine the scales for the horizontal and vertical axes of a scatter plot.

_____

_____

_____

_____

_____

This page intentionally left blank.

Investigating Patterns - Clustering and Outliers

CCSS: 8.SP.A.1: … Describe patterns such as clustering, outliers, positive or negative association, linear association, and nonlinear association.

Launch

MP3, MP4

The scatter plot shows the spine widths and the page counts of 10 books. Which two books stand out from the rest? What makes them unique?

Book Spine Width and Page Count

Reflect How would the problem be different if the data were in a table not a scatter plot? Explain.

_____

_____

_____

Got It?

PART 1 Got It

Which statement(s) about the scatter plot are true?

I.   There are two clusters.
II. The point (2, 12) is an outlier.
III. There are three outliers.

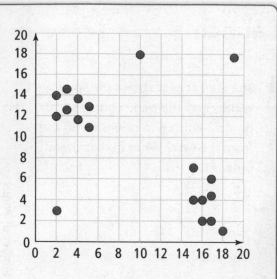

PART 2 Got It

Make a scatter plot to represent the age and number of pets of each person in your classroom. Then describe any features of the scatter plot that represents the data for your class.

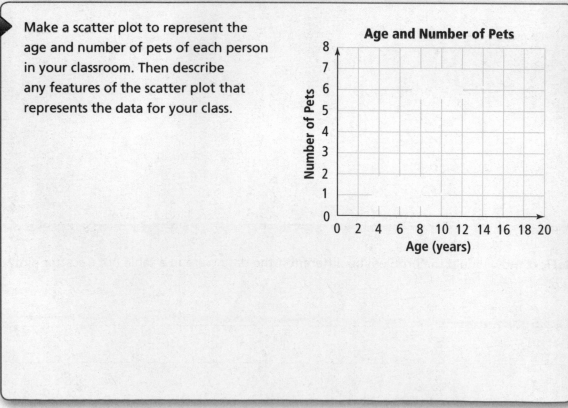

Close and Check

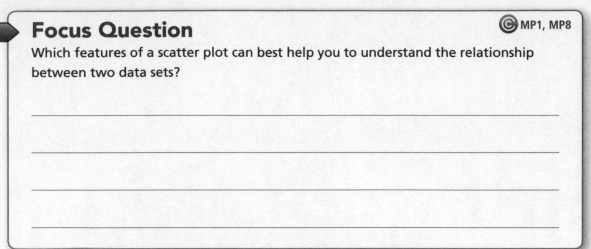

Focus Question

MP1, MP8

Which features of a scatter plot can best help you to understand the relationship between two data sets?

_____

_____

_____

_____

 ## Do you know **HOW?**

1. Circle the true statement(s) about the scatter plot.

Restaurant Business

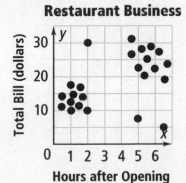

A. Point (2, 30) is an outlier.

B. Most customers spend about the same amount of money.

C. There are two outliers.

D. There are two clusters.

2. What are the coordinates of the outlier(s) in the scatter plot?

Do you **UNDERSTAND?**

3. Writing Explain the meanings of the clusters and outliers in the scatter plot in Exercise 1.

_____

_____

_____

_____

_____

4. Reasoning Explain how the information in the scatter plot might be useful to the restaurant owner.

_____

_____

_____

_____

_____

_____

This page intentionally left blank.

Investigating Patterns – Association

CCSS: 8.SP.A.1: … Describe patterns such as clustering, outliers, positive or negative association, linear association, and nonlinear association.

Launch

© MP2, MP4

Place 16 coins of several different values in a bag. Remove some coins without looking. Graph the results and put the coins back. Repeat five more times. Tell if you see a relationship between the number of coins you remove and the value of the coins.

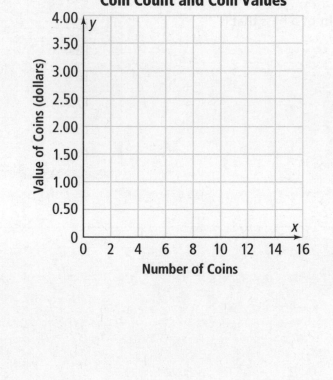

Coin Count and Coin Values

y-axis: Value of Coins (dollars): 0, 0.50, 1.00, 1.50, 2.00, 2.50, 3.00, 3.50, 4.00

x-axis: Number of Coins: 0, 2, 4, 6, 8, 10, 12, 14, 16

Reflect Compare your results with those of a friend. Do you have similar results? What could account for the differences?

_____

_____

_____

_____

_____

Got It?

PART 1 Got It

Biologists recorded the lengths and weights of some largemouth bass. The table shows the results.

a. Make a scatter plot to represent the data.

b. Does an association exist between the length and weight of a largemouth bass? Explain.

c. Predict the weight of a bass that is 19 inches long.

Length (in.)	Weight (lb)
9.2	0.5
10.9	0.8
12.3	0.9
12.0	1.3
14.1	1.7
15.5	2.2
16.4	2.5
16.9	3.2
17.7	3.6
18.4	4.1
19.8	4.8

Got It?

PART 2 Got It

Determine whether a scatter plot of data for the temperature outside and the number of layers of clothing would show a *positive*, a *negative*, or *no association*. Explain your reasoning.

PART 3 Got It

The following graph shows the winning speed for different distances women ran in the 2008 Olympic games. Describe any clusters, outliers, or associations that you see in the graph.

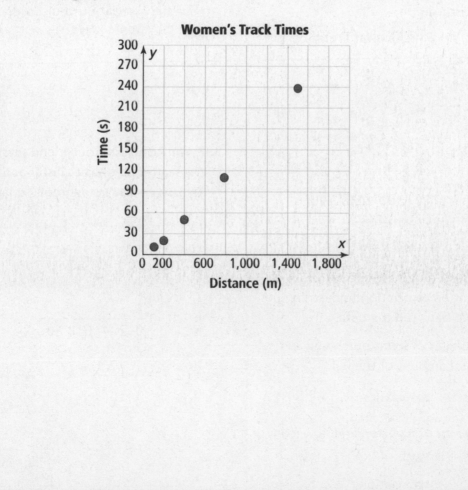

Women's Track Times

Close and Check

 Focus Question

MP2, MP8

Scatter plots show how two sets of data are related. What types of associations result from making a scatter plot? How will you know them when you see them?

_____

_____

_____

_____

_____

Do you know HOW?

1. Determine whether the data in the scatter plot have a *positive*, *negative*, or *no association*.

Educational Trends

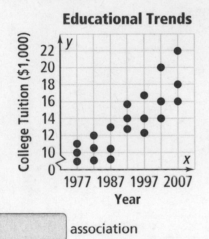

[_____] association

For Exercises 2 and 3, write *positive*, *negative*, or *no* association to describe the relationship between the data.

2. The number of items purchased and the total amount of the bill

[_____] association

3. The height of a person and how many pets he/she owns

[_____] association

Do you UNDERSTAND?

4. **Writing** Explain your answer to Exercise 1. Why do you think the data have the association you chose?

_____

_____

_____

5. **Error Analysis** Your friend says that the scatter plot has a cluster and no association. Do you agree? Explain

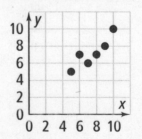

_____

_____

_____

_____

Linear Models – Fitting a Straight Line

CCSS: 8.SP.A.2: ... For scatter plots that suggest a linear association, informally fit a straight line, and informally assess the model fit by judging the closeness of the data points to the line.

Launch

Ⓒ MP3, MP6

Your friend starts drawing lines to connect the results of picking coins from a bag. He says the data show no association between the number of coins and the value of the coins because the lines are so different. Do you agree with your friend? Explain.

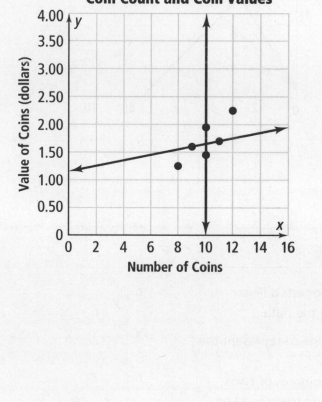

Coin Count and Coin Values

Reflect How are points on any line related? Explain.

_____

_____

_____

_____

Got It?

PART 1 Got It

Which of the lines shown are reasonable trend lines for the scatter plot?

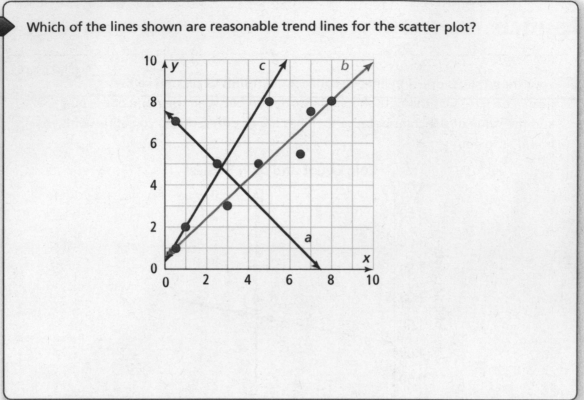

PART 2 Got It

The scatter plot suggests a linear association among the data.

a. Draw a trend line to represent the data.

b. Write the coordinates of two points that lie on the trend line.

c. Write the equation of your trend line.

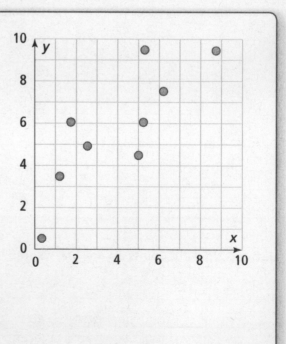

Got It?

The scatter plot suggests a linear association among the data.

Column A	Column B
4	1.1
5	1.3
8	2.2
9	2.3
10	2.4
10	2.6
11	2.8
12	3.3
15	4.7
18	5.1
20	5.8
24	6.8

a. Draw a trend line to represent the data.
b. Find the equation of your trend line.

Discuss with a classmate

Compare the trend lines that you drew to represent the data.
Is one of your trend lines more accurate than the other? Explain.
How similar are the equations that you found using your trend lines?
Explain by observing the slopes and *y*-intercepts.

Close and Check

Focus Question

MP4, MP6

How can a scatter plot have more than one linear model? How do you decide which model to use?

Do you know HOW?

1. Which trend line is the most appropriate for the scatter plot?

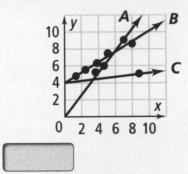

2. Find a trend line and its equation using the scatter plot.

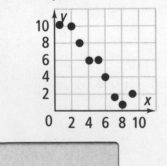

Do you UNDERSTAND?

3. **Writing** Is it easier to draw the trend line first, and then select two points on the line, or to select two points first, then draw the trend line? Explain.

4. **Reasoning** Where would be the most accurate placement of a trend line for the scatter plot shown? Explain.

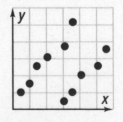

Using the Equation of a Linear Model

CCSS: 8.SP.A.3: Use the equation of a linear model to solve problems in the context of bivariate measurement data, interpreting the slope and intercept ... . Also, **8.SP.A.2.**

Digital Resources

Launch

© MP2, MP7

Which scatter plot would be most useful and which would be least useful for making a prediction of what sales at week 5 might be?

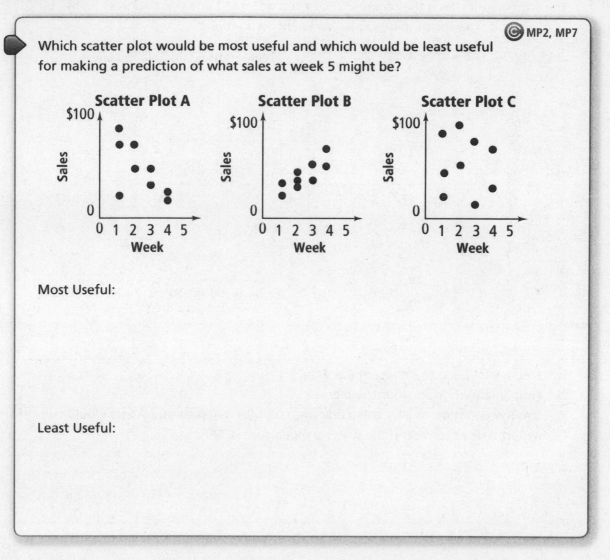

Most Useful:

Least Useful:

Reflect What was most important for you in the scatter plots for making a prediction?

_____

_____

_____

_____

Got It?

Scuba divers wear wet suits to maintain a comfortable body temperature as they dive. The scatter plot shows the temperature of the water (°F) and the thickness (mm) of a wet suit. The scatter plot suggests a linear association.

Temperature	Suit Thickness
76	1.6
69	3.0
64	5.0
49	6.5
33	9.5
80	3.0
70	6.5
65	9.5
45	9.5
80	6.5

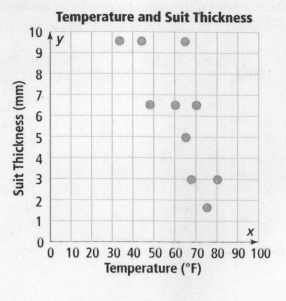

Temperature and Suit Thickness

a. Find a trend line to represent the data.

b. Find an equation for your trend line.

c. Use the equation of your trend line from part (b). What suit thickness would you expect a diver to wear if the water temperature is 30°F?

Got It?

Scuba divers wear wet suits to maintain a comfortable body temperature as they dive. The equation $y = -0.1x + 14.7$ models this relationship, where x represents the temperature of the water in degrees Fahrenheit (°F) and y represents the thickness of the wet suit in millimeters (mm). What does the slope of the line represent in this situation?

Got It?

PART 2 Got It

The scatter plot shows the calories and sugar content in several fruits. The scatter plot suggests a linear association.

Calories	Sugars (g)
15	2
20	0
50	0
50	8
50	9
50	10
50	11
60	11
60	13
70	16
80	14
80	20
90	13
90	20
98	16
110	19

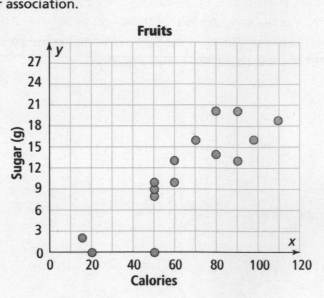

a. Find a trend line to represent the data.

b. Find an equation for your trend line.

c. How many grams of sugar would you expect in a serving of fruit that has 150 calories?

d. How many calories would you expect in a serving of fruit that contains 20 grams of sugar?

Close and Check

Focus Question

© MP1, MP3

How can scatter plots help you to make predictions or draw conclusions?

_____

_____

_____

_____

Do you know HOW?

1. Use the scatter plot to write an equation for a trend line.

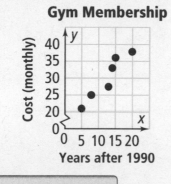

Gym Membership

Cost (monthly)

Years after 1990

_____

2. Using the linear model from Exercise 1, what would you expect the gym membership to have cost in 1993?

_____

3. Using the linear model from Exercise 1, what year would you expect the gym membership to cost $60 per month?

_____

Do you UNDERSTAND?

4. Writing Based on the linear model from Exercise 1, is the expected cost of gym membership the same as the actual cost in 2010? Explain.

_____

_____

_____

_____

_____

5. Reasoning Your friend draws a trend line for the scatter plot in Exercise 1 using the points (5, 20) and (20, 37.5). Would you use his points or the points (5, 21) and (15, 36) to draw a trend line? Explain.

_____

_____

_____

_____

_____

_____

This page intentionally left blank.

Problem Solving

CCSS: 8.SP.A.2: … For scatter plots that suggest a linear association, informally fit a straight line, and informally assess the model fit by judging the closeness of the data points to the line.

Launch

© MP2, MP6

Befuddled botanists bemoan the growth of a venomous giant hogweed in their beautiful botanical garden. The biennial plant literally bolts skyward in its Year 2 growing season.

Predict the plant's height at week 12 of Year 2. Justify your reasoning.

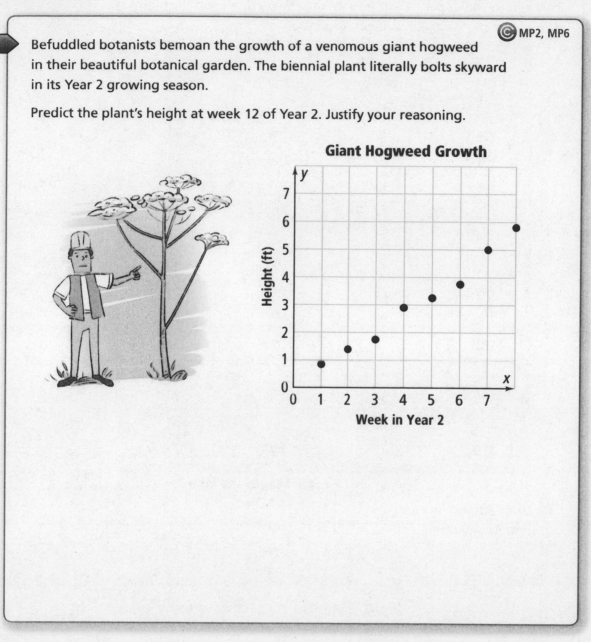

Giant Hogweed Growth

Reflect What is most critical to making an accurate prediction of the plant's height at Week 12?

_____

_____

_____

Got It?

PART 1 Got It

The table and scatter plot show the length of certain models of cars and the miles per gallon they average when driven on the highway. The scatter plot suggests a linear association.

Length (in.)	Highway (mpg)	Length (in.)	Highway (mpg)
194	26	200	27
183	31	196	25
194	29	176	34
191	29	190	30
198	30	197	25
196	27	215	25
200	27	177	32
188	32	190	37
197	25	192	29
200	25	189	32
191	30	185	32
212	25	197	31
190	34	178	38
177	32	188	31
193	25	190	27

a. Draw a trend line and find its equation.

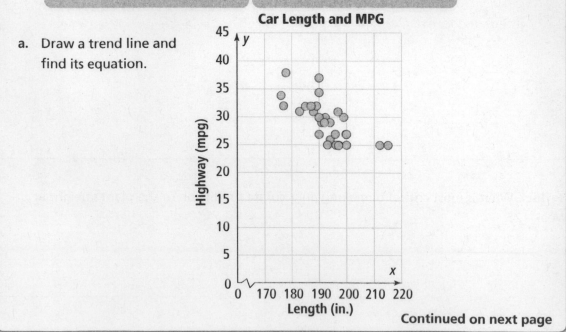

Car Length and MPG

Continued on next page

Got It?

PART 1 Got It

Continued

b. Remove the outliers, (212, 25) and (215, 25), from the
    table. Draw a new trend line for the adjusted data set.
    Then find the equation for this trend line.

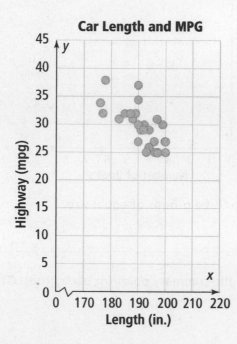

Car Length and MPG

c. How do the outliers affect the position of a trend line? Explain your
    reasoning by examining the highway mpg for a car that is 205 inches long.

Got It?

PART 2 Got It

The scatter plot represents the number of books in a book bag
and the weight, in pounds, of the book bag. The scatter plot suggests
a linear association.
Find the median-median trend line and define its equation to model the data.

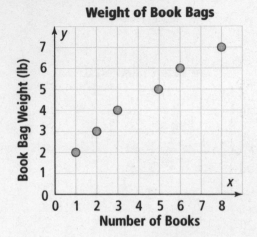

Weight of Book Bags

a. Separate the points into three groups of equal size.

b. Find the coordinates of the summary point for each group. Then graph the
points.

c. Draw a line through the first and third summary points.

d. Find the equation of the line through the first and third summary points.

Continued on next page

Got It?

PART 2 Got It

Continued

e. Find the vertical distance from the line through the first and third summary points to the middle summary point.

f. Find one third of the distance from the line to the middle summary point.

g. Write the equation of the median-median trend line.

h. How many books would you expect to find in a book bag that weighs 10 pounds? Use the equation of your median-median trend line to estimate.

Close and Check

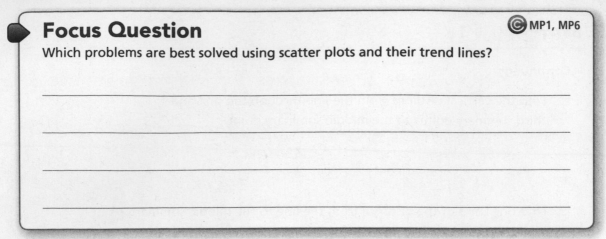

Focus Question

MP1, MP6

Which problems are best solved using scatter plots and their trend lines?

Do you know HOW?

1. Separate the points in the scatter plot into three equal groups. Find the summary point for each group.

Berry Flake Cereal

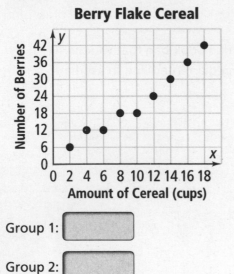

Group 1:

Group 2:

Group 3:

2. Write an equation for the line through the first and third summary points.

3. Write the equation for the median-median trend line for the berry cereal data.

Do you UNDERSTAND?

4. **Reasoning** Line A is a trend line including all the data points and Line B is a trend line that excludes outliers. How do the outliers affect the position of the line? Explain.

Apartment Rent

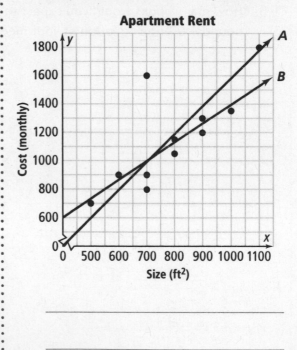

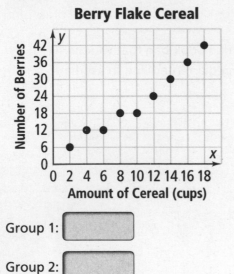

Vocabulary Review

Identify two challenging vocabulary terms from this topic. Write one vocabulary term in the center oval, and fill in the surrounding boxes with details that will help you better understand the term.

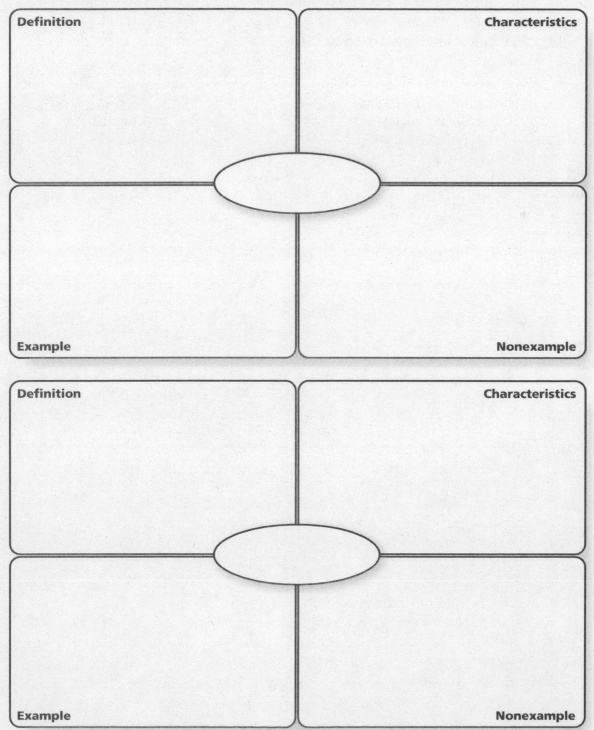

Definition

Characteristics

Example

Nonexample

Definition

Characteristics

Example

Nonexample

Pull It All Together

TASK 1

In music, lower notes have lower frequencies, and higher notes have higher frequencies. This scatter plot shows frequencies for the female singer's vocals (▲) and the guitar part (•) in a song.

Vocal and Guitar Frequencies

a. What type of association is shown in the guitar part?

b. What type of association is shown in the vocal part?

c. How do you interpret the last eight seconds, in which the triangles appear directly above the circles?

Pull It All Together

TASK 2

In music, lower notes have lower frequencies, and higher notes have higher frequencies. This scatter plot shows frequencies for the female singer's vocals (▲) and the guitar part (•) in a song.

a. Write an equation of a trend line for the guitar part.

b. Use the trend line to predict the frequency of the guitar part at 20 seconds.

c. Why would it be impractical to predict the frequency of the guitar part at five minutes, using the trend line?

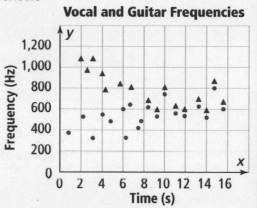

Vocal and Guitar Frequencies

This page intentionally left blank.

Bivariate Categorical Data

Digital Resources

CCSS: 8.SP.A.4: Understand that patterns of association can also be seen in bivariate categorical data by displaying frequencies and relative frequencies in a two-way table . . . .

Launch

© MP1, MP3

Two competing Web-radio rock stations blast listeners with the online surveys shown. Why do you think Station B asked the second question? Explain your reasoning.

Station A

Station A
ROCKS

What type of rock rocks you?
☐ Punk   ☐ Soft
☐ Classic   ☐ Metal

Station B

What type of rock rocks you?
☐ Punk   ☐ Soft
☐ Classic   ☐ Metal
When do you listen most?
☐ A.M.
☐ P.M.

Station B ROCKS

Reflect Are there benefits to both surveys? If so, what are they?

_____

_____

_____

_____

Got It?

PART 1 Got It

Will data about Telephone Area Codes be *categorical data* or *measurement data*? Explain.

PART 2 Got It

Tell which survey(s) you can use to collect bivariate categorical data.

Survey 1

- What is your favorite type of movie?

- How many siblings do you have?

Survey 2

- Do you play a sport?

- Do you want to go to college?

Got It?

PART 3 Got It

You want to see if there is an association between playing sports and being left-handed.

Design a survey to collect bivariate categorical data. Identify the variables, the categories, and the groups in which the data will fall.

Close and Check

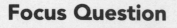

Focus Question

MP3, MP4

What does it mean to have bivariate categorical data? What does the data tell you about a population?

_____

_____

_____

_____

 Do you know HOW?

1. Indicate whether each variable has values that are *categorical data* or *measurement data*.

   Grade Level: [   ]

   Weight: [   ]

   Song Length: [   ]

2. Circle the survey you can use to collect bivariate categorical data.

   Survey 1
   What grade are you in?
   How long did you spend on homework last night?

   Survey 2
   What is your favorite subject in school?
   What is your favorite sport?

   Survey 3
   How many siblings do you have?
   What is your favorite snack?

Do you UNDERSTAND?

3. **Writing** You want to see whether there is an association between gender and wearing shoes with laces. Design a survey to collect bivariate categorical data.

   _____

   _____

   _____

   _____

   _____

4. **Vocabulary** Identify the variables, the categories, and the groups the data will fall in for your survey.

   _____

   _____

   _____

   _____

   _____

   _____

Constructing Two-Way Frequency Tables

CCSS: 8.SP.A.4: Understand that patterns of association can also be seen in bivariate categorical data by displaying frequencies … in a two-way table. Construct … a two-way table summarizing data on two categorical variables collected from the same subjects … .

Digital Resources

Launch

© MP1, MP3

The tables show the survey results on the type of rock music listeners prefer and the time of day they most often listen.

What do you like about how the tables display the results? How could Station B have made a better table?

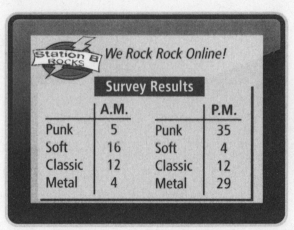

We Rock Rock Online!

Survey Results

	A.M.		P.M.
Punk	5	Punk	35
Soft	16	Soft	4
Classic	12	Classic	12
Metal	4	Metal	29

What I Like:

What Could Be Better:

Reflect What matters most about how you display survey data?

_____

_____

_____

_____

Got It?

PART 1 Got It

You asked your neighbors who donate to charity how often they donate. Two men and 8 women said they donated weekly. Five men and 7 women said they donated monthly. Three men and 15 women said they donated yearly.

Construct a two-way frequency table to show the results of your survey. Show *Gender* as the column variable.

PART 2 Got It

A college granted 2,466 degrees last year. Complete the two-way frequency table.

		Degree				
		Associate	**Bachelor's**	**Master's**	**Doctorate**	**Total**
Gender	**Male**		553	197		1,006
	Female	401	769			
	Total	632		467	45	2,466

Got It?

PART 3 Got It (1 of 2)

You and a friend survey people about car ownership and where they live. Construct a single two-way frequency table that combines the results.

Survey #1

		Own a Car?	
		Yes	No
Property	House	~~||||~~ ~~||||~~ ~~||||~~ |	||
	Apartment	||	~~||||~~ ~~||||~~ ||

Survey #2

		Property	
		House	Apartment
Own a Car?	Yes	~~||||~~ ~~||||~~ ~~||||~~ ||||	
	No	||||	~~||||~~ ~~||||~~ ~~||||~~ ~~||||~~ ~~||||~~ |

PART 3 Got It (2 of 2)

You and a friend are collecting data about whether people have a library card and if they watch movies online.

You record that 45 people have a library card and 15 people do not. Your friend records that 22 people watch movies online and 38 do not.

Is it possible to construct a two-way frequency table to show your results? Why or why not?

Close and Check

Focus Question

What is a two-way table? When you construct a two-way frequency table, what does the table show?

Do you know HOW?

1. You ask 80 students whether they own a portable music player. Half of the 50 eighth graders said yes, and 28 seventh graders said yes. Complete the two-way frequency table.

Grade Level	Music Player?		
	Yes	No	Total
7th			
8th			
Total			

2. You ask all 8th graders whether they participate in an after-school activity. Complete the two-way frequency table.

Gender	After-School Activity?		
	Yes	No	Total
Male		40	
Female			95
Total	102		187

Do you UNDERSTAND?

3. Reasoning Explain how you found the number of 7th graders who do not have a portable music player in Exercise 1.

4. Error Analysis You and a friend take turns interviewing 35 people at the mall. You record that 18 download apps online. Your friend records that 25 own a tablet computer. Can you claim that 18 people download apps onto their tablet computers? Explain.

Interpreting Two-Way Frequency Tables

CCSS: 8.SP.A.4: Understand that patterns of association can also be seen in bivariate categorical data by displaying frequencies … in a two-way table. … interpret a two way table summarizing data on two categorical variables collected from the same subjects … .

Launch

© MP4, MP7

Web-radio rock Station B posts survey results about the type of rock that rocks its male and female listeners.

Describe the two most important things you see in the results. Explain why they are the most important.

We Rock Rock Online!

Station B ROCKS

Type of Rock	Gender		
	Male	Female	Total
Punk	26	10	36
Soft	1	4	5
Classic	18	12	30
Metal	9	8	17
Total	54	34	88

Two Most Important Things

1.

2.

Why They Are The Most Important

Reflect Do you like the way the station shows the survey results in this table? Explain.

_____

_____

Got It?

PART 1 Got It

The two-way frequency table shows the results of a survey at a local high school. Students responded to the question "Do you volunteer anywhere?" How many sophomores said they volunteer?

		Volunteer?		
		Yes	No	Total
Class	Freshman	18	38	56
	Sophomore	22	35	57
	Junior	29	31	60
	Senior	34	29	63
	Total	103	133	236

PART 2 Got It

Based on the table, which statements are true?

I.   More men own 2-door cars than 4-door cars.

II. More women than men own 2-door cars.

III. More men than women were surveyed.

		Gender		
		Male	Female	Total
Car Model	2-door	81	44	125
	4-door	39	36	75
	Total	120	80	200

Got It?

PART 3 Got It

Your friend decides to show two movies in different rooms. Which two types of movies would you choose to show? Explain your reasoning.

		Movie Type			
		Action	**Drama**	**Comedy**	**Total**
Age	**Child**	14	6	19	39
	Adult	10	16	7	33
	Total	24	22	26	72

Close and Check

Focus Question

What can a two-way frequency table tell you about a population?

_____

_____

_____

_____

Do you know HOW?

The table below shows the results of a survey about the subject engineers said was their favorite in middle school.

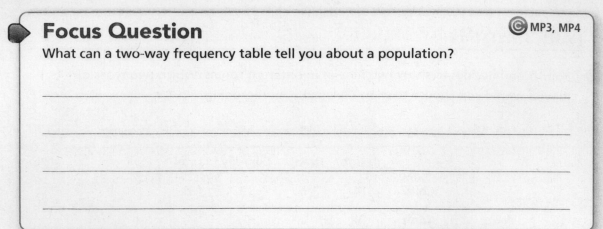

	Subject		
	Math	Science	Total
Electrical	85	90	175
Chemical	80	91	171
Mechanical	89	81	170
Total	254	262	516

(Engineer)

1. How many chemical engineers chose science?

   [ ]

2. How many engineers chose math?

   [ ]

3. Based on the table above, write T or F to classify each statement as true or false.

   [ ] More engineers chose science than chose math.

   [ ] More chemical engineers were surveyed than electrical or mechanical engineers.

Do you UNDERSTAND?

4. **Reasoning** You survey friends about the type of party they enjoy most. What type of party would you plan for them? Explain.

Party Type?	Gender		
	Male	Female	Total
Bowling	6	2	8
Skating	3	11	14
Dancing	1	3	4
Total	10	16	26

_____

_____

_____

5. **Reasoning** Your friend uses the data and plans a bowling party. Explain why he may have chosen bowling.

_____

_____

_____

Constructing Two-Way Relative Frequency Tables

CCSS: 8.SP.A.4: Understand that patterns of association can also be seen in bivariate categorical data by displaying ... relative frequencies in a two-way table. Construct ... a two-way table summarizing data on two categorical variables collected from the same subjects ... .

Launch

©MP5, MP8

Web-radio Station J surveys DJs about the type of jazz to jazz on Saturday. The station manager wants to use percents instead of raw numbers in the table.

She thinks she can use 50% or 100% for the male total. Explain how both percents could be correct.

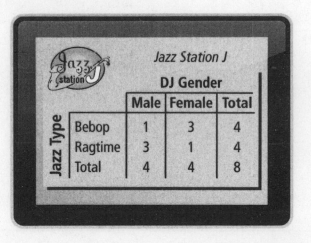

Jazz Station J

Jazz Type	DJ Gender		
	Male	Female	Total
Bebop	1	3	4
Ragtime	3	1	4
Total	4	4	8

Reflect Does the choice of 50% or 100% for the male total affect the percents used for bebop and ragtime for males? Explain.

_____

_____

_____

_____

_____

Got It?

PART 1 Got It

The two-way frequency table shows recent data about Internet connection types in the United States. Construct a two-way relative frequency table to show the distribution of the data with respect to the total population.

Internet Users (in millions)

Location	Internet Connection		
	Dial-up	**Broadband**	**Total**
Rural	4	31	35
Urban	6	141	147
Total	10	172	182

PART 2 Got It

The two-way frequency table shows recent data about Internet connection types in the United States. Construct a two-way relative frequency table to show how Internet connections are distributed with respect to location.

Internet Users (in millions)

Location	Internet Connection		
	Dial-up	**Broadband**	**Total**
Rural	4	31	35
Urban	6	141	147
Total	10	172	182

Got It?

PART 3 Got It

The two-way frequency table shows recent data about Internet connection types in the United States. Use the data from the table to construct a two-way relative frequency table to show how the locations are distributed with respect to type of Internet connection.

Internet Users (in millions)

		Internet Connection		
		Dial-up	Broadband	Total
Location	**Rural**	4	31	35
	Urban	6	141	147
	Total	10	172	182

Close and Check

Focus Question

What is a two-way relative frequency table? How is a two-way relative frequency table different from a two-way frequency table?

_____

_____

_____

_____

Do you know HOW?

A recent poll asked whether customers liked a restaurant's new lunch menu. Use the results shown below for Exercise 1.

Frequency Table

		New Menu?		
		Yes	No	Total
Gender	Male	13	15	28
	Female	18	25	43
	Total	31	40	71

1. Complete the corresponding relative frequency table with respect to the total population.

Total Relative Frequency Table

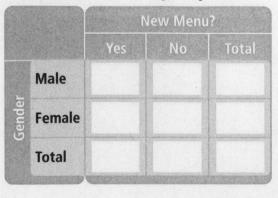

		New Menu?		
		Yes	No	Total
Gender	Male			
	Female			
	Total			

Do you UNDERSTAND?

2. **Vocabulary** You create a frequency table based on survey results about club membership in a middle school. Explain what the shaded box would represent for each type of relative frequency table.

		Club		
		Drama	Debate	Total
Grade Level	6th			
	7th			
	8th			
	Total			

a. Row Relative Frequency Table

_____

_____

_____

b. Column Relative Frequency Table

_____

_____

_____

Interpreting Two-Way Relative Frequency Tables

CCSS: 8.SP.A.4: … Interpret a two-way table summarizing data on two categorical variables collected from the same subjects. Use relative frequencies calculated for rows or columns to describe possible association between the two variables.

Launch

© MP3, MP7

Web-radio Station J plans an online music store. It surveys equal numbers of its two main listener groups—teenagers and adults—about their preferred format for buying jazz.

Provide two pieces of advice to Station J about setting up its online store based on the data.

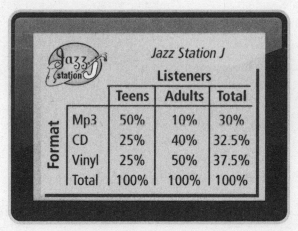

Jazz Station J

Listeners

Format		Teens	Adults	Total
	Mp3	50%	10%	30%
	CD	25%	40%	32.5%
	Vinyl	25%	50%	37.5%
	Total	100%	100%	100%

Two Pieces of Advice

1.

2.

Reflect Could a classmate have different pieces of advice about the same data? Explain.

_____

_____

_____

Got It?

PART 1 Got It

Before an election, voters were polled about how they planned to vote. The relative frequency table shows the relative frequencies with respect to the total population.

a. What percent of the voters plan to vote for the Republican candidate and *No* on Question 1?

b. Based on this table, which candidate would win the election? How do you know?

Total Relative Frequency Table

Candidate	Question 1?		
	Yes	No	Total
Democrat	20.0%	29.6%	49.6%
Republican	32.8%	17.6%	50.4%
Total	52.8%	47.2%	100%

Got It?

PART 2 Got It

Before an election, voters were polled about how they planned to vote. This table shows the relative frequencies with respect to the candidate the voters plan to vote for.

a. What percent of the voters who plan to vote for the Democrat plan to vote *No* on Question 1?

b. Is there evidence of an association between a voter's choice of candidate and how they plan to vote on Question 1? Explain.

Row Relative Frequency Table

		Question 1?		
		Yes	No	Total
Candidate	Democrat	40.4%	59.6%	100%
	Republican	65.1%	34.9%	100%
	Total	52.8%	47.2%	100%

Got It?

PART 3 Got It (1 of 2)

Before an election, voters were polled about how they planned to vote. This table shows the relative frequencies with respect to how voters plan to vote on Question 1.

a. What percent of the voters who plan to vote *No* on Question 1 also plan to vote for the Democratic candidate?

b. Is there evidence of an association between how voters plan to vote on Question 1 and their choice of candidate? Explain.

Column Relative Frequency Table

		Question 1?		
		Yes	**No**	**Total**
Candidate	**Democrat**	37.9%	62.7%	49.6%
	Republican	62.1%	37.3%	50.4%
	Total	100%	100%	100%

Got It?

PART 3 Got It (2 of 2)

Which table would you use to see if voting Yes on Question 1 would be popular with the supporters of the Republican candidate? Explain.

Row Relative Frequency Table

Candidate		Question 1?		
		Yes	**No**	**Total**
	Democrat	40.4%	59.6%	100%
	Republican	65.1%	34.9%	100%
	Total	52.8%	47.2%	100%

Column Relative Frequency Table

Candidate		Question 1?		
		Yes	**No**	**Total**
	Democrat	37.9%	62.7%	49.6%
	Republican	62.1%	37.3%	50.4%
	Total	100%	100%	100%

Close and Check

Focus Question

What can a two-way relative frequency table tell you about a population?

_____

_____

_____

_____

Do you know HOW?

1. What percent of those who studied for 2–4 hours passed the test?

Total Relative Frequency Table

		Hours Studied		
		1–2	2–4	Total
Test Results	Passed	16%	42%	58%
	Failed	30%	12%	42%
	Total	46%	54%	100%

[   ]

2. Complete the column relative frequency table.

Column Total Relative Frequency Table

		Handedness		
		Left	Right	Total
Hair Color	Blonde	25%	21.2%	22.2%
	Brunette		36.4%	
	Redhead	12.5%	12.2%	12.2%
	Other	29.2%		30%
	Total	100%	100%	

Do you UNDERSTAND?

3. Writing Describe the association between hours studied and test results, if any.

_____

_____

_____

_____

_____

4. Reasoning According to the table in Exercise 2, is there any evidence that hair color and handedness are related? Explain.

_____

_____

_____

_____

_____

_____

Choosing a Measure of Frequency

CCSS: 8.SP.A.4: Understand that patterns of association can also be seen in bivariate categorical data by displaying frequencies and relative frequencies in a two-way table. ... Use relative frequencies ... to describe possible association between the two variables.

Launch

© MP3, MP6

Station J asks salespeople (S) and disc jockeys (DJ) to vote on whether a horn or saxophone on the new logo would better communicate that the station plays jazz.

Show the results in a frequency table or a relative frequency table. Justify your choice of table.

New Logo

Votes for Sax	Votes for Horn
DJ DJ S	DJ S
DJ S DJ	DJ S
DJ DJ	

Frequency Table

	Station Workers		
	Sales	DJs	Total
Horn			
Sax			
Total			

Logo

Reflect What conclusions can you draw from your table?

_____

_____

_____

_____

_____

Got It?

PART 1 Got It

You also want to know if a male student is more likely than a female student to have a season ticket. Which table will be more helpful in finding that information? Explain your choice.

Frequency Table

		Season Ticket?		
		Yes	No	Total
Gender	Male	120	30	150
	Female	80	20	100
	Total	200	50	250

Row Relative Frequency Table

		Season Ticket?		
		Yes	No	Total
Gender	Male	80%	20%	100%
	Female	80%	20%	100%
	Total	80%	20%	100%

Got It?

PART 2 Got It

The table shows responses to the statement, "A new student center should be built."

What type of relative frequency table shows the percent of juniors who responded *No Opinion*? What percent of the juniors surveyed responded *No opinion*?

Frequency Table

		Freshman	Sophomore	Junior	Senior	Total
Response	Agree	432	336	264	168	1,200
	Disagree	288	144	216	120	768
	No Opinion	192	120	24	96	432
	Total	912	600	504	384	2,400

PART 3 Got It

You suspect that there is a relationship between having siblings and having chores. You gather data from members of your class.

Based on the data in the table, is there evidence of an association between having siblings and having chores? Explain.

		Have Siblings?		
		Yes	No	Total
Chores?	Yes	35	15	50
	No	25	15	40
	Total	60	30	90

Close and Check

> ## Focus Question
>
> When might you want to use a two-way frequency table? When might you want to use a two-way relative frequency table?
>
> _____
>
> _____
>
> _____
>
> _____

Do you know HOW?

1. Circle the table that will be more helpful in finding whether male or female teenagers are more likely to own a car.

Frequency Table

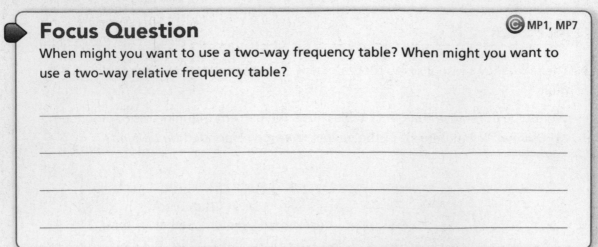

Survey Results	Car Ownership		
	Yes	No	Total
Male	49	126	175
Female	48	102	150
Total	97	228	325

Row Relative Frequency Table

Survey Results	Car Ownership		
	Yes	No	Total
Male	28%	72%	100%
Female	32%	68%	100%
Total	29.8%	70.2%	100%

2. You want to compare the number of male students in marching band to the number of female students in marching band. Would a frequency table or relative frequency table be more useful?

Do you UNDERSTAND?

3. Writing Explain how you decided the answer to Exercise 2.

_____

_____

_____

_____

4. Error Analysis A classmate wants to know if age influences movie attendance. He decides to analyze the data using a frequency table. Do you agree with his choice? Explain.

_____

_____

_____

_____

_____

_____

Problem Solving

CCSS: 8.SP.A.4: ... Construct and interpret a two way table summarizing data on two categorical variables collected from the same subjects. Use relative frequencies calculated for rows or columns to describe possible association between the two variables.

Launch

© MP3, MP5

The table shows survey results from big city and small town residents about their favorite type of Web-radio music.

What's the most important conclusion about city size and music choice you can make? What's the evidence supporting it? Explain.

Type of Music	Listener Location		
	Big City	Small Town	Total
Rock	27%	20%	23.5%
R & B	25%	20%	22.5%
Country	23%	55%	39%
Jazz	25%	5%	15%
Total	100%	100%	100%

Most Important Conclusion:

Evidence:

Reflect Could someone else come up with a different most important conclusion? Explain.

_____

_____

_____

_____

Got It?

PART 1 Got It

The ticket agency notes whether people are buying tickets for an upcoming event for themselves or as a gift. The two tables display the same data. Complete each table.

Frequency Table

Ticket Section	Purpose		
	Self	**Gift**	**Total**
A			
B		70	180
C			100
Total	200		400

Relative Frequency Table

Ticket Section	Purpose		
	Self	**Gift**	**Total**
A			30%
B	55%	35%	
C	25%		
Total		100%	

Got It?

PART 2 Got It

The table shows on-time arrival statistics for two different pilots. Which pilot would you hire? Explain your reasoning.

Pilot A

Result		Time of Flight		
		Night	Day	Total
	On-Time	10	90	100
	Late	10	10	20
	Total	20	100	120

Pilot B

Result		Time of Flight		
		Night	Day	Total
	On-Time	75	19	94
	Late	25	1	26
	Total	100	20	120

Close and Check

Focus Question

How can you determine which two-way table will be most useful in answering a certain question?

_____

_____

_____

_____

Do you know HOW?

1. A city planner conducts a survey of adult residents on whether they have a library card and whether they have an interest in buying an eReader. Complete the tables.

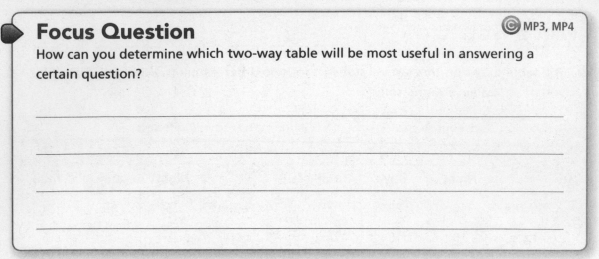

Frequency Table

	Interest in eReader		
Library Card		Yes	No	Total
Yes			75	
No		45		
Total		130		325

Total Relative Frequency Table

	Interest in eReader		
Library Card		Yes	No	Total
Yes		26%		
No				51%
Total		40%		100%

Do you UNDERSTAND?

2. **Reasoning** Is there evidence that having a library card makes you more or less interested in buying an eReader? Explain.

_____

_____

_____

3. **Reasoning** What could explain the interest or lack of interest in buying eReaders among library-card holders?

_____

_____

New Vocabulary: bivariate categorical data, bivariate data, categorical data, measurement data, two-way frequency table, two-way relative frequency table
Review Vocabulary: population, variable

Vocabulary Review

 Identify two challenging vocabulary terms from this topic. Write one vocabulary term in the center oval, and fill in the surrounding boxes with details that will help you better understand the term.

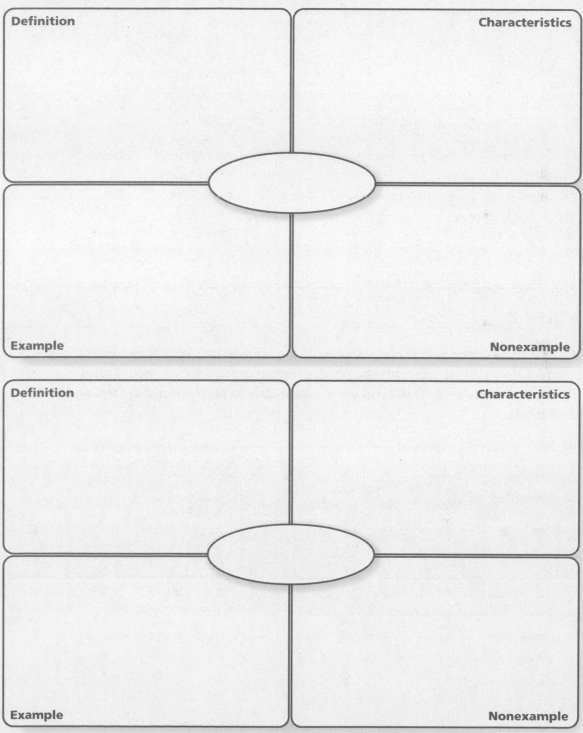

Definition

Characteristics

Example

Nonexample

Definition

Characteristics

Example

Nonexample

Pull It All Together

TASK 1

You need 5 musicians to play at a benefit concert. You have already selected 1 rock singer and 1 rock guitarist.

You want 60% of the musicians to be guitarists and 40% to be singers. You also want 40% of the musicians to be rock musicians and 60% to be country musicians.

What type of musicians do you still need?

TASK 2

You and a friend are deciding which cold medicine to buy. Your friend used the frequency table to construct the relative frequency table shown. Your friend chooses Medicine A. Could you use the same data to justify choosing Medicine B? Explain.

Frequency Table

Medicine		Improvement?		
		Yes	No	Total
	A	27	23	50
	B	13	7	20
	Total	40	30	70

Relative Frequency Table

Medicine		Improvement?		
		Yes	No	Total
	A	67.5%	76.7%	71.4%
	B	32.5%	23.3%	28.6%
	Total	100%	100%	100%

English/Spanish Glossary

········· **A** ·········

Absolute deviation from the mean Absolute deviation measures the distance that the data value is from the mean. You find the absolute deviation by taking the absolute value of the deviation of a data value. Absolute deviations are always nonnegative.

Desviación absoluta de la media La desviación absoluta mide la distancia a la que un valor se encuentra de la media. Para hallar la desviación absoluta, tomas el valor absoluto de la desviación de un valor. Las desviaciones absolutas siempre son no negativas.

Absolute value The absolute value of a number a is the distance between a and zero on a number line. The absolute value of a is written as $|a|$.

Valor absoluto El valor absoluto de un número a es la distancia entre a y cero en la recta numérica. El valor absoluto de a se escribe como $|a|$.

Accuracy The accuracy of an estimate or measurement is the degree to which it agrees with an accepted or actual value of that measurement.

Exactitud La exactitud de una estimación o medición es el grado de concordancia con un valor aceptado o real de esa medición.

Action In a probability situation, an action is a process with an uncertain result.

Acción En una situación de probabilidad, una acción es el proceso con un resultado incierto.

Acute angle An acute angle is an angle with a measure between 0° and 90°.

Ángulo agudo Un ángulo agudo es un ángulo que mide entre 0° y 90°.

Acute triangle An acute triangle is a triangle with three acute angles.

Triángulo acutángulo Un triángulo acutángulo es un triángulo que tiene tres ángulos agudos.

Addend Addends are the numbers that are added together to find a sum.

Sumando Los sumandos son los números que se suman para hallar un total.

English/Spanish Glossary

Additive inverses Two numbers that have a sum of 0.

Inversos de suma Dos números cuya suma es 0.

Adjacent angles Two angles are adjacent angles if they share a vertex and a side, but have no interior points in common.

Ángulos adyacentes Dos ángulos son adyacentes si tienen un vértice y un lado en común, pero no comparten puntos internos.

Algebraic expression An algebraic expression is a mathematical phrase that consists of variables, numbers, and operation symbols.

Expresión algebraica Una expresión algebraica es una frase matemática que consiste en variables, números y símbolos de operaciones.

Analyze To analyze is to think about and understand facts and details about a given set of information. Analyzing can involve providing a written summary supported by factual information, diagrams, charts, tables, or any combination of these.

Analizar Analizar es pensar en los datos y detalles de cierta información y comprenderlos. El análisis puede incluir la presentación de un resumen escrito sustentado por información objetiva, diagramas, tablas o una combinación de esos elementos.

Angle An angle is a figure formed by two rays with a common endpoint.

Ángulo Un ángulo es una figura formada por dos semirrectas que tienen un extremo en común.

Angle of rotation The angle of rotation is the number of degrees a figure is rotated.

Ángulo de rotación El ángulo de rotación es el número de grados que se rota una figura.

Annual salary The amount of money earned at a job in one year.

Salario annual La cantidad de dinero ganó en un trabajo en un año.

Area The area of a figure is the number of square units the figure encloses.

Área El área de una figura es el número de unidades cuadradas que ocupa.

English/Spanish Glossary

Area of a circle The formula for the area of a circle is $A = \pi r^2$, where A represents the area and r represents the radius of the circle.

Área de un círculo La fórmula del área de un círculo es $A = \pi r^2$, donde A representa el área y r representa el radio del círculo.

Area of a parallelogram The formula for the area of a parallelogram is $A = bh$, where A represents the area, b represents a base, and h is the corresponding height.

Área de un paralelogramo La fórmula del área de un paralelogramo es $A = bh$, donde A representa el área, b representa una base y h es la altura correspondiente.

Area of a rectangle The formula for the area of a rectangle is $A = bh$, where A represents the area, b represents the base, and h represents the height of the rectangle.

Área de un rectángulo La fórmula del área de un rectángulo es $A = bh$, donde A representa el área, b representa la base y h representa la altura del rectángulo.

Area of a square The formula for the area of a square is $A = s^2$, where A represents the area and s represents a side length.

Área de un cuadrado La fórmula del área de un cuadrado es $A = s^2$, donde A representa el área y l representa la longitud de un lado.

Area of a trapezoid The formula for the area of a trapezoid is $A = \frac{1}{2}h(b_1 + b_2)$, where A represents the area, b_1 and b_2 represent the bases, and h represents the height between the bases.

El área de un trapezoide La fórmula para el área de un trapezoide es $A = \frac{1}{2}h(b_1 + b_2)$, donde A representa el área, b_1 y b_2 representan las bases, y h representa la altura entre las bases.

Area of a triangle The formula for the area of a triangle is $A = \frac{1}{2}bh$, where A represents the area, b represents the length of a base, and h represents the corresponding height.

Área de un triángulo La fórmula del área de un triángulo es $A = \frac{1}{2}bh$, donde A representa el área, b representa la longitud de una base y h representa la altura correspondiente.

Asset An asset is money you have or property of value that you own.

Ventaja Una ventaja es dinero que tiene o la propiedad de valor que usted posee.

English/Spanish Glossary

Associative Property of Addition For any numbers a, b, and c:
$(a + b) + c = a + (b + c)$

Propiedad asociativa de la suma Para los números cualesquiera a, b y c:
$(a + b) + c = a + (b + c)$

Associative Property of Multiplication For any numbers a, b, and c:
$(a \cdot b) \cdot c = a \cdot (b \cdot c)$

Propiedad asociativa de la multiplicación Para los números cualesquiera a, b y c:
$(a \cdot b) \cdot c = a \cdot (b \cdot c)$

Average of two numbers The average of two numbers is the value that represents the middle of two numbers. It is found by adding the two numbers together and dividing by 2.

Promedio de dos números El promedio de dos números es el valor que está justo en el medio de esos dos números. Se halla sumando los dos números y dividiendo el resultado por 2.

B

Balance The balance in an account is the principal amount plus the interest earned.

Saldo El saldo de una cuenta es el capital más el interés ganado.

Balance of a checking account The balance of a checking account is the amount of money in the checking account.

El equilibrio de una Cuenta Corriente Bancaria El equilibrio de una cuenta corriente bancaria es la cantidad de dinero en la cuenta corriente bancaria.

Balance of a loan The balance of a loan is the remaining unpaid principal.

El equilibrio de un préstamo El equilibrio de un préstamo es el director impagado restante.

Bar diagram A bar diagram is a way to represent part to whole relationships.

Diagrama de barras Un diagrama de barras es una forma de representar una relación de parte a entero.

Base The base is the repeated factor of a number written in exponential form.

Base La base es el factor repetido de un número escrito en forma exponencial.

English/Spanish Glossary

Base area of a cone The base area of a cone is the area of a circle. Base Area = πr^2.

Área de la base de un cono El área de la base de un cono es el área de un círculo. El área de la base = πr^2.

Base of a cone The base of a cone is a circle with radius r.

Base de un cono La base de un cono es un círculo con radio r.

Base of a cylinder A base of a cylinder is one of a pair of parallel circular faces that are the same size.

Base de un cilindro Una base de un cilindro es una de dos caras circulares paralelas que tienen el mismo tamaño.

Base of a parallelogram A base of a parallelogram is any side of the parallelogram.

Base de un paralelogramo La base de un paralelogramo es cualquiera de los lados del paralelogramo.

Base of a prism A base of a prism is one of a pair of parallel polygonal faces that are the same size and shape. A prism is named for the shape of its bases.

Base de un prisma La base de un prisma es una de las dos caras poligonales paralelas que tienen el mismo tamaño y la misma forma. El nombre de un prisma depende de la forma de sus bases.

Base of a pyramid A base of a pyramid is a polygonal face that does not connect to the vertex.

Base de una pirámide La base de una pirámide es una cara poligonal que no se conecta con el vértice.

Base of a triangle The base of a triangle is any side of the triangle.

Base de un triángulo La base de un triángulo es cualquiera de los lados del triángulo.

Benchmark A benchmark is a number you can use as a reference point for other numbers.

Referencia Una referencia es un número que usted puede utilizar como un punto de referencia para otros números.

English/Spanish Glossary

Bias A bias is a tendency toward a particular perspective that is different from the overall perspective of the population.

Sesgo Un sesgo es una tendencia hacia una perspectiva particular que es diferente de la perspectiva general de la población.

Biased sample In a biased sample, the number of subjects in the sample with the trait that you are studying is not proportional to the number of members in the population with that trait. A biased sample does not accurately represent the population.

Muestra sesgada En una muestra sesgada, el número de sujetos de la muestra que tiene la característica que se está estudiando no es proporcional al número de miembros de la población que tienen esa característica. Una muestra sesgada no representa con exactitud la población.

Bivariate categorical data Bivariate categorical data pairs categorical data collected about two variables of the same population.

Datos bivariados por categorías Los datos bivariados por categorías agrupan pares de datos obtenidos acerca de dos variables de la misma población.

Bivariate data Bivariate data is comprised of pairs of linked observations about a population.

Datos bivariados Los datos bivariados se forman a partir de pares de observaciones relacionadas sobre una población.

Box plot A box plot is a statistical graph that shows the distribution of a data set by marking five boundary points where data occur along a number line. Unlike a dot plot or a histogram, a box plot does not show frequency.

Diagrama de cajas Un diagrama de cajas es un diagrama de estadísticas que muestra la distribución de un conjunto de datos al marcar cinco puntos de frontera donde se hallan los datos sobre una recta numérica. A diferencia del diagrama de puntos o el histograma, el diagrama de cajas no muestra la frecuencia.

Budget A budget is a plan for how you will spend your money.

Presupuesto Un presupuesto es un plan para cómo gastará su dinero.

English/Spanish Glossary

C

Categorical data Categorical data consist of data that fall into categories.

Datos por categorías Los datos por categorías son datos que se pueden clasificar en categorías.

Center of a circle The center of a circle is the point inside the circle that is the same distance from all points on the circle. Name a circle by its center.

Centro de un círculo El centro de un círculo es el punto dentro del círculo que está a la misma distancia de todos los puntos del círculo. Un círculo se identifica por su centro.

Center of a regular polygon The center of a regular polygon is the point that is equidistant from its vertices.

Centro de un polígono regular El centro de un polígono regular es el punto equidistante de todos sus vértices.

Center of rotation The center of rotation is a fixed point about which a figure is rotated.

Centro de rotación El centro de rotación es el punto fijo alrededor del cual se rota una figura.

Check register A record that shows all of the transactions for a bank account, including withdrawals, deposits, and transfers. It also shows the balance of the account after each transaction.

Verifique registro Un registro que muestra todas las transacciones para una cuenta bancaria, inclusive retiradas, los depósitos, y las transferencias. También muestra el equilibrio de la cuenta después de cada transacción.

Circle A circle is the set of all points in a plane that are the same distance from a given point, called the center.

Círculo Un círculo es el conjunto de todos los puntos de un plano que están a la misma distancia de un punto dado, llamado centro.

Circle graph A circle graph is a graph that represents a whole divided into parts.

Gráfica circular Una gráfica circular es una gráfica que representa un todo dividido en partes.

English/Spanish Glossary

Circumference of a circle The circumference of a circle is the distance around the circle. The formula for the circumference of a circle is $C = \pi d$, where C represents the circumference and d represents the diameter of the circle.

Circunferencia de un círculo La circunferencia de un círculo es la distancia alrededor del círculo. La fórmula de la circunferencia de un círculo es $C = \pi d$, donde C representa la circunferencia y d representa el diámetro del círculo.

Cluster A cluster is a group of points that lie close together on a scatter plot.

Grupo Un grupo es un conjunto de puntos que están agrupados en un diagrama de dispersión.

Coefficient A coefficient is the number part of a term that contains a variable.

Coeficiente Un coeficiente es la parte numérica de un término que contiene una variable.

Common denominator A common denominator is a number that is the denominator of two or more fractions.

Común denominador Un común denominador es un número que es el denominador de dos o más fracciones.

Common multiple A common multiple is a multiple that two or more numbers share.

Múltiplo común Un múltiplo común es un múltiplo que comparten dos o más números.

Commutative Property of Addition For any numbers a and b: $a + b = b + a$

Propiedad conmutativa de la suma Para los números cualesquiera a y b: $a + b = b + a$

Commutative Property of Multiplication For any numbers a and b: $a \cdot b = b \cdot a$

Propiedad conmutativa de la multiplicación Para los números cualesquiera a y b: $a \cdot b = b \cdot a$

Comparative inference A comparative inference is an inference made by interpreting and comparing two sets of data.

Inferencia comparativa Una inferencia comparativa es una inferencia que se hace al interpretar y comparar dos conjuntos de datos.

English/Spanish Glossary

Compare To compare is to tell or show how two things are alike or different.

Comparar Comparar es describir o mostrar en qué se parecen o en qué se diferencian dos cosas.

Compatible numbers Compatible numbers are numbers that are easy to compute mentally.

Números compatibles Los números compatibles son números fáciles de calcular mentalmente.

Complementary angles Two angles are complementary angles if the sum of their measures is 90°. Complementary angles that are adjacent form a right angle.

Ángulos complementarios Dos ángulos son complementarios si la suma de sus medidas es 90°. Los ángulos complementarios que son adyacentes forman un ángulo recto.

Complex fraction A complex fraction is a fraction $\frac{A}{B}$ where A and/or B are fractions and B is not zero.

Fracción compleja Una fracción compleja es una fracción $\frac{A}{B}$ donde A y/o B son fracciones y B es distinto de cero.

Compose a shape To compose a shape, join two (or more) shapes so that there is no gap or overlap.

Componer una figura Para componer una figura, debes unir dos (o más) figuras de modo que entre ellas no queden espacios ni superposiciones.

Composite figure A composite figure is the combination of two or more figures into one object.

Figura compuesta Una figura compuesta es la combinación de dos o más figuras en un objeto.

Composite number A composite number is a whole number greater than 1 with more than two factors.

Número compuesto Un número compuesto es un número entero mayor que 1 con más de dos factores.

Compound event A compound event is an event associated with a multi-step action. A compound event is composed of events that are the outcomes of the steps of the action.

Evento compuesto Un evento compuesto es un evento que se relaciona con una acción de varios pasos. Un evento compuesto se compone de eventos que son los resultados de los pasos de una acción.

English/Spanish Glossary

Compound interest Compound interest is interest paid on both the principal and the interest earned in previous interest periods. To calculate compound interest, use the formula $B = p(1 + r)^n$, where B is the balance in the account, p is the principal, r is the annual interest rate, and n is the time in years that the account earns interest.

Interés compuesto El interés compuesto es el interés que se paga sobre el capital y el interés obtenido en períodos de interés anteriores. Para calcular el interés compuesto, usa la fórmula $B = c(1 + r)^n$ donde B es el saldo de la cuenta, c es el capital, r es la tasa de interés anual y n es el tiempo en años en que la cuenta obtiene un interés.

Cone A cone is a three-dimensional figure with one circular base and one vertex.

Cono Un cono es una figura tridimensional con una base circular y un vértice.

Congruent figures Two two-dimensional figures are congruent $\cong$ if the second can be obtained from the first by a sequence of rotations, reflections, and translations.

Figuras congruentes Dos figuras bidimensionales son congruentes $\cong$ si la segunda puede obtenerse a partir de la primera mediante una secuencia de rotaciones, reflexiones y traslaciones.

Conjecture A conjecture is a statement that you believe to be true but have not yet proved to be true.

Conjetura Una conjetura es un enunciado que crees que es verdadero, pero que todavía no has comprobado que sea verdadero.

Constant A constant is a term that only contains a number.

Constante Una constante es un término que solamente contiene un número.

Constant of proportionality In a proportional relationship, one quantity y is a constant multiple of the other quantity x. The constant multiple is called the constant of proportionality. The constant of proportionality is equal to the ratio $\frac{y}{x}$.

Constante de proporcionalidad En una relación proporcional, una cantidad y es un múltiplo constante de la otra cantidad x. El múltiplo constante se llama constante de proporcionalidad. La constante de proporcionalidad es igual a la razón $\frac{y}{x}$.

English/Spanish Glossary

Construct To construct is to make something, such as an argument, by organizing ideas. Constructing an argument can involve a written response, equations, diagrams, charts, tables, or a combination of these.

Construir Construir es hacer o crear algo, como se construye un argumento al organizar ideas. Para construir un argumento puede usarse una respuesta escrita, ecuaciones, diagramas, tablas o una combinación de esos elementos.

Convenience sampling Convenience sampling is a sampling method in which a researcher chooses members of the population that are convenient and available. Many researchers use this sampling technique because it is fast and inexpensive. It does not require the researcher to keep track of everyone in the population.

Muestra de conveniencia Una muestra de conveniencia es un método de muestreo en el que un investigador escoge miembros de la población que están convenientemente disponibles. Muchos investigadores usan esta técnica de muestreo porque es rápida y no es costosa. No requiere que el investigador lleve un registro de cada miembro de la población.

Cost of attendance The cost of attendance of one year of college is the sum of all of your expenses during the year.

El costo de asistencia El costo de asistencia de un año del colegio es la suma de todos sus gastos durante el año.

Cost of credit The cost of credit for a loan is the difference between the total cost and the principal.

El costo de crédito El costo de crédito para un préstamo es la diferencia entre el coste total y el director.

Converse of the Pythagorean Theorem If the sum of the squares of the lengths of two sides of a triangle equals the square of the length of the third side, then the triangle is a right triangle. If $a^2 + b^2 = c^2$, then the triangle is a right triangle.

Expresión recíproca del Teorema de Pitágoras Si la suma del cuadrado de la longitud de dos lados de un triángulo es igual al cuadrado de la longitud del tercer lado, entonces el triángulo es un triángulo rectángulo. $a^2 + b^2 = c^2$, entonces el triángulo es un triángulo rectángulo.

Conversion factor A conversion factor is a rate that equals 1.

Factor de conversión Un factor de conversión es una tasa que es igual a 1.

English/Spanish Glossary

Coordinate plane A coordinate plane is formed by a horizontal number line called the *x*-axis and a vertical number line called the *y*-axis.

Plano de coordenadas Un plano de coordenadas está formado por una recta numérica horizontal llamada eje de las *x* y una recta numérica vertical llamada eje de las *y*.

Corresponding angles Corresponding angles lie on the same side of a transversal and in corresponding positions.

Ángulos correspondientes Los ángulos correspondientes se ubican al mismo lado de una secante y en posiciones correspondientes.

Counterexample A counterexample is a specific example that shows that a conjecture is false.

Contraejemplo Un contraejemplo es un ejemplo específico que muestra que una conjetura es falsa.

Counting Principle If there are *m* possible outcomes of one action and *n* possible outcomes of a second action, then there are *m · n* outcomes of the first action followed by the second action.

Principio de conteo Si hay *m* resultados posibles de una acción y *n* resultados posibles de una segunda acción, entonces hay *m · n* resultados de la primera acción seguida de la segunda acción.

Coupon A coupon is part of a printed or online advertisement entitling the holder to a discount at checkout.

Cupón Un cupón forma parte de un anuncio impreso o en línea que permite al poseedor a un descuento en comprueba.

Credit card A credit card is a card issued by a lender that can be used to borrow money or make purchases on credit.

Tarjeta de crédito Una tarjeta de crédito es una tarjeta publicada por un prestamista que puede ser utilizado para pedir dinero prestado o compras de marca a cuenta.

Credit history A credit history shows how a consumer has managed credit in the past.

Acredite la historia Una historia del crédito muestra cómo un consumidor ha manejado crédito en el pasado.

 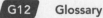

English/Spanish Glossary

Credit report A report that shows personal information about a consumer and details about the consumer's credit history.

Acredite reporte Un reporte que muestra información personal sobre un consumidor y detalles acerca de la historia del crédito del consumidor.

Critique A critique is a careful judgment in which you give your opinion about the good and bad parts of something, such as how a problem was solved.

Crítica Una crítica es una evaluación cuidadosa en la que das tu opinión acerca de las partes positivas y negativas de algo, como la manera en la que se resolvió un problema.

Cross section A cross section is the intersection of a three-dimensional figure and a plane.

Corte transversal Un corte transversal es la intersección de una figura tridimensional y un plano.

Cube A cube is a rectangular prism whose faces are all squares.

Cubo Un cubo es un prisma rectangular cuyas caras son todas cuadrados.

Cube root The cube root of a number, *n*, is a number whose cube equals *n*.

Raíz cúbica La raíz cúbica de un número, *n*, es un número que elevado al cubo es igual a *n*.

Cubic unit A cubic unit is the volume of a cube that measures 1 unit on each edge.

Unidad cúbica Una unidad cúbica es el volumen de un cubo en el que cada arista mide 1 unidad.

Cylinder A cylinder is a three-dimensional figure with two parallel circular bases that are the same size.

Cilindro Un cilindro es una figura tridimensional con dos bases circulares paralelas que tienen el mismo tamaño.

D

Data Data are pieces of information collected by asking questions, measuring, or making observations about the real world.

Datos Los datos son información reunida mediante preguntas, mediciones u observaciones sobre la vida diaria.

 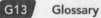

English/Spanish Glossary

Debit card A debit card is a card issued by a bank that is linked a customer's bank account, normally a checking account. A debit card can normally be used to withdraw money from an ATM or to make a purchase.

Tarjeta de débito Una tarjeta de débito es una tarjeta publicada por un banco que es ligado la cuenta bancaria de un cliente, normalmente una cuenta corriente bancaria. Una tarjeta de débito puede ser utilizada normalmente retirar dinero de una ATM o para hacer una compra.

Decimal A decimal is a number with one or more places to the right of a decimal point.

Decimal Un decimal es un número que tiene uno o más lugares a la derecha del punto decimal.

Decimal places The digits after the decimal point are called decimal places.

Lugares decimales Los dígitos que están después del punto decimal se llaman lugares decimales.

Decompose a shape To decompose a shape, break it up to form other shapes.

Descomponer una figura Para descomponer una figura, debes separarla para formar otras figuras.

Deductive reasoning Deductive reasoning is a process of reasoning logically from given facts to a conclusion.

Razonamiento deductivo El razonamiento deductivo es un proceso de razonamiento lógico que parte de hechos dados hasta llegar a una conclusión.

Denominator The denominator is the number below the fraction bar in a fraction.

Denominador El denominador es el número que está debajo de la barra de fracción en una fracción.

Dependent events Two events are dependent events if the occurrence of the first event affects the probability of the second event.

Eventos dependientes Dos eventos son dependientes si el resultado del primer evento afecta la probabilidad del segundo evento.

Deposit A transaction that adds money to a bank account is a deposit.

Depósito Una transacción que agrega dinero a una cuenta bancaria es un depósito.

English/Spanish Glossary

Dependent variable A dependent variable is a variable whose value changes in response to another (independent) variable.

Variable dependiente Una variable dependiente es una variable cuyo valor cambia en respuesta a otra variable (independiente).

Describe To describe is to explain or tell in detail. A written description can contain facts and other information needed to communicate your answer. A diagram or a graph may also be included.

Describir Describir es explicar o indicar algo en detalle. Una descripción escrita puede incluir hechos y otra información necesaria para comunicar tu respuesta. También puede incluir un diagrama o una gráfica.

Design To design is to make using specific criteria.

Diseñar Diseñar es crear algo a partir de criterios específicos.

Determine To determine is to use the given information and any related facts to find a value or make a decision.

Determinar Determinar es usar la información dada y cualquier otro dato relacionado para hallar un valor o tomar una decisión.

Deviation from the mean Deviation indicates how far away and in which direction a data value is from the mean. Data values that are less than the mean have a negative deviation. Data values that are greater than the mean have a positive deviation.

Desviación de la media La desviación indica a qué distancia y en qué dirección un valor se aleja de la media. Los valores menores que la media tienen una desviación negativa. Los valores mayores que la media tienen una desviación positiva.

Diagonal A diagonal of a figure is a segment that connects two nonconsecutive vertices of the figure.

Diagonal La diagonal de una figura es un segmento que conecta dos vértices no consecutivos de la figura.

Diameter A diameter is a segment that passes through the center of a circle and has both endpoints on the circle. The term diameter can also mean the length of this segment.

Diámetro Un diámetro es un segmento que atraviesa el centro de un círculo y tiene sus dos extremos en el círculo. El término diámetro también puede referirse a la longitud de este segmento.

English/Spanish Glossary

Difference The difference is the answer you get when subtracting two numbers.

Diferencia La diferencia es la respuesta que obtienes cuando restas dos números.

Dilation A dilation is a transformation that moves each point along the ray through the point, starting from a fixed center, and multiplies distances from the center by a common scale factor. If a vertex of a figure is the center of dilation, then the vertex and its image after the dilation are the same point.

Dilatación Una dilatación es una transformación que mueve cada punto a lo largo de la semirrecta a través del punto, a partir de un centro fijo, y multiplica las distancias desde el centro por un factor de escala común. Si un vértice de una figura es el centro de dilatación, entonces el vértice y su imagen después de la dilatación son el mismo punto.

Direct variation A linear relationship that can be represented by an equation in the form $y = kx$, where $x \neq 0$.

Dirija variación Una relación lineal que puede ser representada por una ecuación en la forma $y = kx$, donde x no iguale 0.

Distribution (of a data set) The distribution of a data set describes the way that its data values are spread out over all possible values. This includes describing the frequencies of each data value. The shape of a data display shows the distribution of a data set.

Distribución (de un conjunto de datos) La distribución de un conjunto de datos describe la manera en que sus valores se esparcen sobre todos los valores posibles. Eso incluye la descripción de las frecuencias de cada valor. La forma de una exhibición de datos muestra la distribución de un conjunto de datos.

Distributive Property Multiplying a number by a sum or difference gives the same result as multiplying that number by each term in the sum or difference and then adding or subtracting the corresponding products.
$a \cdot (b + c) = a \cdot b + a \cdot c$ and
$a \cdot (b - c) = a \cdot b - a \cdot c$

Propiedad distributiva Multiplicar un número por una suma o una diferencia da el mismo resultado que multiplicar ese mismo número por cada uno de los términos de la suma o la diferencia y después sumar o restar los productos obtenidos.
$a \cdot (b + c) = a \cdot b + a \cdot c$ and
$a \cdot (b - c) = a \cdot b - a \cdot c$

Dividend The dividend is the number to be divided.

Dividendo El dividendo es el número que se divide.

English/Spanish Glossary

Divisible A number is divisible by another number if there is no remainder after dividing.

Divisible Un número es divisible por otro número si no hay residuo después de dividir.

Divisor The divisor is the number used to divide another number.

Divisor El divisor es el número por el cual se divide otro número.

Dot plot A dot plot is a statistical graph that shows the shape of a data set with stacked dots above each data value on a number line. Each dot represents one data value.

Diagrama de puntos Un diagrama de puntos es una gráfica estadística que muestra la forma de un conjunto de datos con puntos marcados sobre cada valor de una recta numérica. Cada punto representa un valor.

E

Earned wages Earned wages are the income you receive from an employer for doing a job. Earned wages are also called gross pay.

Sueldos ganados Los sueldos ganados son los ingresos que usted recibe de un empleador para hacer un trabajo. Los sueldos ganados también son llamados la paga bruta.

Easy-access loan The term easy-access loan refers to a wide variety of loans with a streamlined application process. Many easy-access loans are short-term loans of relatively small amounts of money. They often have high interest rates.

Préstamo de fácil-acceso El préstamo del fácil-acceso del término se refiere a una gran variedad de préstamos con un proceso simplificado de aplicación. Muchos préstamos del fácil-acceso son préstamos a corto plazo de cantidades relativamente pequeñas de dinero. Ellos a menudo tienen los tipos de interés altos.

Edge of a three-dimensional figure An edge of a three-dimensional figure is a segment formed by the intersection of two faces.

Arista de una figura tridimensional Una arista de una figura tridimensional es un segmento formado por la intersección de dos caras.

English/Spanish Glossary

Enlargement An enlargement is a dilation with a scale factor greater than 1. After an enlargement, the image is bigger than the original figure.

Aumento Un aumento es una dilatación con un factor de escala mayor que 1. Después de un aumento, la imagen es más grande que la figura original.

Equation An equation is a mathematical sentence that includes an equals sign to compare two expressions.

Ecuación Una ecuación es una oración matemática que incluye un signo igual para comparar dos expresiones.

Equilateral triangle An equilateral triangle is a triangle whose sides are all the same length.

Triángulo equilátero Un triángulo equilátero es un triángulo que tiene todos sus lados de la misma longitud.

Equivalent equations Equivalent equations are equations that have exactly the same solutions.

Ecuaciones equivalentes Las ecuaciones equivalentes son ecuaciones que tienen exactamente la misma solución.

Equivalent expressions Equivalent expressions are expressions that always have the same value.

Expresiones equivalentes Las expresiones equivalentes son expresiones que siempre tienen el mismo valor.

Equivalent fractions Equivalent fractions are fractions that name the same number.

Fracciones equivalentes Las fracciones equivalentes son fracciones que representan el mismo número.

Equivalent inequalities Equivalent inequalities are inequalities that have the same solution.

Desigualdades equivalentes Las desigualdades equivalentes son desigualdades que tienen la misma solución.

Equivalent ratios Equivalent ratios are ratios that express the same relationship.

Razones equivalentes Las razones equivalentes son razones que expresan la misma relación.

Estimate To estimate is to find a number that is close to an exact answer.

Estimar Estimar es hallar un número cercano a una respuesta exacta.

English/Spanish Glossary

Evaluate a numerical expression To evaluate a numerical expression is to follow the order of operations.

Evaluar una expresión numérica Evaluar una expresión numérica es seguir el orden de las operaciones.

Evaluate an algebraic expression To evaluate an algebraic expression, replace each variable with a number, and then follow the order of operations.

Evaluar una expresión algebraica Para evaluar una expresión algebraica, reemplaza cada variable con un número y luego sigue el orden de las operaciones.

Event An event is a single outcome or group of outcomes from a sample space.

Evento Un evento es un resultado simple o un grupo de resultados de un espacio muestral.

Expand an algebraic expression To expand an algebraic expression, use the Distributive Property to rewrite a product as a sum or difference of terms.

Desarrollar una expresión algebraica Para desarrollar una expresión algebraica, usa la propiedad distributiva para reescribir el producto como una suma o diferencia de términos.

Expected family contribution The amount of money a student's family is expected to contribute towards the student's cost of attendance for school.

Contribución familiar esperado La cantidad de dinero que la familia de un estudiante es esperada contribuir hacia el estudiante es costado de asistencia para la escuela.

Expense Money that a business or a person needs to spend to pay for or buy something.

Gasto El dinero que un negocio o una persona debe gastar para pagar por o comprar algo.

Experiment To experiment is to try to gather information in several ways.

Experimentar Experimentar es intentar reunir información de varias maneras.

English/Spanish Glossary

Experimental probability You find the experimental probability of an event by repeating an experiment many times and using this ratio: $P(\text{event}) =$ $\dfrac{\text{number of times event occurs}}{\text{total number of trials}}$

Probabilidad experimental Para hallar la probabilidad experimental de un evento, debes repetir un experimento muchas veces y usar esta razón: $P(\text{evento}) =$ $\dfrac{\text{número de veces que sucede el evento}}{\text{número total de pruebas}}$

Explain To explain is to give facts and details that make an idea easier to understand. Explaining can involve a written summary supported by a diagram, chart, table, or a combination of these.

Explicar Explicar es brindar datos y detalles para que una idea sea más fácil de comprender. Para explicar algo se puede usar un resumen escrito sustentado por un diagrama, una tabla o una combinación de esos elementos.

Exponent An exponent is a number that shows how many times a base is used as a factor.

Exponente Un exponente es un número que muestra cuántas veces se usa una base como factor.

Expression An expression is a mathematical phrase that can involve variables, numbers, and operations. See algebraic expression or numerical expression.

Expresión Una expresión es una frase matemática que puede tener variables, números y operaciones. Ver expresión algebraica o expresión numérica.

Exterior angle of a triangle An exterior angle of a triangle is an angle formed by a side and an extension of an adjacent side.

Ángulo externo de un triángulo Un ángulo externo de un triángulo es un ángulo formado por un lado y una extensión de un lado adyacente.

F

Face of a three-dimensional figure A face of a three-dimensional figure is a flat surface shaped like a polygon.

Cara de una figura tridimensional La cara de una figura tridimensional es una superficie plana con forma de polígono.

English/Spanish Glossary

Factor an algebraic expression To factor an algebraic expression, write the expression as a product.

Descomponer una expresión algebraica en factores Para descomponer una expresión algebraica en factores, escribe la expresión como un producto.

Factors Factors are numbers that are multiplied to give a product.

Factores Los factores son los números que se multiplican para obtener un producto.

False equation A false equation has values that do not equal each other on each side of the equals sign.

Ecuación falsa Una ecuación falsa tiene valores a cada lado del signo igual que no son iguales entre sí.

Financial aid Financial aid is any money offered to a student to assist with the cost of attendance.

Ayuda financiera La ayuda financiera es cualquier dinero ofreció a un estudiante para ayudar con el costo de asistencia.

Financial need A student's financial need is the difference between the student's cost of attendance and the student's expected family contribution.

Necesidad financiera Una necesidad financiera del estudiante es la diferencia entre el estudiante es costada de asistencia y la contribución esperado de familia de estudiante.

Find To find is to calculate or determine.

Hallar Hallar es calcular o determinar.

First quartile For an ordered set of data, the first quartile is the median of the lower half of the data set.

Primer cuartil Para un conjunto ordenado de datos, el primer cuartil es la mediana de la mitad inferior del conjunto de datos.

Fixed expenses Fixed expenses are expenses that do not change from one budget period to the next.

Gastos fijos Los gastos fijos son los gastos que no cambian de un período económico al próximo.

English/Spanish Glossary

Fraction A fraction is a number that can be written in the form $\frac{a}{b}$, where a is a whole number and b is a positive whole number. A fraction is formed by a parts of size $\frac{1}{b}$.

Fracción Una fracción es un número que puede expresarse de forma $\frac{a}{b}$, donde a es un entero y b es un número entero positivo. La fracción está formada por a partes de tamaño $\frac{1}{b}$.

Frequency Frequency describes the number of times a specific value occurs in a data set.

Frecuencia La frecuencia describe el número de veces que aparece un valor específico en un conjunto de datos.

Function A function is a rule for taking each input value and producing exactly one output value.

Función Una función es una regla por la cual se toma cada valor de entrada y se produce exactamente un valor de salida.

G

Gap A gap is an area of a graph that contains no data points.

Espacio vacío o brecha Un espacio vacío o brecha es un área de una gráfica que no contiene ningún valor.

Grant A type of monetary award a student can use to pay for his or her education. The student does not need to repay this money.

Grant Un tipo de premio monetario que un estudiante puede utilizar para pagar por su educación. El estudiante no debe devolver este dinero.

Greater than > The greater-than symbol shows a comparison of two numbers with the number of greater value shown first, or on the left.

Mayor que > El símbolo de mayor que muestra una comparación de dos números con el número de mayor valor que aparece primero, o a la izquierda.

Greatest common factor The greatest common factor (GCF) of two or more whole numbers is the greatest number that is a factor of all of the numbers.

Máximo común divisor El máximo común divisor (M.C.D.) de dos o más números enteros no negativos es el número mayor que es un factor de todos los números.

English/Spanish Glossary

H

Height of a cone The height of a cone, *h*, is the length of a segment perpendicular to the base that joins the vertex and the base.

Altura de un cono La altura de un cono, *h*, es la longitud de un segmento perpendicular a la base que une el vértice y la base.

Height of a cylinder The height of a cylinder is the length of a perpendicular segment that joins the planes of the bases.

Altura de un cilindro La altura de un cilindro es la longitud de un segmento perpendicular que une los planos de las bases.

Height of a parallelogram A height of a parallelogram is the perpendicular distance between opposite bases.

Altura de un paralelogramo La altura de un paralelogramo es la distancia perpendicular que existe entre las bases opuestas.

Height of a prism The height of a prism is the length of a perpendicular segment that joins the bases.

Altura de un prisma La altura de un prisma es la longitud de un segmento perpendicular que une a las bases.

Height of a pyramid The height of a pyramid is the length of a segment perpendicular to the base that joins the vertex and the base.

Altura de una pirámide La altura de una pirámide es la longitud de un segmento perpendicular a la base que une al vértice con la base.

Height of a triangle The height of a triangle is the length of the perpendicular segment from a vertex to the base opposite that vertex.

Altura de un triángulo La altura de un triángulo es la longitud del segmento perpendicular desde un vértice hasta la base opuesta a ese vértice.

Hexagon A hexagon is a polygon with six sides.

Hexágono Un hexágono es un polígono de seis lados.

English/Spanish Glossary

Histogram A histogram is a statistical graph that shows the shape of a data set with vertical bars above intervals of values on a number line. The intervals are equal in size and do not overlap. The height of each bar shows the frequency of data within that interval.

Histograma Un histograma es una gráfica de estadísticas que muestra la forma de un conjunto de datos con barras verticales encima de intervalos de valores en una recta numérica. Los intervalos tienen el mismo tamaño y no se superponen. La altura de cada barra muestra la frecuencia de los datos dentro de ese intervalo.

Hundredths One hundredth is one part of 100 equal parts of a whole.

Centésima Una centésima es 1 de las 100 partes iguales de un todo.

Hypotenuse In a right triangle, the longest side, which is opposite the right angle, is the hypotenuse.

Hipotenusa En un triángulo rectángulo, el lado más largo, que es opuesto al ángulo recto, es la hipotenusa.

I

Identify To identify is to match a definition or description to an object or to recognize something and be able to name it.

Identificar Identificar es unir una definición o una descripción con un objeto, o reconocer algo y poder nombrarlo.

Identity Property of Addition The sum of 0 and any number is that number. For any number n, $n + 0 = n$ and $0 + n = n$.

Propiedad de identidad de la suma La suma de 0 y cualquier número es ese número. Para cualquier número n, $n + 0 = n$ and $0 + n = n$.

Identity Property of Multiplication The product of 1 and any number is that number. For any number n, $n \cdot 1 = n$ and $1 \cdot n = n$.

Propiedad de identidad de la multiplicación El producto de 1 y cualquier número es ese número. Para cualquier número n, $n \cdot 1 = n$ and $1 \cdot n = n$.

Illustrate To illustrate is to show or present information, usually as a drawing or a diagram. You can also illustrate a point using a written explanation.

Ilustrar Ilustrar es mostrar o presentar información, generalmente en forma de dibujo o diagrama. También puedes usar una explicación escrita para ilustrar un punto.

English/Spanish Glossary

Image An image is the result of a transformation of a point, line, or figure.

Imagen Una imagen es el resultado de una transformación de un punto, una recta o una figura.

Improper fraction An improper fraction is a fraction in which the numerator is greater than or equal to its denominator.

Fracción impropia Una fracción impropia es una fracción en la cual el numerador es mayor que o igual a su denominador.

Included angle An included angle is an angle that is between two sides.

Ángulo incluido Un ángulo incluido es un ángulo que está entre dos lados.

Included side An included side is a side that is between two angles.

Lado incluido Un lado incluido es un lado que está entre dos ángulos.

Income Money that a business receives. The money that a person earns from working is also called income.

Ingresos El dinero que un negocio recibe. El dinero que una persona gana de trabajar también es llamado los ingresos.

Income tax Income tax is money collected by the government based on how much you earn.

Impuesto de renta El impuesto de renta es dinero completo por el gobierno basado en cuánto gana.

Independent events Two events are independent events if the occurrence of one event does not affect the probability of the other event.

Eventos independientes Dos eventos son eventos independientes cuando el resultado de un evento no altera la probabilidad del otro.

Independent variable An independent variable is a variable whose value determines the value of another (dependent) variable.

Variable independiente Una variable independiente es una variable cuyo valor determina el valor de otra variable (dependiente).

Indicate To indicate is to point out or show.

Indicar Indicar es señalar o mostrar.

English/Spanish Glossary

Indirect measurement Indirect measurement uses proportions and similar triangles to measure distances that would be difficult to measure directly.

Medición indirecta La medición indirecta usa proporciones y triángulos semejantes para medir distancias que serían difíciles de medir de forma directa.

Inequality An inequality is a mathematical sentence that uses $<$, $\leq$, $>$, $\geq$, or $\neq$ to compare two quantities.

Desigualdad Una desigualdad es una oración matemática que usa $<$, $\leq$, $>$, $\geq$, o $\neq$ para comparar dos cantidades.

Inference An inference is a judgment made by interpreting data.

Inferencia Una inferencia es una opinión que se forma al interpretar datos.

Infinitely many solutions A linear equation in one variable has infinitely many solutions if any value of the variable makes the two sides of the equation equal.

Número infinito de soluciones Una ecuación lineal en una variable tiene un número infinito de soluciones si cualquier valor de la variable hace que los dos lados de la ecuación sean iguales.

Initial value The initial value of a linear function is the value of the output when the input is 0.

Valor inicial El valor inicial de una función lineal es el valor de salida cuando el valor de entrada es 0.

Integers Integers are the set of positive whole numbers, their opposites, and 0.

Enteros Los enteros son el conjunto de los números enteros positivos, sus opuestos y 0.

Interest When you deposit money in a bank account, the bank pays you interest for the right to use your money for a period of time.

Interés Cuando depositas dinero en una cuenta bancaria, el banco te paga un interés por el derecho a usar tu dinero por un período de tiempo.

Interest period The length of time on which compound interest is based. The total number of interest periods that you keep the money in the account is represented by the variable n.

Período de interés La cantidad de tiempo sobre la que se calcula el interés compuesto. El número total de períodos de interés que mantienes el dinero en la cuenta se representa con la variable n.

English/Spanish Glossary

Interest rate Interest is calculated based on a percent of the principal. That percent is called the interest rate (*r*).

Tasa de interés El interés se calcula con base en un porcentaje del capital. Ese porcentaje se llama tasa de interés, (*r*).

Interest rate for an interest period The interest rate for an interest period is the annual interest rate divided by the number of interest periods per year.

El tipo de interés por un período de interés El tipo de interés por un período de interés es el tipo de interés anual dividido por el número de períodos de interés por año.

Interquartile range The interquartile range (IQR) is the distance between the first and third quartiles of the data set. It represents the spread of the middle 50% of the data values.

Rango intercuartil El rango intercuartil es la distancia entre el primer y el tercer cuartil del conjunto de datos. Representa la ubicación del 50% del medio de los valores.

Interval An interval is a period of time between two points of time or events.

Intervalo Un intervalo es un período de tiempo entre dos puntos en el tiempo o entre dos sucesos.

Invalid inference An invalid inference is false about the population, or does not follow from the available data. A biased sample can lead to invalid inferences.

Inferencia inválida Una inferencia inválida es una inferencia falsa acerca de una población, o no se deduce a partir de los datos disponibles. Una muestra sesgada puede llevar a inferencias inválidas.

Inverse operations Inverse operations are operations that undo each other.

Operaciones inversas Las operaciones inversas son operaciones que se cancelan entre sí.

Inverse Property of Addition Every number has an additive inverse. The sum of a number and its additive inverse is zero.

Propiedad inversa de la suma Todos los números tienen un inverso de suma. La suma de un número y su inverso de suma es cero.

English/Spanish Glossary

Irrational numbers An irrational number is a number that cannot be written in the form $\frac{a}{b}$, where a and b are integers and $b \neq 0$. In decimal form, an irrational number cannot be written as a terminating or repeating decimal.

Números irracionales Un número irracional es un número que no se puede escribir en la forma $\frac{a}{b}$ donde a y b, son enteros y $b \neq 0$. Los números racionales en forma decimal no son finitos y no son periódicos.

Isolate a variable When solving equations, to isolate a variable means to get a variable with a coefficient of 1 alone on one side of an equation. Use the properties of equality and inverse operations to isolate a variable.

Aislar una variable Cuando resuelves ecuaciones, aislar una variable significa poner una variable con un coeficiente de 1 sola a un lado de la ecuación. Usa las propiedades de igualdad y las operaciones inversas para aislar una variable.

Isosceles triangle An isosceles triangle is a triangle with at least two sides that are the same length.

Triángulo isósceles Un triángulo isósceles es un triángulo que tiene al menos dos lados de la misma longitud.

J

Justify To justify is to support your answer with reasons or examples. A justification may include a written response, diagrams, charts, tables, or a combination of these.

Justificar Justificar es apoyar tu respuesta con razones o ejemplos. Una justificación puede incluir una respuesta escrita, diagramas, tablas o una combinación de esos elementos.

L

Lateral area of a cone The lateral area of a cone is the area of its lateral surface. The formula for the lateral area of a cone is L.A. $= \pi r \ell$, where r represents the radius of the base and ℓ represents the slant height of the cone.

Área lateral de un cono El área lateral de un cono es el área de su superficie lateral. La fórmula del área lateral de un cono es A.L. $= \pi r \ell$, donde r representa el radio de la base y ℓ representa la altura inclinada del cono.

English/Spanish Glossary

Lateral area of a cylinder The lateral area of a cylinder is the area of its lateral surface. The formula for the lateral area of a cylinder is L.A. $= 2\pi rh$, where r represents the radius of a base and h represents the height of the cylinder.

Área lateral de un cilindro El área lateral de un cilindro es el área de su superficie lateral. La fórmula del área lateral de un cilindro es A.L. $= 2\pi rh$, donde r representa el radio de una base y h representa la altura del cilindro.

Lateral area of a prism The lateral area of a prism is the sum of the areas of the lateral faces of the prism. The formula for the lateral area, L.A., of a prism is L.A. $= ph$, where p represents the perimeter of the base and h represents the height of the prism.

Área lateral de un prisma El área lateral de un prisma es la suma de las áreas de las caras laterales del prisma. La fórmula del área lateral, A.L., de un prisma es A.L. $= ph$, donde p representa el perímetro de la base y h representa la altura del prisma.

Lateral area of a pyramid The lateral area of a pyramid is the sum of the areas of the lateral faces of the pyramid. The formula for the lateral area, L.A., of a pyramid is L.A. $= \frac{1}{2}p\ell$ where p represents the perimeter of the base and ℓ represents the slant height of the pyramid.

Área lateral de una pirámide El área lateral de una pirámide es la suma de las áreas de las caras laterales de la pirámide. La fórmula del área lateral, A.L., de una pirámide es A.L. $= \frac{1}{2}p\ell$ donde p representa el perímetro de la base y ℓ representa la altura inclinada de la pirámide.

Lateral face of a prism A lateral face of a prism is a face that joins the bases of the prism.

Cara lateral de un prisma La cara lateral de un prisma es la cara que une a las bases del prisma.

Lateral face of a pyramid A lateral face of a pyramid is a triangular face that joins the base and the vertex.

Cara lateral de una pirámide La cara lateral de una pirámide es una cara lateral que une a la base con el vértice.

Lateral surface of a cone The lateral surface of a cone is the curved surface that is not included in the base.

Superficie lateral de un cono La superficie lateral de un cono es la superficie curva que no está incluida en la base.

English/Spanish Glossary

Lateral surface of a cylinder The lateral surface of a cylinder is the curved surface that is not included in the bases.

Superficie lateral de un cilindro La superficie lateral de un cilindro es la superficie curva que no está incluida en las bases.

Least common multiple The least common multiple (LCM) of two or more numbers is the least multiple shared by all of the numbers.

Mínimo común múltiplo El mínimo común múltiplo (MCM) de dos o más números es el múltiplo menor compartido por todos los números.

Leg of a right triangle In a right triangle, the two shortest sides are legs.

Cateto de un triángulo rectángulo En un triángulo rectángulo, los dos lados más cortos son los catetos.

Less than < The less-than symbol shows a comparison of two numbers with the number of lesser value shown first, or on the left.

Menor que < El símbolo de menor que muestra una comparación de dos números con el número de menor valor que aparece primero, o a la izquierda.

Liability A liability is money that you owe.

Obligación Una obligación es dinero que usted debe.

Lifetime income The amount of money earned over a lifetime of working.

Ingresos para toda la vida La cantidad de dinero ganó sobre una vida de trabajar.

Like terms Terms that have identical variable parts are like terms.

Términos semejantes Los términos que tienen partes variables idénticas son términos semejantes.

Line of reflection A line of reflection is a line across which a figure is reflected.

Eje de reflexión Un eje de reflexión es una línea a través de la cual se refleja una figura.

Linear equation An equation is a linear equation if the graph of all of its solutions is a line.

Ecuación lineal Una ecuación es lineal si la gráfica de todas sus soluciones es una línea recta.

English/Spanish Glossary

Linear function A linear function is a function whose graph is a straight line. The rate of change for a linear function is constant.

Función lineal Una función lineal es una función cuya gráfica es una línea recta. La tasa de cambio en una función lineal es constante.

Linear function rule A linear function rule is an equation that describes a linear function.

Regla de la función lineal La ecuación que describe una función lineal es la regla de la función lineal.

Loan A loan is an amount of money borrowed for a period of time with the promise of paying it back.

Préstamo Un préstamo es una cantidad de dinero pedido prestaddo por un espacio de tiempo con la promesa de pagarlo apoya.

Loan length Loan length is the period of time set to repay a loan.

Preste longitud La longitud del préstamo es el conjunto de espacio de tiempo de devolver un préstamo.

Loan term The term of a loan is the period of time set to repay the loan.

Preste término El término de un préstamo es el conjunto de espacio de tiempo de devolver el préstamo.

Locate To locate is to find or identify a value, usually on a number line or coordinate graph.

Ubicar Ubicar es hallar o identificar un valor, generalmente en una recta numérica o en una gráfica de coordenadas.

Loss When a business's expenses are greater than the business's income, there is a loss.

Pérdida Cuando los gastos de un negocio son más que los ingresos del negocio, hay una pérdida.

English/Spanish Glossary

M

Mapping diagram A mapping diagram describes a relation by linking the input values to the corresponding output values using arrows.

Diagrama de correspondencia Un diagrama de correspondencia describe una relación uniendo con flechas los valores de entrada con sus correspondientes valores de salida.

Markdown Markdown is the amount of decrease from the selling price to the sale price. The markdown as a percent decrease of the original selling price is called the percent markdown.

Rebaja La rebaja es la cantidad de disminución de un precio de venta a un precio rebajado. La rebaja como una disminución porcentual del precio de venta original se llama porcentaje de rebaja.

Markup Markup is the amount of increase from the cost to the selling price. The markup as a percent increase of the original cost is called the percent markup.

Margen de ganancia El margen de ganancia es la cantidad de aumento del costo al precio de venta. El margen de ganancia como un aumento porcentual del costo original se llama porcentaje del margen de ganancia.

Mean The mean represents the center of a numerical data set. To find the mean, sum the data values and then divide by the number of values in the data set.

Media La media representa el centro de un conjunto de datos numéricos. Para hallar la media, suma los valores y luego divide por el número de valores del conjunto de datos.

Mean absolute deviation The mean absolute deviation is a measure of variability that describes how much the data values are spread out from the mean of a data set. The mean absolute deviation is the average distance that the data values are spread around the mean.

$$\text{mean absolute deviation} = \frac{\text{sum of the absolute deviations of the data values}}{\text{total number of data values}}$$

Desviación absoluta media La desviación absoluta media es una medida de variabilidad que describe cuánto se alejan los valores de la media de un conjunto de datos. La desviación absoluta media es la distancia promedio que los valores se alejan de la media.

$$\text{desviación absoluta media} = \frac{\text{suma de las desviaciones absolutas de los valores}}{\text{número total de valores}}$$

English/Spanish Glossary

Measure of variability A measure of variability describes the spread of values in a data set. There may be more than one measure of variability for a data set.

Medida de variabilidad Una medida de variabilidad describe la distribución de los valores de un conjunto de datos. Puede haber más de una medida de variabilidad para un conjunto de datos.

Measurement data Measurement data consist of data that are measures.

Datos de mediciones Los datos de mediciones son datos que son medidas.

Measures of center A measure of center is a value that represents the middle of a data set. There may be more than one measure of center for a data set.

Medida de tendencia central Una medida de tendencia central es un valor que representa el centro de un conjunto de datos. Puede haber más de una medida de tendencia central para un conjunto de datos.

Median The median represents the center of a numerical data set. For an odd number of data values, the median is the middle value when the data values are arranged in numerical order. For an even number of data values, the median is the average of the two middle values when the data values are arranged in numerical order.

Mediana La mediana representa el centro de un conjunto de datos numéricos. Para un número impar de valores, la mediana es el valor del medio cuando los valores están organizados en orden numérico. Para un número par de valores, la mediana es el promedio de los dos valores del medio cuando los valores están organizados en orden numérico.

Median-median line The median-median line, or median trend line, is a method of finding a fit line for a scatter plot that suggests a linear association. This method involves dividing the data into three subgroups and using medians to find a summary point for each subgroup. The summary points are used to find the equation of the fit line.

Recta mediana-mediana La recta mediana-mediana es un método que se usa para hallar una línea de ajuste para un diagrama de dispersión que sugiere una asociación lineal. Este método implica dividir los datos en tres subgrupos y usar medianas para hallar un punto medio para cada subgrupo. Los puntos medios se usan para hallar la ecuación de la línea de ajuste.

Million Whole numbers in the millions have 7, 8, or 9 digits.

Millón Los números enteros no negativos que están en los millones tienen 7, 8 ó 9 dígitos.

English/Spanish Glossary

Mixed number A mixed number combines a whole number and a fraction.

Número mixto Un número mixto combina un número entero no negativo con una fracción.

Mode The item, or items, in a data set that occurs most frequently.

Modo El artículo, o los artículos, en un conjunto de datos que ocurre normalmente.

Model To model is to represent a situation using pictures, diagrams, or number sentences.

Demostrar Demostrar es usar ilustraciones, diagramas o enunciados numéricos para representar una situación.

Monetary incentive A monetary incentive is an offer that might encourage customers to buy a product.

Estímulo monetario Un estímulo monetario es una oferta que quizás favorezca a clientes para comprar un producto.

Multiple A multiple of a number is the product of the number and a whole number.

Múltiplo El múltiplo de un número es el producto del número y un número entero no negativo.

N

Natural numbers The natural numbers are the counting numbers.

Números naturales Los números naturales son los números que se usan para contar.

Negative exponent property For every nonzero number a and integer n, $a^{-n} = \frac{1}{a^n}$.

Propiedad del exponente negativo Para todo número distinto de cero a y entero n, $a^{-n} = \frac{1}{a^n}$.

Negative numbers Negative numbers are numbers less than zero.

Números negativos Los números negativos son números menores que cero.

English/Spanish Glossary

Net A net is a two-dimensional pattern that you can fold to form a three-dimensional figure. A net of a figure shows all of the surfaces of that figure in one view.

Modelo plano Un modelo plano es un diseño bidimensional que puedes doblar para formar una figura tridimensional. Un modelo plano de una figura muestra todas las superficies de la figura en una vista.

Net worth Net worth is the total value of all assets minus the total value of all liabilities.

Patrimonio neto El patrimonio neto es el valor total de todas las ventajas menos el valor total de todas las obligaciones.

Net worth statement Net worth is the total value of all assets minus the total value of all liabilities.

Declaración de patrimonio neto El patrimonio neto es el valor total de todas las ventajas menos el valor total de todas las obligaciones.

No solution A linear equation in one variable has no solution if no value of the variable makes the two sides of the equation equal.

Sin solución Una ecuación lineal en una variable no tiene solución si ningún valor de la variable hace que los dos lados de la ecuación sean iguales.

Nonlinear function A nonlinear function is a function that does not have a constant rate of change.

Función no lineal Una función no lineal es una función que no tiene una tasa de cambio constante.

Numerator The numerator is the number above the fraction bar in a fraction.

Numerador El numerador es el número que está arriba de la barra de fracción en una fracción.

Numerical expression A numerical expression is a mathematical phrase that consists of numbers and operation symbols.

Expresión numérica Una expresión numérica es una frase matemática que contiene números y símbolos de operaciones.

English/Spanish Glossary

O

Obtuse angle An obtuse angle is an angle with a measure greater than 90° and less than 180°.

Ángulo obtuso Un ángulo obtuso es un ángulo con una medida mayor que 90° y menor que 180°.

Obtuse triangle An obtuse triangle is a triangle with one obtuse angle.

Triángulo obtusángulo Un triángulo obtusángulo es un triángulo que tiene un ángulo obtuso.

Octagon An octagon is a polygon with eight sides.

Octágono Un octágono es un polígono de ocho lados.

Online payment system An online payment system allows money to be exchanged electronically between buyer and seller, usually using credit card or bank account information.

Sistema en línea de pago Un sistema en línea del pago permite dinero para ser cambiado electrónicamente entre comprador y vendedor, utilizando generalmente información de tarjeta de crédito o cuenta bancaria.

Open sentence An open sentence is an equation with one or more variables.

Enunciado abierto Un enunciado abierto es una ecuación con una o más variables.

Opposites Opposites are two numbers that are the same distance from 0 on a number line, but in opposite directions.

Opuestos Los opuestos son dos números que están a la misma distancia de 0 en la recta numérica, pero en direcciones opuestas.

Order of operations The order of operations is the order in which operations should be performed in an expression. Operations inside parentheses are done first, followed by exponents. Then, multiplication and division are done in order from left to right, and finally addition and subtraction are done in order from left to right.

Orden de las operaciones El orden de las operaciones es el orden en el que se deben resolver las operaciones de una expresión. Las operaciones que están entre paréntesis se resuelven primero, seguidas de los exponentes. Luego, se multiplica y se divide en orden de izquierda a derecha, y finalmente se suma y se resta en orden de izquierda a derecha.

English/Spanish Glossary

Ordered pair An ordered pair identifies the location of a point in the coordinate plane. The *x*-coordinate shows a point's position left or right of the *y*-axis. The *y*-coordinate shows a point's position up or down from the *x*-axis.

Par ordenado Un par ordenado identifica la ubicación de un punto en el plano de coordenadas. La coordenada *x* muestra la posición de un punto a la izquierda o a la derecha del eje de las *y*. La coordenada *y* muestra la posición de un punto arriba o abajo del eje de las *x*.

Origin The origin is the point of intersection of the *x*- and *y*-axes on a coordinate plane.

Origen El origen es el punto de intersección del eje de las *x* y el eje de las *y* en un plano de coordenadas.

Outcome An outcome is a possible result of an action.

Resultado Un resultado es un desenlace posible de una acción.

Outlier An outlier is a piece of data that doesn't seem to fit with the rest of a data set.

Valor extremo Un valor extremo es un valor que parece no ajustarse al resto de los datos de un conjunto.

P

Parallel lines Parallel lines are lines in the same plane that never intersect.

Rectas paralelas Las rectas paralelas son rectas que están en el mismo plano y nunca se intersecan.

Parallelogram A parallelogram is a quadrilateral with both pairs of opposite sides parallel.

Paralelogramo Un paralelogramo es un cuadrilátero en el cual los dos pares de lados opuestos son paralelos.

Partial product A partial product is part of the total product. A product is the sum of the partial products.

Producto parcial Un producto parcial es una parte del producto total. Un producto es la suma de los productos parciales.

English/Spanish Glossary

Pay period Wages for many jobs are paid at regular intervals, such a weekly, biweekly, semimonthly, or monthly. The interval of time is called a pay period.

Pague el período Los sueldos para muchos trabajos son pagados con regularidad, tal semanal, quincenal, quincenal, o mensual. El intervalo de tiempo es llamado un período de la paga.

Payroll deductions Your employer can deduct your income taxes from your wages before you receive your paycheck. The amounts deducted are called payroll deductions.

Deducciones de nómina Su empleador puede descontar sus impuestos de renta de sus sueldos antes que reciba su cheque de pago. Las cantidades descontadas son llamadas nómina deducciones.

Percent A percent is a ratio that compares a number to 100.

Porcentaje Un porcentaje es una razón que compara un número con 100.

Percent bar graph A percent bar graph is a bar graph that shows each category as a percent of the total number of data items.

Gráfico de barras de por ciento Un gráfico de barras del por ciento es un gráfico de barras que muestra cada categoría como un por ciento del número total de artículos de datos.

Percent decrease When a quantity decreases, the percent of change is called a percent decrease. percent decrease = $\dfrac{\text{amount of decrease}}{\text{original quantity}}$

Disminución porcentual Cuando una cantidad disminuye, el porcentaje de cambio se llama disminución porcentual. disminución porcentual = $\dfrac{\text{cantidad de disminución}}{\text{cantidad original}}$

Percent equation The percent equation describes the relationship between a part and a whole. You can use the percent equation to solve percent problems. part = percent · whole

Ecuación de porcentaje La ecuación de porcentaje describe la relación entre una parte y un todo. Puedes usar la ecuación de porcentaje para resolver problemas de porcentaje. parte = por ciento · todo

Percent error Percent error describes the accuracy of a measured or estimated value compared to an actual or accepted value.

Error porcentual El error porcentual describe la exactitud de un valor medido o estimado en comparación con un valor real o aceptado.

English/Spanish Glossary

Percent increase When a quantity increases, the percent of change is called a percent increase.

Aumento porcentual Cuando una cantidad aumenta, el porcentaje de cambio se llama aumento porcentual.

Percent of change Percent of change is the percent something increases or decreases from its original measure or amount. You can find the percent of change by using the equation: percent of change $= \dfrac{\text{amount of change}}{\text{original quantity}}$

Porcentaje de cambio El porcentaje de cambio es el porcentaje en que algo aumenta o disminuye en relación a la medida o cantidad original. Puedes hallar el porcentaje de cambio con la siguiente ecuación: porcentaje de cambio $= \dfrac{\text{cantidad de cambio}}{\text{cantidad original}}$

Perfect cube A perfect cube is the cube of an integer.

Cubo perfecto Un cubo perfecto es el cubo de un entero.

Perfect square A perfect square is a number that is the square of an integer.

Cuadrado perfecto Un cuadrado perfecto es un número que es el cuadrado de un entero.

Perimeter Perimeter is the distance around a figure.

Perímetro El perímetro es la distancia alrededor de una figura.

Period A period is a group of 3 digits in a number. Periods are separated by a comma and start from the right of a number.

Período Un período es un grupo de 3 dígitos en un número. Los períodos están separados por una coma y empiezan a la derecha del número.

Periodic savings plan A periodic savings plan is a method of saving that involves making deposits on a regular basis.

Plan de ahorros periódico Un plan de ahorros periódico es un método de guardar que implica depósitos que hace con regularidad.

Perpendicular lines Perpendicular lines intersect to form right angles.

Rectas perpendiculares Las rectas perpendiculares se intersecan para formar ángulos rectos.

English/Spanish Glossary

Pi Pi (π) is the ratio of a circle's circumference, *C*, to its diameter, *d*.

Pi Pi (π) es la razón de la circunferencia de un círculo, *C*, a su diámetro, *d*.

Place value Place value is the value given to an individual digit based on its position within a number.

Valor posicional El valor posicional es el valor asignado a determinado dígito según su posición en un número.

Plane A plane is a flat surface that extends indefinitely in all directions.

Plano Un plano es una superficie plana que se extiende indefinidamente en todas direcciones.

Polygon A polygon is a closed figure formed by three or more line segments that do not cross.

Polígono Un polígono es una figura cerrada compuesta por tres o más segmentos que no se cruzan.

Population A population is the complete set of items being studied.

Población Una población es todo el conjunto de elementos que se estudian.

Positive numbers Positive numbers are numbers greater than zero.

Números positivos Los números positivos son números mayores que cero.

Power A power is a number expressed using an exponent.

Potencia Una potencia es un número expresado con un exponente.

Predict To predict is to make an educated guess based on the analysis of real data.

Predecir Predecir es hacer una estimación informada según el análisis de datos reales.

Prime factorization The prime factorization of a composite number is the expression of the number as a product of its prime factors.

Descomposición en factores primos La descomposición en factores primos de un número compuesto es la expresión del número como un producto de sus factores primos.

English/Spanish Glossary

Prime number A prime number is a whole number greater than 1 with exactly two factors, 1 and the number itself.

Número primo Un número primo es un número entero mayor que 1 con exactamente dos factores, 1 y el número mismo.

Principal The original amount of money deposited or borrowed in an account.

Capital La cantidad original de dinero que se deposita o se pide prestada en una cuenta.

Prism A prism is a three-dimensional figure with two parallel polygonal faces that are the same size and shape.

Prisma Un prisma es una figura tridimensional con dos caras poligonales paralelas que tienen el mismo tamaño y la misma forma.

Probability model A probability model consists of an action, its sample space, and a list of events with their probabilities. The events and probabilities in the list have these characteristics: each outcome in the sample space is in exactly one event, and the sum of all of the probabilities must be 1.

Modelo de probabilidad Un modelo de probabilidad consiste en una acción, su espacio muestral y una lista de eventos con sus probabilidades. Los eventos y las probabilidades de la lista tienen estas características: cada resultado del espacio muestral está exactamente en un evento, y la suma de todas las probabilidades debe ser 1.

Probability of an event The probability of an event is a number from 0 to 1 that measures the likelihood that the event will occur. The closer the probability is to 0, the less likely it is that the event will happen. The closer the probability is to 1, the more likely it is that the event will happen. You can express probability as a fraction, decimal, or percent.

Probabilidad de un evento La probabilidad de un evento es un número de 0 a 1 que mide la probabilidad de que suceda el evento. Cuanto más se acerca la probabilidad a 0, menos probable es que suceda el evento. Cuanto más se acerca la probabilidad a 1, más probable es que suceda el evento. Puedes expresar la probabilidad como una fracción, un decimal o un porcentaje.

Product A product is the value of a multiplication or an expression showing multiplication.

Producto Un producto es el valor de una multiplicación o una expresión que representa la multiplicación.

English/Spanish Glossary

Profit When a business's expenses are less than the business's income, there is a profit.

Ganancia Cuando los gastos de un negocio son menos que los ingresos del negocio, hay una ganancia.

Proof A proof is a logical, deductive argument in which every statement of fact is supported by a reason.

Comprobación Una comprobación es un argumento lógico y deductivo en el que cada enunciado de un hecho está apoyado por una razón.

Proper fraction A proper fraction has a numerator that is less than its denominator.

Fracción propia Una fracción propia tiene un numerador que es menor que su denominador.

Proportion A proportion is an equation stating that two ratios are equal.

Proporción Una proporción es una ecuación que establece que dos razones son iguales.

Proportional relationship Two quantities x and y have a proportional relationship if y is always a constant multiple of x. A relationship is proportional if it can be described by equivalent ratios.

Relación de proporción Dos cantidades x y y tienen una relación de proporción si y es siempre un múltiplo constante de x. Una relación es de proporción si se puede describir con razones equivalentes.

Pyramid A pyramid is a three-dimensional figure with a base that is a polygon and triangular faces that meet at a vertex. A pyramid is named for the shape of its base.

Pirámide Una pirámide es una figura tridimensional con una base que es un polígono y caras triangulares que se unen en un vértice. El nombre de la pirámide depende de la forma de su base.

English/Spanish Glossary

Pythagorean Theorem In any right triangle, the sum of the squares of the lengths of the legs equals the square of the length of the hypotenuse. If a triangle is a right triangle, then $a^2 + b^2 = c^2$, where a and b represent the lengths of the legs, and c represents the length of the hypotenuse.

Teorema de Pitágoras En cualquier triángulo rectángulo, la suma del cuadrado de la longitud de los catetos es igual al cuadrado de la longitud de la hipotenusa. Si un triángulo es un triángulo rectángulo, entonces $a^2 + b^2 = c^2$, donde a y b representan la longitud de los catetos, y c representa la longitud de la hipotenusa.

Q

Quadrant The x- and y-axes divide the coordinate plane into four regions called quadrants.

Cuadrante Los ejes de las x y de las y dividen el plano de coordenadas en cuatro regiones llamadas cuadrantes.

Quadrilateral A quadrilateral is a polygon with four sides.

Cuadrilátero Un cuadrilátero es un polígono de cuatro lados.

Quarter circle A quarter circle is one fourth of a circle.

Círculo cuarto Un círculo cuarto es la cuarta parte de un círculo.

Quartile The quartiles of a data set divide the data set into four parts with the same number of data values in each part.

Cuartil Los cuartiles de un conjunto de datos dividen el conjunto de datos en cuatro partes que tienen el mismo número de valores cada una.

Quotient The quotient is the answer to a division problem. When there is a remainder, "quotient" sometimes refers to the whole-number portion of the answer.

Cociente El cociente es el resultado de una división. Cuando queda un residuo, "cociente" a veces se refiere a la parte de la solución que es un número entero.

English/Spanish Glossary

R

Radius A radius of a circle is a segment that has one endpoint at the center and the other endpoint on the circle. The term radius can also mean the length of this segment.

Radio Un radio de un círculo es un segmento que tiene un extremo en el centro y el otro extremo en el círculo. El término radio también puede referirse a la longitud de este segmento.

Radius of a sphere The radius of a sphere, r, is a segment that has one endpoint at the center and the other endpoint on the sphere.

Radio de una esfera El radio de una esfera, r, es un segmento que tiene un extremo en el centro y el otro extremo en la esfera.

Random sample In a random sample, each member in the population has an equal chance of being selected.

Muestra aleatoria En una muestra aleatoria, cada miembro en la población tiene una oportunidad igual de ser seleccionado.

Range The range is a measure of variability of a numerical data set. The range of a data set is the difference between the greatest and least values in a data set.

Rango El rango es una medida de la variabilidad de un conjunto de datos numéricos. El rango de un conjunto de datos es la diferencia que existe entre el mayor y el menor valor del conjunto.

Rate A rate is a ratio involving two quantities measured in different units.

Tasa Una tasa es una razón que relaciona dos cantidades medidas con unidades diferentes.

Rate of change The rate of change of a linear function is the ratio $\frac{\text{vertical change}}{\text{horizontal change}}$ between any two points on the graph of the function.

Tasa de cambio La tasa de cambio de una función lineal es la razón del $\frac{\text{cambio vertical}}{\text{cambio horizontal}}$ que existe entre dos puntos cualesquiera de la gráfica de la función.

Ratio A ratio is a relationship in which for every x units of one quantity there are y units of another quantity.

Razón Una razón es una relación en la cual por cada x unidades de una cantidad hay y unidades de otra cantidad.

English/Spanish Glossary

Rational numbers A rational number is a number that can be written in the form $\frac{a}{b}$ or $-\frac{a}{b}$, where a is a whole number and b is a positive whole number. The rational numbers include the integers.

Números racionales Un número racional es un número que se puede escribir como $\frac{a}{b}$ or $-\frac{a}{b}$, donde a es un número entero no negativo y b es un número entero positivo. Los números racionales incluyen los enteros.

Real numbers The real numbers are the set of rational and irrational numbers.

Números reales Los números reales son el conjunto de los números racionales e irracionales.

Reason To reason is to think through a problem using facts and information.

Razonar Razonar es usar hechos e información para estudiar detenidamente un problema.

Rebate A rebate returns part of the purchase price of an item after the buyer provides proof of purchase through a mail-in or online form.

Reembolso Un reembolso regresa la parte del precio de compra de un artículo después de que el comprador proporcione comprobante de compra por un correo-en o forma en línea.

Recall To recall is to remember a fact quickly.

Recordar Recordar es traer a la memoria un hecho rápidamente.

Reciprocals Two numbers are reciprocals if their product is 1. If a nonzero number is named as a fraction, , then its reciprocal is .

Recíprocos Dos números son recíprocos si su producto es 1. Si un número distinto de cero se expresa como una fracción, , entonces su recíproco es .

Rectangle A rectangle is a quadrilateral with four right angles.

Rectángulo Un rectángulo es un cuadrilátero que tiene cuatro ángulos rectos.

Rectangular prism A rectangular prism is a prism with bases in the shape of a rectangle.

Prisma rectangular Un prisma rectangular es un prisma cuyas bases tienen la forma de un rectángulo.

 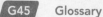

English/Spanish Glossary

Reduction A reduction is a dilation with a scale factor less than 1. After a reduction, the image is smaller than the original figure.

Reducción Una reducción es una dilatación con un factor de escala menor que 1. Después de una reducción, la imagen es más pequeña que la figura original.

Reflection A reflection, or flip, is a transformation that flips a figure across a line of reflection.

Reflexión Una reflexión, o inversión, es una transformación que invierte una figura a través de un eje de reflexión.

Regular polygon A regular polygon is a polygon with all sides of equal length and all angles of equal measure.

Polígono regular Un polígono regular es un polígono que tiene todos los lados de la misma longitud y todos los ángulos de la misma medida.

Relate To relate two different things, find a connection between them.

Relacionar Para relacionar dos cosas diferentes, halla una conexión entre ellas.

Relation Any set of ordered pairs is called a relation.

Relación Todo conjunto de pares ordenados se llama relación.

Relative frequency relative frequency

of an event $= \dfrac{\text{number of times event occurs}}{\text{total number of trials}}$

Frecuencia relativa frecuencia relativa de un evento $=$
$\dfrac{\text{número de veces que sucede el evento}}{\text{número total de pruebas}}$

Relative frequency table A relative frequency table shows the ratio of the number of data in each category to the total number of data items. The ratio can be expressed as a fraction, decimal, or percent.

Mesa relativa de frecuencia Una mesa relativa de la frecuencia muestra la proporción del número de datos en cada categoría al número total de artículos de datos. La proporción puede ser expresada como una fracción, el decimal, o el por ciento.

Remainder In division, the remainder is the number that is left after the division is complete.

Residuo En una división, el residuo es el número que queda después de terminar la operación.

 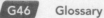

English/Spanish Glossary

Remote interior angles Remote interior angles are the two nonadjacent interior angles corresponding to each exterior angle of a triangle.

Ángulos internos no adyacentes Los ángulos internos no adyacentes son los dos ángulos internos de un triángulo que se corresponden con el ángulo externo que está más alejado de ellos.

Repeating decimal A repeating decimal has a decimal expansion that repeats the same digit, or block of digits, without end.

Decimal periódico Un decimal periódico tiene una expansión decimal que repite el mismo dígito, o grupo de dígitos, sin fin.

Represent To represent is to stand for or take the place of something else. Symbols, equations, charts, and tables are often used to represent particular situations.

Representar Representar es sustituir u ocupar el lugar de otra cosa. A menudo se usan símbolos, ecuaciones y tablas para representar determinadas situaciones.

Representative sample A representative sample is a sample of a population in which the number of subjects in the sample with the trait that you are studying is proportional to the number of members in the population with that trait. A representative sample accurately represents the population and does not have bias.

Muestra representativa Una muestra representativa es una muestra de una población en la que el número de sujetos de la muestra que tiene la característica que se estudia es proporcional al número de miembros de la población que tienen esa característica. Una muestra representativa representa la población con exactitud y no está sesgada.

Rhombus A rhombus is a parallelogram whose sides are all the same length.

Rombo Un rombo es un paralelogramo que tiene todos sus lados de la misma longitud.

Right angle A right angle is an angle with a measure of 90°.

Ángulo recto Un ángulo recto es un ángulo que mide 90°.

Right cone A right cone is a cone in which the segment representing the height connects the vertex and the center of the base.

Cono recto Un cono recto es un cono en el que el segmento que representa la altura une el vértice y el centro de la base.

English/Spanish Glossary

Right cylinder A right cylinder is a cylinder in which the height joins the centers of the bases.

Cilindro recto Un cilindro recto es un cilindro en el que la altura une los centros de las bases.

Right prism In a right prism, all lateral faces are rectangles.

Prisma recto En un prisma recto, todas las caras laterales son rectángulos.

Right pyramid In a right pyramid, the segment that represents the height intersects the base at its center.

Pirámide recta En una pirámide recta, el segmento que representa la altura interseca la base en el centro.

Right triangle A right triangle is a triangle with one right angle.

Triángulo rectángulo Un triángulo rectángulo es un triángulo que tiene un ángulo recto.

Rigid motion A rigid motion is a transformation that changes only the position of a figure.

Movimiento rígido Un movimiento rígido es una transformación que sólo cambia la posición de una figura.

Rotation A rotation is a rigid motion that turns a figure around a fixed point, called the center of rotation.

Rotación Una rotación es un movimiento rígido que hace girar una figura alrededor de un punto fijo, llamado centro de rotación.

Rounding Rounding a number means replacing the number with a number that tells about how much or how many.

Redondear Redondear un número significa reemplazar ese número por un número que indica más o menos cuánto o cuántos.

S

Sale A sale is a discount offered by a store. A sale does not require the customer to have a coupon.

Venta Una venta es un descuento ofreció por una tienda. Una venta no requiere al cliente a tener un cupón.

English/Spanish Glossary

Sales tax A tax added to the price of goods and services.

Las ventas tasan Un impuesto añadió al precio de bienes y servicios.

Sample of a population A sample of a population is part of the population. A sample is useful when you want to find out about a population but you do not have the resources to study every member of the population.

Muestra de una población Una muestra de una población es una parte de la población. Una muestra es útil cuando quieres saber algo acerca de una población, pero no tienes los recursos para estudiar a cada miembro de esa población.

Sample space The sample space for an action is the set of all possible outcomes of that action.

Espacio muestral El espacio muestral de una acción es el conjunto de todos los resultados posibles de esa acción.

Sampling method A sampling method is the method by which you choose members of a population to sample.

Método de muestreo Un método de muestreo es el método por el cual escoges miembros de una población para muestrear.

Savings Savings is money that a person puts away for use at a later date.

Ahorros Los ahorros son dinero que una persona guarda para el uso en una fecha posterior.

Scale A scale is a ratio that compares a length in a scale drawing to the corresponding length in the actual object.

Escala Una escala es una razón que compara una longitud en un dibujo a escala con la longitud correspondiente en el objeto real.

Scale drawing A scale drawing is an enlarged or reduced drawing of an object that is proportional to the actual object.

Dibujo a escala Un dibujo a escala es un dibujo ampliado o reducido de un objeto que es proporcional al objeto real.

English/Spanish Glossary

Scale factor The scale factor is the ratio of a length in the image to the corresponding length in the original figure.

Factor de escala El factor de escala es la razón de una longitud de la imagen a la longitud correspondiente en la figura original.

Scalene triangle A scalene triangle is a triangle in which no sides have the same length.

Triángulo escaleno Un triángulo escaleno es un triángulo que no tiene lados de la misma longitud.

Scatter plot A scatter plot is a graph that uses points to display the relationship between two different sets of data. Each point can be represented by an ordered pair.

Diagrama de dispersión Un diagrama de dispersión es una gráfica que usa puntos para mostrar la relación entre dos conjuntos de datos diferentes. Cada punto se puede representar con un par ordenado.

Scholarship A type of monetary award a student can use to pay for his or her education. The student does not need to repay this money.

Beca Un tipo de premio monetario que un estudiante puede utilizar para pagar por su educación. El estudiante no debe devolver este dinero.

Scientific notation A number in scientific notation is written as the product of two factors, one greater than or equal to 1 and less than 10, and the other a power of 10.

Notación científica Un número en notación científica está escrito como el producto de dos factores, uno mayor que o igual a 1 y menor que 10, y el otro una potencia de 10.

Segment A segment is part of a line. It consists of two endpoints and all of the points on the line between the endpoints.

Segmento Un segmento es una parte de una recta. Está formado por dos extremos y todos los puntos de la recta que están entre los extremos.

Semicircle A semicircle is one half of a circle.

Semicírculo Un semicírculo es la mitad de un círculo.

English/Spanish Glossary

Similar figures A two-dimensional figure is similar to another two-dimensional figure if you can map one figure to the other by a sequence of rotations, reflections, translations, and dilations.

Figuras semejantes Una figura bidimensional es semejante a otra figura bidimensional si puedes hacer corresponder una figura con otra mediante una secuencia de rotaciones, reflexiones, traslaciones y dilataciones.

Simple interest Simple interest is interest paid only on an original deposit. To calculate simple interest, use the formula where I is the simple interest, p is the principal, r is the annual interest rate, and t is the number of years that the account earns interest.

Interés simple El interés simple es el interés que se paga sobre un depósito original solamente. Para calcular el interés simple, usa la fórmula donde I es el interés simple, c es el capital, r es la tasa de interés anual y t es el número de años en que la cuenta obtiene un interés.

Simple random sampling Simple random sampling is a sampling method in which every member of the population has an equal chance of being chosen for the sample.

Muestreo aleatorio simple El muestreo aleatorio simple es un método de muestreo en el que cada miembro de la población tiene la misma probabilidad de ser seleccionado para la muestra.

Simpler form A fraction is in simpler form when it is equivalent to a given fraction and has smaller numbers in the numerator and denominator.

Forma simplificada Una fracción está en su forma simplificada cuando es equivalente a otra fracción dada, pero tiene números más pequeños en el numerador y el denominador.

Simplest form A fraction is in simplest form when the only common factor of the numerator and denominator is one.

Mínima expresión Una fracción está en su mínima expresión cuando el único factor común del numerador y el denominador es 1.

Simplify an algebraic expression To simplify an algebraic expression, combine the like terms of the expression.

Simplificar una expresión algebraica Para simplificar una expresión algebraica, combina los términos semejantes de la expresión.

English/Spanish Glossary

Simulation A simulation is a model of a real-world situation that is used to find probabilities.

Simulación Una simulación es un modelo de una situación de la vida diaria que se usa para hallar probabilidades.

Sketch To sketch a figure, draw a rough outline. When a sketch is asked for, it means that a drawing needs to be included in your response.

Bosquejo Para hacer un bosquejo, dibuja un esquema simple. Si se pide un bosquejo, tu respuesta debe incluir un dibujo.

Slant height of a cone The slant height of a cone, ℓ, is the length of its lateral surface from base to vertex.

Altura inclinada de un cono La altura inclinada de un cono, ℓ, es la longitud de su superficie lateral desde la base hasta el vértice.

Slant height of a pyramid The slant height of a pyramid is the height of a lateral face.

Altura inclinada de una pirámide La altura inclinada de una pirámide es la altura de una cara lateral.

Slope Slope is a ratio that describes steepness.

$$\text{slope} = \frac{\text{vertical change}}{\text{horizontal change}} = \frac{\text{rise}}{\text{run}}$$

Pendiente La pendiente es una razón que describe la inclinación.

$$\text{pendiente} = \frac{\text{cambio vertical}}{\text{cambio horizontal}}$$
$$= \frac{\text{distancia vertical}}{\text{distancia horizontal}}$$

Slope of a line slope =

$$\frac{\text{change in } y\text{-coordinates}}{\text{change in } x\text{-coordinates}} = \frac{\text{rise}}{\text{run}}$$

Pendiente de una recta pendiente =
$$\frac{\text{cambio en las coordenadas } y}{\text{cambio en las coordenadas } x}$$
$$= \frac{\text{distancia vertical}}{\text{distancia horizontal}}$$

Slope-intercept form An equation written in the form $y = mx + b$ is in slope-intercept form. The graph is a line with slope m and y-intercept b.

Forma pendiente-intercepto Una ecuación escrita en la forma $y = mx + b$ está en forma de pendiente-intercepto. La gráfica es una línea recta con pendiente m e intercepto en y b.

English/Spanish Glossary

Solution of a system of linear equations A solution of a system of linear equations is any ordered pair that makes all the equations of that system true.

Solución de un sistema de ecuaciones lineales Una solución de un sistema de ecuaciones lineales es cualquier par ordenado que hace que todas las ecuaciones de ese sistema sean verdaderas.

Solution of an equation A solution of an equation is a value of the variable that makes the equation true.

Solución de una ecuación Una solución de una ecuación es un valor de la variable que hace que la ecuación sea verdadera.

Solution of an inequality The solutions of an inequality are the values of the variable that make the inequality true.

Solución de una desigualdad Las soluciones de una desigualdad son los valores de la variable que hacen que la desigualdad sea verdadera.

Solution set A solution set contains all of the numbers that satisfy an equation or inequality.

Conjunto solución Un conjunto solución contiene todos los números que satisfacen una ecuación o desigualdad.

Solve To solve a given statement, determine the value or values that make the statement true. Several methods and strategies can be used to solve a problem, including estimating, isolating the variable, drawing a graph, or using a table of values.

Resolver Para resolver un enunciado dado, determina el valor o los valores que hacen que ese enunciado sea verdadero. Para resolver un problema se pueden usar varios métodos y estrategias, como estimar, aislar la variable, dibujar una gráfica o usar una tabla de valores.

Sphere A sphere is the set of all points in space that are the same distance from a center point.

Esfera Una esfera es el conjunto de todos los puntos en el espacio que están a la misma distancia de un punto central.

Square A square is a quadrilateral with four right angles and all sides the same length.

Cuadrado Un cuadrado es un cuadrilátero que tiene cuatro ángulos rectos y todos los lados de la misma longitud.

English/Spanish Glossary

Square root A square root of a number is a number that, when multiplied by itself, equals the original number.

Raíz cuadrada La raíz cuadrada de un número es un número que, cuando se multiplica por sí mismo, es igual al número original.

Square unit A square unit is the area of a square that has sides that are 1 unit long.

Unidad cuadrada Una unidad cuadrada es el área de un cuadrado en el que cada lado mide 1 unidad de longitud.

Standard form A number written using digits and place value is in standard form.

Forma estándar Un número escrito con dígitos y valor posicional está escrito en forma estándar.

Statistical question A statistical question is a question that investigates an aspect of the real world and can have variety in the responses.

Pregunta estadística Una pregunta estadística es una pregunta que investiga un aspecto de la vida diaria y puede tener varias respuestas.

Statistics Statistics is the study of collecting, organizing, graphing, and analyzing data to draw conclusions about the real world.

Estadística La estadística es el estudio de la recolección, organización, representación gráfica y análisis de datos para sacar conclusiones sobre la vida diaria.

Stem-and-leaf plot A stem-and-leaf plot is a graph that uses the digits of each number to show the data distribution. Each data item is broken into a stem and into a leaf. The leaf is the last digit of the data value. The stem is the other digit or digits of the data value.

Complot de tallo y hoja Un complot del tallo y la hoja es un gráfico que utiliza los dígitos de cada número para mostrar la distribución de datos. Cada artículo de datos es roto en un tallo y en una hoja. La hoja es el último dígito de los datos valora. El tallo es el otro dígito o los dígitos de los datos valoran.

Stored-value card A stored-value card is a prepaid card electronically coded to be worth a specified amount of money.

Tarjeta de almacenado-valor Una tarjeta del almacenado-valor es una tarjeta pagada por adelantado codificó electrónicamente valer una cantidad especificado de dinero.

English/Spanish Glossary

Straight angle A straight angle is an angle with a measure of 180°.

Ángulo llano Un ángulo llano es un ángulo que mide 180°.

Student loan A student loan provides money to a student to pay for college. The student needs to repay the loan after leaving college. Often the student will need to pay interest on the amount of the loan.

Crédito personal para estudiantes Un crédito personal para estudiantes le proporciona dinero a un estudiante para pagar por el colegio. El estudiante debe devolver el préstamo después de dejar el colegio. A menudo el estudiante deberá pagar interés en la cantidad del préstamo.

Subject Each member in a sample is a subject.

Sujeto Cada miembro de una muestra es un sujeto.

Sum The sum is the answer to an addition problem.

Suma o total La suma o total es el resultado de una operación de suma.

Summarize To summarize an explanation or solution, go over or review the most important points.

Resumir Para resumir una explicación o solución, revisa o repasa los puntos más importantes.

Supplementary angles Two angles are supplementary angles if the sum of their measures is 180°. Supplementary angles that are adjacent form a straight angle.

Ángulos suplementarios Dos ángulos son suplementarios si la suma de sus medidas es 180°. Los ángulos suplementarios que son adyacentes forman un ángulo llano.

Surface area of a cone The surface area of a cone is the sum of the lateral area and the area of the base. The formula for the surface area of a cone is S.A. = L.A. + B.

Área total de un cono El área total de un cono es la suma del área lateral y el área de la base. La fórmula del área total de un cono es A.T. = A.L. + B.

English/Spanish Glossary

Surface area of a cube The surface area of a cube is the sum of the areas of the faces of the cube. The formula for the surface area, S.A., of a cube is S.A. , where s represents the length of an edge of the cube.

Área total de un cubo El área total de un cubo es la suma de las áreas de las caras del cubo. La fórmula del área total, A.T., de un cubo es A.T. , donde s representa la longitud de una arista del cubo.

Surface area of a cylinder The surface area of a cylinder is the sum of the lateral area and the areas of the two circular bases. The formula for the surface area of a cylinder is S.A.   L.A.   2B, where L.A. represents the lateral area of the cylinder and B represents the area of a base of the cylinder.

Área total de un cilindro El área total de un cilindro es la suma del área lateral y las áreas de las dos bases circulares. La fórmula del área total de un cilindro es A.T.   A.L.   2B, donde A.L. representa el área lateral del cilindro y B representa el área de una base del cilindro.

Surface area of a pyramid The surface area of a pyramid is the sum of the areas of the faces of the pyramid. The formula for the surface area, S.A., of a pyramid is S.A. = L.A. + B, where L.A. represents the lateral area of the pyramid and B represents the area of the base of the pyramid.

Área total de una pirámide El área total de una pirámide es la suma de las áreas de las caras de la pirámide. La fórmula del área total, A.T., de una pirámide es A.T. = A.L. + B, donde A.L. representa el área lateral de la pirámide y B representa el área de la base de la pirámide.

Surface area of a sphere The surface area of a sphere is equal to the lateral area of a cylinder that has the same radius, r, and height 2r. The formula for the surface area of a sphere is S.A. = $4\pi r^2$, where r represents the radius of the sphere.

Área total de una esfera El área total de una esfera es igual al área lateral de un cilindro que tiene el mismo radio, r, y una altura de 2r. La fórmula del área total de una esfera es A.T. = $4\pi r^2$, donde r representa el radio de la esfera.

Surface area of a three-dimensional figure The surface area of a three-dimensional figure is the sum of the areas of its faces. You can find the surface area by finding the area of the net of the three-dimensional figure.

Área total de una figura tridimensional El área total de una figura tridimensional es la suma de las áreas de sus caras. Puedes hallar el área total si hallas el área del modelo plano de la figura tridimensional.

English/Spanish Glossary

System of linear equations A system of linear equations is formed by two or more linear equations that use the same variables.

Sistema de ecuaciones lineales Un sistema de ecuaciones lineales está formado por dos o más ecuaciones lineales que usan las mismas variables.

Systematic sampling Systematic sampling is a sampling method in which you choose every nth member of the population, where *n* is a predetermined number. A systematic sample is useful when the researcher is able to approach the population in a systematic, or methodical, way.

Muestreo sistemático El muestreo sistemático es un método de muestreo en el que se escoge cada enésimo miembro de la población, donde *n* es un número predeterminado. Una muestra sistemática es útil cuando el investigador puede enfocarse en la población de manera sistemática o metódica.

T

Taxable wages For federal income tax purposes, your taxable wages are the difference between your earned wages and your withholding allowance. Your employer divides your withholding allowance equally among the pay periods of one year.

Sueldos imponibles Para propósitos federales de impuesto de renta, sus sueldos imponibles son la diferencia entre sus sueldos ganados y su concesión que retienen. Su empleador divide su concesión que retiene igualmente entre los períodos de paga de un año.

Tenths One tenth is one out of ten equal parts of a whole.

Décimas Una décima es 1 de 10 partes iguales de un todo.

Term A term is a number, a variable, or the product of a number and one or more variables.

Término Un término es un número, una variable o el producto de un número y una o más variables.

Terminating decimal A terminating decimal has a decimal expansion that terminates in 0.

Decimal finito Un decimal finito tiene una expansión decimal que termina en 0.

English/Spanish Glossary

Terms of a ratio The terms of a ratio are the quantities *x* and *y* in the ratio.

Términos de una razón Los términos de una razón son la cantidad *x* y la cantidad *y* de la razón.

Theorem A theorem is a conjecture that is proven.

Teorema Un teorema es una conjetura que se ha comprobado.

Theoretical probability When all outcomes of an action are equally likely,

$$P(\text{event}) = \frac{\text{number of favourable outcomes}}{\text{number of possible outcomes}}.$$

Probabilidad teórica Cuando todos los resultados de una acción son igualmente probables, $P(\text{evento}) =$

$$\frac{\text{número de resultados favorables}}{\text{número de resultados posibles}}.$$

Third quartile For an ordered set of data, the third quartile is the median of the upper half of the data set.

Tercer cuartil Para un conjunto de datos ordenados, el tercer cuartil es la mediana de la mitad superior del conjunto de datos.

Thousandths One thousandth is one part of 1,000 equal parts of a whole.

Milésimas Una milésima es 1 de 1,000 partes iguales de un todo.

Three-dimensional figure A three-dimensional (3-D) figure is a figure that does not lie in a plane.

Figura tridimensional Una figura tridimensional es una figura que no está en un plano.

Total cost of a loan The total cost of a loan is the total amount spent to repay the loan. Total cost includes the principal and all interest paid over the length of the loan. Total cost also includes any fees charged.

El coste total de un préstamo El coste total de un préstamo es el cantidad total que es gastado para devolver el préstamo. El coste total incluye al director y todo el interés pagó sobre la longitud del préstamo. El coste total también incluye cualquier honorario cargado.

Transaction A banking transaction moves money into or out of a bank account.

Transacción Una transacción bancaria mueve dinero en o fuera de una cuenta bancaria.

English/Spanish Glossary

Transfer A transaction that moves money from one bank account to another is a transfer. The balance of one account increases by the same amount the other account decreases.

Transferencia Una transacción que mueve dinero de una cuenta bancaria a otro es una transferencia. El equilibrio de un aumentos de cuenta por la misma cantidad que la otra cuenta disminuye.

Transformation A transformation is a change in position, shape, or size of a figure. Three types of transformations that change position only are translations, reflections, and rotations.

Transformación Una transformación es un cambio en la posición, la forma o el tamaño de una figura. Tres tipos de transformaciones que cambian sólo la posición son las traslaciones, las reflexiones y las rotaciones.

Translation A translation, or slide, is a rigid motion that moves every point of a figure the same distance and in the same direction.

Traslación Una traslación, o deslizamiento, es un movimiento rígido que mueve cada punto de una figura a la misma distancia y en la misma dirección.

Transversal A transversal is a line that intersects two or more lines at different points.

Transversal o secante Una transversal o secante es una línea que interseca dos o más líneas en distintos puntos.

Trapezoid A trapezoid is a quadrilateral with exactly one pair of parallel sides.

Trapecio Un trapecio es un cuadrilátero que tiene exactamente un par de lados paralelos.

Trend line A trend line is a line on a scatter plot, drawn near the points, that approximates the association between the data sets.

Línea de tendencia Una línea de tendencia es una línea en un diagrama de dispersión, trazada cerca de los puntos, que se aproxima a la relación entre los conjuntos de datos.

Trial In a probability experiment, you carry out or observe an action repeatedly. Each observation of the action is a trial.

Prueba En un experimento de probabilidad, realizas u observas una acción varias veces. Cada observación de la acción es una prueba.

Triangle A triangle is a polygon with three sides.

Triángulo Un triángulo es un polígono de tres lados.

English/Spanish Glossary

Triangular prism A triangular prism is a prism with bases in the shape of a triangle.

Prisma triangular Un prisma triangular es un prisma cuyas bases tienen la forma de un triángulo.

True equation A true equation has equal values on each side of the equals sign.

Ecuación verdadera En una ecuación verdadera, los valores a ambos lados del signo igual son iguales.

Two-way frequency table A two-way frequency table displays the counts of the data in each group.

Tabla de frecuencia con dos variables Una tabla de frecuencia con dos variables muestra el conteo de los datos de cada grupo.

Two-way relative frequency table A two-way relative frequency table shows the ratio of the number of data in each group to the size of the population. The relative frequencies can be calculated with respect to the entire population, the row populations, or the column populations. The relative frequencies can be expressed as fractions, decimals, or percents.

Tabla de frecuencias relativas con dos variables Una tabla de frecuencias relativas con dos variables muestra la razón del número de datos de cada grupo al tamaño de la población. Las frecuencias relativas se pueden calcular respecto de la población entera, las poblaciones de las filas o las poblaciones de las columnas. Las frecuencias relativas se pueden expresar como fracciones, decimales o porcentajes.

Two-way table A two-way table shows bivariate categorical data for a population.

Tabla con dos variables Una tabla con dos variables muestra datos bivariados por categorías de una población.

U

Uniform probability model A uniform probability model is a probability model based on using the theoretical probability of equally likely outcomes.

Modelo de probabilidad uniforme Un modelo de probabilidad uniforme es un modelo de probabilidad que se basa en el uso de la probabilidad teórica de resultados igualmente probables.

 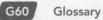

English/Spanish Glossary

Unit fraction A unit fraction is a fraction with a numerator of 1 and a denominator that is a whole number greater than 1.

Fracción unitaria Una fracción unitaria es una fracción con un numerador 1 y un denominador que es un número entero mayor que 1.

Unit price A unit price is a unit rate that gives the price of one item.

Precio por unidad El precio por unidad es una tasa por unidad que muestra el precio de un artículo.

Unit rate The rate for one unit of a given quantity is called the unit rate.

Tasa por unidad Se llama tasa por unidad a la tasa que corresponde a 1 unidad de una cantidad dada.

Use To use given information, draw on it to help you determine something else.

Usar Para usar una información dada, apóyate en ella para determinar otra cosa.

V

Valid inference A valid inference is an inference that is true about the population. Valid inferences can be made when they are based on data from a representative sample.

Inferencia válida Una inferencia válida es una inferencia verdadera acerca de una población. Se pueden hacer inferencias válidas si están basadas en los datos de una muestra representativa.

Variability Variability describes how much the items in a data set differ (or vary) from each other. On a data display, variability is shown by how much the data on the horizontal scale are spread out.

Variabilidad La variabilidad describe qué diferencia (o variación) existe entre los elementos de un conjunto de datos. Al exhibir datos, la variabilidad queda representada por la distancia que separa los datos en la escala horizontal.

Variable A variable is a letter that represents an unknown value.

Variable Una variable es una letra que representa un valor desconocido.

Variable expenses Variable expenses are expenses that change from one budget period to the next.

Gastos variables Los gastos variables son los gastos que cambian de un período económico al próximo.

English/Spanish Glossary

Vertex of a cone The vertex of a cone is the point farthest from the base.

Vértice de un cono El vértice de un cono es el punto más alejado de la base.

Vertex of a polygon The vertex of a polygon is any point where two sides of a polygon meet.

Vértice de un polígono El vértice de un polígono es cualquier punto donde se encuentran dos lados de un polígono.

Vertex of a three-dimensional figure A vertex of a three-dimensional figure is a point where three or more edges meet.

Vértice de una figura tridimensional El vértice de una figura tridimensional es un punto donde se unen tres o más aristas.

Vertex of an angle The vertex of an angle is the point of intersection of the rays that make up the sides of the angle.

Vértice de un ángulo El vértice de un ángulo es el punto de intersección de las semirrectas que forman los lados del ángulo.

Vertical angles Vertical angles are formed by two intersecting lines and are opposite each other. Vertical angles have equal measures.

Ángulos opuestos por el vértice Los ángulos opuestos por el vértice están formados por dos rectas secantes y están uno frente a otro. Los ángulos opuestos por el vértice tienen la misma medida.

Vertical-line test The vertical-line test is a method used to determine if a relation is a function or not. If a vertical line passes through a graph more than once, the graph is not the graph of a function.

Prueba de recta vertical La prueba de recta vertical es un método que se usa para determinar si una relación es una función o no. Si una recta vertical atraviesa la gráfica más de una vez, la gráfica no es la gráfica de una función.

Volume Volume is the number of cubic units needed to fill a solid figure.

Volumen El volumen es el número de unidades cúbicas que se necesitan para llenar un cuerpo geométrico.

English/Spanish Glossary

Volume of a cone The volume of a cone is the number of unit cubes, or cubic units, needed to fill the cone. The formula for the volume of a cone is $V = \frac{1}{3}Bh$, where B represents the area of the base and h represents the height of the cone.

Volumen de un cono El volumen de un cono es el número de bloques de unidades, o unidades cúbicas, que se necesitan para llenar el cono. La fórmula del volumen de un cono $V = \frac{1}{3}Bh$, donde B representa el área de la base y h representa la altura del cono.

Volume of a cube The volume of a cube is the number of unit cubes, or cubic units, needed to fill the cube. The formula for the volume V of a cube is $V = s^3$, where s represents the length of an edge of the cube.

Volumen de un cubo El volumen de un cubo es el número de bloques de unidades, o unidades cúbicas, que se necesitan para llenar el cubo. La fórmula del volumen, V, de un cubo es $V = s^3$, donde s representa la longitud de una arista del cubo.

Volume of a cylinder The volume of a cylinder is the number of unit cubes, or cubic units, needed to fill the cylinder. The formula for the volume of a cylinder is $V = \pi r^2 h$, where r represents the radius of a base and h represents the height of the cylinder.

Volumen de un cilindro El volumen de un cilindro es el número de bloques de unidades, o unidades cúbicas, que se necesitan para llenar el cilindro. La fórmula del volumen de un cilindro es $V = \pi r^2 h$, donde r representa el radio de una base y h representa la altura del cilindro.

Volume of a prism The volume of a prism is the number of unit cubes, or cubic units, needed to fill the prism. The formula for the volume V of a prism is $V = Bh$, where B represents the area of a base and h represents the height of the prism.

Volumen de un prisma El volumen de un prisma es el número de bloques de unidades, o unidades cúbicas, que se necesitan para llenar el prisma. La fórmula del volumen, V, de un prisma $V = Bh$, donde B representa el área de una base y h representa la altura del prisma.

Volume of a pyramid The volume of a pyramid is the number of unit cubes needed to fill the pyramid. The formula for the volume V of a pyramid is $V = \frac{1}{3}Bh$, where B represents the area of the base and h represents the height of the pyramid.

Volumen de una pirámide El volumen de una pirámide es el número de bloques de unidades, o unidades cúbicas, que se necesitan para llenar la pirámide. La fórmula del volumen, V, de una pirámide es $V = \frac{1}{3}Bh$, donde B representa el área de la base y h representa la altura de la pirámide.

English/Spanish Glossary

Volume of a sphere The volume of a sphere is the number of unit cubes, or cubic units, needed to fill the sphere. The formula for the volume of a sphere is $V = \frac{4}{3}\pi r^3$.

Volumen de una esfera El volumen de una esfera es el número de bloques de unidades, o unidades cúbicas, que se necesitan para llenar la esfera. La fórmula del volumen de una esfera es $V = \frac{4}{3}\pi r^3$.

W

Whole numbers The whole numbers consist of the number 0 and all of the natural numbers.

Números enteros no negativos Los números enteros no negativos son el número 0 y todos los números naturales.

Withdrawal A transaction that takes money out of a bank account is a withdrawal.

Retirada Una transacción que toma dinero fuera de una cuenta bancaria es una retirada.

Withholding allowance You can exclude a portion of your earned wages, called a withholding allowance, from federal income tax. You can claim one withholding allowance for yourself and one for each person dependent upon your income.

Retener concesión Puede excluir una porción de sus sueldos ganados, llamó una concesión que retiene, del impuesto de renta federal. Puede reclamar una concesión que retiene para usted mismo y para uno para cada dependiente de persona sobre sus ingresos.

Word form of a number The word form of a number is the number written in words.

Número en palabras Un número en palabras es un número escrito con palabras en lugar de dígitos.

Work-Study Work-study is a type of need-based aid that schools might offer to a student. A student must earn work-study money by working certain jobs.

Práctica estudiantil La práctica estudiantil es un tipo de ayuda necesidad-basado que escuelas quizás ofrezcan a un estudiante. Un estudiante debe ganar dinero de práctica estudiantil por ciertos trabajos de trabajo.

English/Spanish Glossary

X

x-axis The x-axis is the horizontal number line that, together with the y-axis, forms the coordinate plane.

Eje de las x El eje de las x es la recta numérica horizontal que, junto con el eje de las y, forma el plano de coordenadas.

x-coordinate The x-coordinate is the first number in an ordered pair. It tells the number of horizontal units a point is from 0.

Coordenada x La coordenada x (abscisa) es el primer número de un par ordenado. Indica cuántas unidades horizontales hay entre un punto y 0.

Y

y-axis The y-axis is the vertical number line that, together with the x-axis, forms the coordinate plane.

Eje de las y El eje de las y es la recta numérica vertical que, junto con el eje de las x, forma el plano de coordenadas.

y-coordinate The y-coordinate is the second number in an ordered pair. It tells the number of vertical units a point is from 0.

Coordenada y La coordenada y (ordenada) es el segundo número de un par ordenado. Indica cuántas unidades verticales hay entre un punto y 0.

y-intercept The y-intercept of a line is the y-coordinate of the point where the line crosses the y-axis.

Intercepto en y El intercepto en y de una recta es la coordenada y del punto por donde la recta cruza el eje de las y.

Z

Zero exponent property For any nonzero number a, $a^0 = 1$.

Propiedad del exponente cero Para cualquier número distinto de cero a, $a^0 = 1$.

Zero Property of Multiplication The product of 0 and any number is 0. For any number n, $n \cdot 0 = 0$ and $0 \cdot n = 0$.

Propiedad del cero en la multiplicación El producto de 0 y cualquier número es 0. Para cualquier número n, $n \cdot 0 = 0$ and $0 \cdot n = 0$.

Formulas

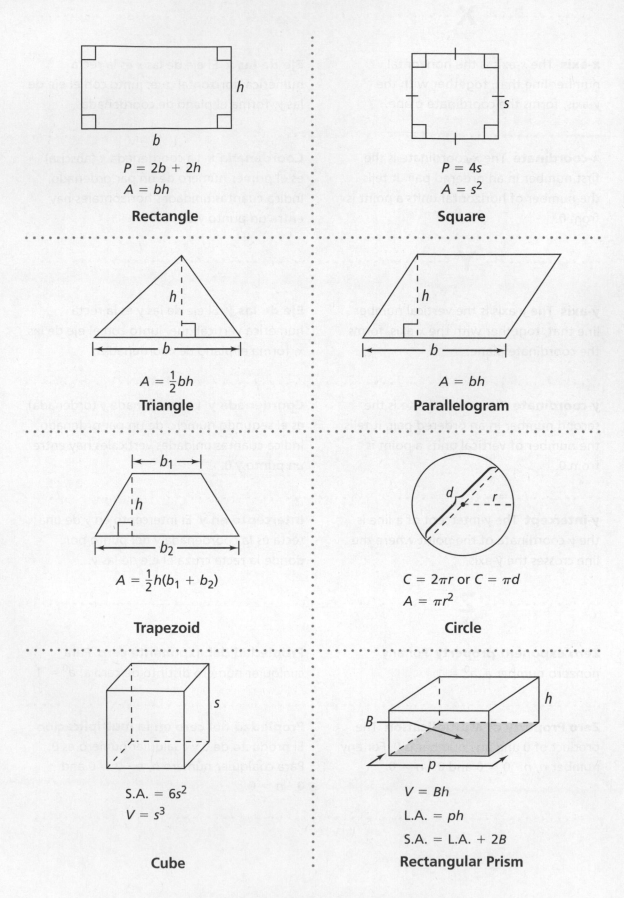

$P = 2b + 2h$
$A = bh$
Rectangle

$P = 4s$
$A = s^2$
Square

$A = \frac{1}{2}bh$
Triangle

$A = bh$
Parallelogram

$A = \frac{1}{2}h(b_1 + b_2)$
Trapezoid

$C = 2\pi r$ or $C = \pi d$
$A = \pi r^2$
Circle

S.A. $= 6s^2$
$V = s^3$
Cube

$V = Bh$
L.A. $= ph$
S.A. $=$ L.A. $+ 2B$
Rectangular Prism

Formulas

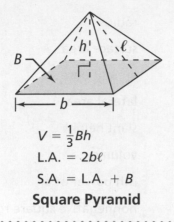

$V = \frac{1}{3}Bh$

L.A. $= 2b\ell$

S.A. $=$ L.A. $+ B$

Square Pyramid

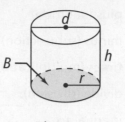

$V = Bh$

L.A. $= 2\pi rh$

S.A. $=$ L.A. $+ 2B$

Cylinder

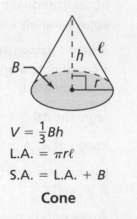

$V = \frac{1}{3}Bh$

L.A. $= \pi r\ell$

S.A. $=$ L.A. $+ B$

Cone

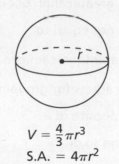

$V = \frac{4}{3}\pi r^3$

S.A. $= 4\pi r^2$

Sphere

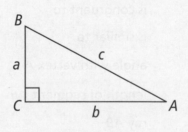

$a^2 + b^2 = c^2$

Pythagorean Theorem

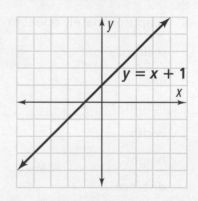

$y = mx + b$, where
$m =$ slope and
$b = y$-intercept

Equation of Line

Math Symbols

$+$	plus (addition)
$-$	minus (subtraction)
$\times$, $\cdot$	times (multiplication)
$\div$, $\sqrt{}$, $\frac{a}{b}$	divide (division)
$=$	is equal to
$<$	is less than
$>$	is greater than
$\leq$	is less than or equal to
$\geq$	is greater than or equal to
$\neq$	is not equal to
$(\ )$	parentheses for grouping
$[\ ]$	brackets for grouping
$-a$	opposite of a
$\ldots$	and so on
$^\circ$	degrees
$\lvert a \rvert$	absolute value of a
$\overset{?}{=}, \overset{?}{<}, \overset{?}{>}$	Is the statement true?
$\approx$	is approximately equal to
$\frac{b}{a}$	reciprocal of $\frac{a}{b}$
A	area
ℓ	length
w	width
h	height
d	distance
r	rate
t	time
P	perimeter
b	base length
C	circumference
d	diameter

r	radius
S.A.	surface area
B	area of base
L.A.	lateral area
ℓ	slant height
V	volume
a^n	nth power of a
$\sqrt{x}$	nonnegative square root of x
π	pi, an irrational number approximately equal to 3.14
(a, b)	ordered pair with x-coordinate a and y-coordinate b
$\overline{AB}$	segment AB
A'	image of A, A prime
$\triangle ABC$	triangle with vertices A, B, and C
$\rightarrow$	arrow notation
$a : b, \frac{a}{b}$	ratio of a to b
$\cong$	is congruent to
$\sim$	is similar to
$\angle A$	angle with vertex A
AB	length of segment $\overline{AB}$
$\overrightarrow{AB}$	ray AB
$\angle ABC$	angle formed by $\overrightarrow{BA}$ and $\overrightarrow{BC}$
$m\angle ABC$	measure of angle ABC
$\perp$	is perpendicular to
$\overleftrightarrow{AB}$	line AB
$\parallel$	is parallel to
$\%$	percent
P (event)	probability of an event

Measures

Customary	Metric
Length	**Length**
1 foot (ft) = 12 inches (in.) 1 yard (yd) = 36 in. 1 yd = 3 ft 1 mile (mi) = 5,280 ft 1 mi = 1,760 yd	1 centimeter (cm) = 10 millimeters (mm) 1 meter (m) = 100 cm 1 kilometer (km) = 1,000 m 1 mm = 0.001 m
Area	**Area**
1 square foot (ft^2) = 144 square inches (in.^{2}) 1 square yard (yd^2) = 9 ft^2 1 square mile (mi^2) = 640 acres	1 square centimeter (cm^2) = 100 square millimeters (mm^2) 1 square meter (m^2) − 10,000 cm^2
Volume	**Volume**
1 cubic foot (ft^3) = 1,728 cubic inches (in.^{3}) 1 cubic yard (yd^3) = 27 ft^3	1 cubic centimeter (cm^3) = 1,000 cubic millimeters (mm^3) 1 cubic meter (m^3) = 1,000,000 cm^3
Mass	**Mass**
1 pound (lb) = 16 ounces (oz) 1 ton (t) = 2,000 lb	1 gram (g) = 1,000 milligrams (mg) 1 kilogram (kg) = 1,000 g
Capacity	**Capacity**
1 cup (c) = 8 fluid ounces (fl oz) 1 pint (pt) = 2 c 1 quart (qt) = 2 pt 1 gallon (gal) = 4 qt	1 liter (L) = 1,000 milliliters (mL) 1000 liters = 1 kiloliter (kL)

Customary Units and Metric Units	
Length	1 in. = 2.54 cm 1 mi ≈ 1.61 km 1 ft ≈ 0.3 m
Capacity	1 qt ≈ 0.94 L
Weight and Mass	1 oz ≈ 28.3 g 1 lb ≈ 0.45 kg

Properties

Unless otherwise stated, the variables a, b, c, m, and n used in these properties can be replaced with any number represented on a number line.

Identity Properties

Addition $n + 0 = n$ and $0 + n = n$

Multiplication $n \cdot 1 = n$ and $1 \cdot n = n$

Zero Property

$a \cdot 0 = 0$ and $0 \cdot a = 0$.

Commutative Properties

Addition $a + b = b + a$

Multiplication $a \cdot b = b \cdot a$

Associative Properties

Addition $(a + b) + c = a + (b + c)$

Multiplication $(a \cdot b) \cdot c = a \cdot (b \cdot c)$

Inverse Properties

Addition

$a + (-a) = 0$ and $-a + a = 0$

Multiplication

$a \cdot \frac{1}{a} = 1$ and $\frac{1}{a} \cdot a = 1$, $(a \neq 0)$

Distributive Properties

$a(b + c) = ab + ac$ $(b + c)a = ba + ca$

$a(b - c) = ab - ac$ $(b - c)a = ba - ca$

Properties of Equality

Addition If $a = b$,

then $a + c = b + c$.

Subtraction If $a = b$,

then $a - c = b - c$.

Multiplication If $a = b$,

then $a \cdot c = b \cdot c$.

Division If $a = b$, and $c \neq 0$,

then $\frac{a}{c} = \frac{b}{c}$.

Substitution If $a = b$, then b can replace a in any expression.

Properties of Inequality

Addition If $a > b$,

then $a + c > b + c$.

If $a < b$,

then $a + c < b + c$.

Subtraction If $a > b$,

then $a - c > b - c$.

If $a < b$,

then $a - c < b - c$.

Multiplication

If $a > b$ and $c > 0$, then $ac > bc$.

If $a < b$ and $c > 0$, then $ac < bc$.

If $a > b$ and $c < 0$, then $ac < bc$.

If $a < b$ and $c < 0$, then $ac > bc$.

Division

If $a > b$ and $c > 0$, then $\frac{a}{c} > \frac{b}{c}$.

If $a < b$ and $c > 0$, then $\frac{a}{c} < \frac{b}{c}$.

If $a > b$ and $c < 0$, then $\frac{a}{c} < \frac{b}{c}$.

If $a < b$ and $c < 0$, then $\frac{a}{c} > \frac{b}{c}$.

Properties of Exponents

For any nonzero number n and any integers m and n:

Zero Exponent $a^0 = 1$

Negative Exponent $a^{-n} = \frac{1}{a^n}$

Product of Powers $a^m \cdot a^n = a^{m+n}$

Power of a Product $(ab)^n = a^n b^n$

Quotient of Powers $\frac{a^m}{a^n} = a^{m-n}$

Power of a Quotient $\left(\frac{a}{b}\right)^n = \frac{a^n}{b^n}$

Power of a Power $(a^m)^n = a^{mn}$